Strathnaver at Sydney after her post-war refit (P&O).

20th CENTURY PASSENGER SHIPS OF THE P&O

20th CENTURY PASSENGER SHIPS OF THE P&O

NEIL McCART

Patrick Stephens, Wellingborough

First published 1985

British Library Cataloguing in Publication Data

McCart, Neil
20th century passenger ships of the P&O.
1. P&O company 2. Merchant ships—Great
Britain—History
I. Title
623.8'243 VM57

ISBN 0-85059-716-1

*Patrick Stephens Limited is part of the
Thorsons Publishing Group*

Text photoset in 10 on 11pt Garamond
by Avocet Marketing Services, Aylesbury, Bucks.
Printed in Great Britain on 115 gsm Fineblade
coated cartridge by St Edmundsbury Press,
Bury St Edmunds, Suffolk, and bound by
Hunter & Foulis Limited, Edinburgh,
for the publishers,
Patrick Stephens Limited, Denington Estate, Wellingborough,
Northants, NN8 2QD, England.

Contents

Introduction

I first became fascinated with the liners of the P&O 27 years ago, when as a young boy I travelled east in that lovely little liner *Carthage*. I can recall that in the tourist class foyer on 'C' deck there was a plaque detailing the ship's history. Reading it set my mind thinking, 'What on earth was this small passenger ship doing as an armed merchant cruiser?', and in fact 'What was an armed merchant cruiser?—And where did the ship carry troops to, for three years from 1944?' Then whilst living in Singapore I was able to see and visit more of those gleaming white liners, with their British officers and Asian crews. They were not as huge as the 'Atlantic Greyhounds', but to my mind were just as glamorous. There was no 'Blue Riband' to run for on each voyage, but then these ships were sailing on voyages which would keep them away from home for up to three months at a time. Nevertheless, records were broken, as in 1929 when *Viceroy of India* reduced the passage time between London and India to 16 days, one hour and 45 minutes.

Right up to the present day the ships of the P&O have served their country well. They have been found in the thick of the action, and in fact 68 years before *Canberra* sailed with the task force for the Falkland Islands, P&O's *Macedonia*, one of the famous pre-1914 'M' Class ships, took a minor but important role in the first 'Battle of the Falkland Islands'. Although the enemy was different, the hostile weather conditions of the South Atlantic were the same. In the Second World War *Rawalpindi* took part in that tragic surface action, and *Canton* hunted U boats in 1940. P&O ships have been bombed by aircraft in places as far apart as Bougie in North Africa, and San Carlos Water in the Falkland Islands. Yet those same ships have carried holiday-makers intent on enjoying a cruise to the sun, emigrants sailing halfway across the globe to a new life in Australia or New Zealand, and British civil servants going out to administer colonial territories in those far-off days of Empire.

Readers may wonder why *Oriana* and the other three Orient Line ships which were transferred to P&O ownership in the 1960s are not included. In my opinion theirs is a separate story, even though the two companies have long been closely linked. I have chosen to cover the period between 1900 and the present day, because it is within living memory of many thousands of men and women who travelled in those great ships, whether as fare-paying passengers, ships' companies, emigrants, or as part of an army unit on their way to a garrison or battle area overseas. The first 50 years cover a period when Kipling's 'Exiles' Line' had passed into history, and when the liner was the only way to travel. From 1950 onwards air travel in jet airliners, increasingly able to carry more and more passengers, was having a severe effect on the profitability of ocean liners, so that in the early 1970s, P&O abandoned their old image and this included the traditional liner voyage. The ships which escaped the breakers' yard were committed to full time cruising and formed a most formidable fleet. The announcement in February 1982 that the company was to build a new 40,000 gross ton cruise liner delighted the shipping world, (even if the

Left *Stern view of* Maloja *whilst under construction at Belfast. Her name was taken from the Swiss town of Maloggia* (Harland & Wolff).

artist's impression of the proposed new vessel was not quite what might have been expected).

There have been books which have related the story of the P&O Company, and books which have told tales of passengers and crews of their ships. But this book is essentially the story of the vessels themselves, and I hope it will appeal to a wide variety of readers who either know these ships already, or perhaps have beome interested in them through watching them enter and leave ports the world over, people who like me want to know more of what happened to them during the years when they plied the oceans of the world.

Moldavia 1903

The opening years of the 20th century saw the entry into service of the first of P&O's 'M' Class of ships. They were perhaps the most celebrated vessels built before the First World War, and were designed for the mail service between London and Brisbane. *Moldavia*, the first of the class, was built at Greenock by Caird & Co, who were to build five of the ten ships. Her launching in March 1903 was certainly a great event at Greenock, as she was the largest P&O liner to be built there. On the day before the launch Sir Thomas Sutherland, the Chairman of P&O, travelled up by train to the port he knew so well. He had been Member of Parliament for the town from 1884 to 1900, and Chairman of the P&O since 1880, during which time he had successfully brought the company through some difficult periods.

So at just after 11.00 am on Saturday March 28 1903, Sir Thomas' daughter gracefully performed the naming ceremony and the *Moldavia* took to the water in fine style. She was then towed to Victoria Harbour for fitting out, and on April 20 at 1.30 pm fire broke out in one of her bunkers. The Greenock Fire Brigade soon extinguished the blaze but not before some damage had been done to her bulkhead plates. During May work was held up for four days because of an engineers' strike, but she was completed on time, and on July 30 1903 she was ready to undertake her trials. She had cost the P&O £336,178 to build, which was some £75,000 more than the company's previous most expensive ship, the *Persia* in 1900.

Moldavia was a fine looking vessel of 9,505 gross registered tons (grt). She was a twin screw ship powered by triple-expansion reciprocating engines, which gave her a service speed of 16 knots. She had accommodation for 348 first and 166 second class passengers and with all her passenger cabins above the level of the main deck, she represented a definite improvement on all earlier tonnage.

In early August she arrived at Tilbury and on the 21st she left Gravesend for a three-day cruise in the English Channel. Sir Thomas Sutherland was on board and among his guests were the Governor of the Bank of England, Major General Sir Redvers Buller of Boer War fame, and Mr Patrick Caird from the builders. She lay off Margate on the first night out and the following day anchored off Netley near Southampton where most of her guests disembarked before she returned to London. It was a satisfactory trip and on a test run in the Channel a speed of 18 knots was recorded. On September 11 she was opened to the public for a day, and two weeks later on the 25th she left London for her maiden voyage to Bombay. It was December that year before she made her first voyage to Australia, via Marseilles and Colombo.

For the next three years she ran an uninterrupted service to Australia, but suddenly on Saturday January 19 1907 she was unexpectedly in the news. She was on the final stages of a voyage from Sydney when, in the early hours of the morning, a dense fog settled over the Channel. Several ships came to grief that day, including the 12,000 ton Red Star liner *Vaderland* which collided wih a small coaster off the Goodwin Sands. Shortly after this *Moldavia* went aground on the Goodwins, not far from one of the lightships. Distress signals were sent out, and the Walmer lifeboat was launched. Tugs were despatched from Dover, but *Moldavia*'s Master did not require assistance at this stage. Fortunately she had stuck on a spit of the Sands and with the tide rising fast she was able to get off by means of her own engines. After a survey at Tilbury it was established that no damage had been done and she was able to sail on her next outward voyage with no delay. Once again *Moldavia* was able to run for the next seven years with no problems. There was an interesting incident in March 1911 when she was docked in Melbourne opposite a German liner belonging to Norddeutscher Lloyd, and *Moldavia*'s band played the German National Anthem, much to the delight of passengers on both ships. Just three and a half years later the playing of that anthem would give anything but pleasure to *Moldavia*'s passengers.

In 1914, in the final tense weeks before the continent of Europe was plunged into war, *Moldavia* was making her last peacetime voyage from India to London. She left Bombay on July 19 and arrived in London on August 3, the day before war was declared on Germany. For the first few months of the war little changed for *Moldavia*, and she sailed for Australia again on August 22 that year. Little changed in the press either, and for the rest of 1914 and during 1915 all liner sailings were still advertised and noted in *The Times*, with *Moldavia* shown as sailing to Australia for most of that time. It was not until 1916, as shipping losses mounted, that effective censorship was applied to the movements of British shipping. By then *Moldavia* had embarked on a new and final phase of her career.

In late 1915 she was requisitioned by the government for use as an armed merchant cruiser, undergoing conversion at the Royal Albert Dock in London. She was commissioned into the Royal Navy as HMS *Moldavia* on February 1 1916, and many of her new crew members were RNR men from HMS *Teutonic* (an ex-White Star Liner converted to an AMC in the first weeks of the war). *Moldavia* arrived in the Solent on February 11 and after drydocking at Southampton she left to join the 10th Cruiser Squadron.

Although it sounded a rather formidable force, the 10th Cruiser Squadron consisted of liners converted into AMCs, and used specifically to enforce a blockade between the north of Scotland and Iceland. The AMCs were not intended to take part in any action with purpose built warships, but to intercept merchant vessels and if necessary put an armed guard on board to ensure that the merchant ship sailed to an Allied port where the cargo could be examined for contraband. It was a role for which the ex-liners were particularly well suited, as they could spend long periods on patrol and had a far greater turn of speed than the average merchantman. The squadron had its northern base at Busta Voe in the Shetland Islands, but this remote outpost was mainly a coaling station, so most maintenance work had to be carried out on the Clyde.

HMS *Moldavia*'s first patrol in those cold northern waters commenced on March 25 1916, and lasted for 12 days during which she sent two Norwegian ships to Lerwick under armed guard. This was to set the pattern for the rest of the year when, apart from three ten-day visits to Glasgow, the whole time was spent on patrol with only one or two days every fortnight coaling at Busta Voe. She intercepted numerous merchant vessels, 31 of these being sent into port for examination. In November 1916 her gunners were given some useful practice when she sank an abandoned merchant ship, SS *Patio*, by gunfire. Also that month the *Moldavia* was compulsorily purchased by the government, but P&O contested the government's right to do so and some months later she reverted to P&O ownership, although it did not affect her ultimate fate. In December, four days before Christmas, she tied up alongside Meadowside Wharf in Glasgow for refit and her ship's company had a well deserved leave. On January 16 1917 she left Glasgow once more for Busta Voe. It was during her second patrol, on February 9 1917, that she intercepted an Italian merchant vessel, SS *Famiglia*. Ironically the Italian ship had already been stopped by a U-boat, which had placed an armed guard aboard her and set course for Germany.

When *Moldavia* stopped her, the Germans detonated four explosive charges and then, with the crew, they abandoned the sinking ship. All were taken on board and landed later that month in Loch Ewe. On May 13 when *Moldavia* was steaming north between the Clyde and Loch Ewe, she sighted an enemy submarine just breaking the surface. However, the submarine had obviously sighted *Moldavia* for she immediately submerged and made good her escape. On July 30 1917 *Moldavia* completed her last patrol in northern waters, sailing ten days later for Dakar to begin her new role of convoy escort between West

Africa and Plymouth. In November 1917 she sailed from Freetown with 609 cases of gold bullion and 11 German prisoners on board and reached Devonport safely with her valuable cargo two weeks later. It was the first of three bullion voyages she was to make between November 1917 and March 1918. The final voyage terminated at Avonmouth on March 1 and a few days later she left for Canada.

By now the USA had been at war on the side of the Allies for 11 months, and many thousands of troops and supplies were being transported across the Atlantic. On May 11 1918 *Moldavia* left Halifax, Nova Scotia, as the ocean escort to a convoy (HC 1) of five merchant vessels. It is of interest that although her role was that of a commissioned RN ship, she had a considerable cargo aboard; 526 tons of frozen meat, 88 tons of butter, 8 tons of wood and 25 tons of stores for Chinese labourers in France. She also had on board 477 troops of the 28th Regiment of the United States Army, as well as 461 naval officers and ratings. The convoy's destination was London. On May 20 five destroyers joined them for the final leg of the passage through the Western Approaches and up the English Channel. On the following day the convoy passed four miles south of Bishop Rock and set a course for the Straits of Dover.

By 2.35 am on May 23 she was in a position, Latitude 50° 24' N Longitude 0° 26' W, off Beachy Head, and 17 miles from the Owers lightship. All seemed to be well and later that day the convoy would be in the safe waters of the Thames Estuary. Suddenly there was a terrific explosion as a torpedo hit the port bow, on a line with number three bulkhead, which was badly damaged. Both number three and number four holds were flooded, as was the stokehold. The ship took a 25° list to port, then uprighted and slowly listed to starboard. The radio was out of action, and with the stokeholds flooded all power was soon lost. By 3.30 am it was clear that *Moldavia* was sinking fast, and her commander, Captain Adrian H. Smyth RN, gave the order to abandon ship which was carried out quickly and efficiently. At 3.50 am the ship was upright and settling by the head. She settled gradually, heeling at the last to port and at 3.55 am she disappeared into the waters of the English Channel.

When the survivors were landed at Dover it became

The first of the long line of 'M' Class ships, Moldavia *of 1903* (P&O).

clear that 56 US soldiers were missing and as they had all been billeted in number three upper hold, it seemed certain they had been killed by the explosion when the torpedo hit the ship. A court martial was held in June 1918, and Captain Smyth was commended for the way he and his ship's company had handled the ship. There was special praise for Captain Henry B. Cordun and his men of the 28th Regiment US Army, for their high state of discipline and excellent conduct. Also commended was Boy First Class W.G.F. Sandell of *Moldavia* who, despite having been injured, rendered invaluable assistance by running messages and standing by his Captain until he left the ship shortly before she sank.

Technical Data
Gross tonnage: 9,505
Net tonnage: 4,928
Length overall: 545 ft (166.12m)
Depth: 58 ft 4 in (17.78m)
Draught: 33 ft 3 in (10.13m)
Cargo capacity: 90,000 cu ft in six holds served by 10 hydraulic cranes
Boilers: Coal-fired, three double-ended and four single-ended boilers, 185 psi
Main engines: Twin screw, two sets compound triple-expansion reciprocating engines, 12,000 IHP, 17 knots
Ship's company: 370
Passengers: First class 348, Second class 166

The first class music room on Moldavia, *the height of Edwardian luxury* (P&O).

Mongolia 1903

The second ship of the 'M' Class to enter service was the *Mongolia*. She was the second company vessel to bear the name, the first being a vessel of 2,000 tons built in 1865 for service between Suez and Calcutta. She was broken up in Zanzibar 23 years later.

The new *Mongolia* was completed on October 29 1903, and she left Greenock for her trials that forenoon. Like *Moldavia* she was built by Caird & Co, this time at a cost of £336,024. Her dimensions and layout were identical to her sister, and indeed, the layout of all the 'M' Class of ships was to be basically the same. There were five passenger decks, the uppermost being the boat deck, with the midships section for the use of first class passengers. Below this was the promenade deck with, once again, first class accommodation amidships, with the aft area reserved for second class saloon passengers. Below this was the hurricane deck, where most of the public rooms for both classes were situated. The first class lounge, music room and smoke room were amidships and the second saloon music room and smoke room aft. Next came the spar deck which ran the whole length of the ship, and on which were situated the dining saloons for both classes, and the galleys. The main deck was beneath this and here there were some passenger cabins for both classes. The decorative scheme of the saloons, music and smoking rooms was designed by Mr T.E. Callcutt. In the first class saloon the woodwork was chiefly English and Austrian oak, while the general effect of the dining room was enhanced by the extra height given to the centre portion.

Mongolia sailed on her maiden voyage to Bombay on Friday November 20 1903. Among her passengers were Lady Cromer, wife of the Comptroller General of Egypt, Sir William Preece who was responsible for the introduction of the postal telegraphic service into England, and Prince Ranjitsinhje, an Indian aristocrat.

The P&O route east in those days was via Plymouth, Marseilles, Suez and Aden, with occasional calls at Gibraltar, Malta and Port Sudan. The outward voyage went without incident, but when she was homeward bound in the Bay of Biscay she ran into severe weather and hurricane force winds battered the ship. At the height of the storm, damage was done to deck fittings and several crew members were injured, the most badly hurt being a joiner who was knocked unconscious. In the stokehold a number of firemen suffered burns as they struggled to feed the furnaces.

Mongolia's next voyage was to Sydney, and on February 20 1904, while outward bound in the Red Sea and 460 miles north of Aden, she encountered a Russian battleship and four destroyers. The Russo-Japanese War had started 12 days earlier and the Russian ships it seems, were hoping to capture Japanese merchant vessels in the area. It can only be surmised that they mistook *Mongolia* for one of them, for one of the destroyers endeavoured to cut her off, but failed. Then the whole Russian squadron gave chase, but, being unable to overtake the liner, they signalled her to stop. *Mongolia* did so at once, after one of the destroyers had subjected the vessel to close scrutiny she signalled 'beg to be excused' and was allowed to proceed. A few days later the BI liner *Mombasa* was stopped and boarded by the same Russian warships.

A year later in January 1905 *Mongolia* arrived in Fremantle from London a day ahead of schedule, and, despite leaving Marseilles two days late because of weather conditions, she had completed the run from Marseilles to Fremantle in a record 23 days and 16 hours.

On February 28 1908 *Mongolia* left London for Australia, and arrived in Marseilles six days later with a fire in one of her holds. Local fire brigades were called and the fire was extinguished, but not before considerable damage had been done to the cargo and to passengers' baggage. However, it did not affect the rest of the voyage and she arrived in Sydney on April 9. Later that year on December 29, while homeward bound and entering Fremantle harbour, *Mongolia* collided with and sank the Customs tug boat. On June 24 1911, she took her place in the Coronation Fleet Review at Spithead along with three other ships from the P&O line, *Mooltan*, *Soudan* and *Dongola*. *Mongolia* anchored with the latter two in 'G' line which had been reserved for privileged merchant vessels representing the great passenger steamship lines.

When war came in August 1914 *Mongolia* continued in P&O service, and she sailed on a voyage to Australia on October 3. On May 17 1915, she had a strange encounter while outward bound for Australia. Off Cape Torinana, shortly after leaving the Bay of Biscay, the Chief Officer sighted what he thought was an enemy submarine about one mile away on the port side. At the same time a suspicious looking vessel on the starboard side turned and headed for *Mongolia*, and it seemed that the submarine and merchant vessel were acting together. Fortunately it was soon dark and *Mongolia* was able to leave both vessels behind at 17½ knots. But she was not always to be so lucky.

In December 1916 a German 'Q' ship, the 5,800 ton SS *Wolf*, left Hamburg with a cargo of 465 mines, one of which was ultimately to seal the fate of *Mongolia*. The *Wolf* was formerly a cargo ship named *Wachtfels*, which had been fitted with two 5.9-in and four 4.1-in guns. In addition she was fitted with torpedo tubes and a scouting seaplane called *Wölfchen* (*Wolfcub*). The *Wolf*'s mission was to break through the Allied blockade, steam down the Atlantic, round the Cape and into the Indian Ocean. Once there she was to cause as much havoc as possible to Allied shipping, and she did in fact sink a dozen merchant vessels by gunfire, while more fell victim to her mines. In December 1917 she rounded the Cape once again, and successfully broke the blockade, reaching her home port of Kiel in February 1918.

It was in June 1917, while the raider *Wolf* was halfway through her destructive mission, that *Mongolia* left London for a voyage to Sydney. Most of her passengers by this time were travelling on government service, and she also had on board a full general cargo in addition to the Indian, China and Australian mails. She was escorted as far as Suez by two destroyers, and a cruiser joined them at Malta. Once she had cleared the Suez Canal it was considered that the main danger was over, although lifeboat drills were still carried out regularly and passengers were advised to keep lifebelts close by all the time. By midday on June 23 she was only 17 miles from Bombay in the Arabian Sea. In an article written in *The Times* of November 14 1962, one of the few women passengers on board, a professor of anatomy from a Delhi college, described how the whole atmosphere on board was relaxed as passengers prepared to disembark at their destination or anticipated seeing the sights of Bombay.

Suddenly at about 12.16 pm a huge explosion rocked the whole ship. One passenger described how the force of the explosion tore one of *Mongolia*'s defensive 6-in guns from its mountings at the stern and the previous witness described how both she and her deck chair were lifted from the deck. *Mongolia* had hit a 'two tier mine' laid by the *Wolf*, and it appeared that the main 'second' charge exploded directly beneath the engine room killing three engineer officers, 17 crew members and three passengers. The professor from Delhi described how, as she hurried down the main staircase to fetch a lifebelt from her cabin, a mass of people were on their way up to the promenade deck where the lifeboats were to be loaded. Although it may have appeared chaotic at the time, the frequent boat drills were to pay off, for only 13 minutes after she struck the mine *Mongolia* sank, and it is a credit to her officers and crew that, other than those killed in the explosion, every soul was got away safely in the ship's boats, a total of 450 people. The same lady passenger describes how, as her boat pulled clear, only the tops of *Mongolia*'s masts were visible above the water. But for all the survivors the main ordeal was only now about to begin, as with all radio equipment destroyed in the explosion, the outside world was ignorant as to the fate of the *Mongolia*.

The Captain decided to take his lifeboat and two

others, one under the command of the Supernumerary Chief Officer, to Bombay under sail, and when they arrived there safely the first news of *Mongolia*'s fate became known. The remaining 11 boats made for the nearest land, and the professor's account tells of how her boat made its way in tropical squalls towards the coast and eventually landed that night on a deserted beach. The other boats arrived shortly afterwards and soon there were hundreds of survivors on the beach. The professor and three Australian nurses tended the injured seamen, while some of the men walked to the nearby village where they obtained supplies and telephoned the bad news to Bombay. The following day they heard that P&O had organised relief in the form of a minesweeper, the *Curlew*, and after a gruelling march of ten miles, with the injured being carried in litters, the survivors were able to join the *Curlew* and other relief ships at Janjira. When they were landed at Bombay, each of the survivors was given £10 and those whose destinations were beyond Bombay were given passages in the P&O liner *Malta*.

The professor gives an interesting postscript to the story. Some years later when the wreck of *Mongolia* was being salvaged, she was given a piece of the woodwork from which she had a small trinket box made, and in it she kept a small handful of shells from the beach where the survivors were so thankful to land.

Technical data
Gross tonnage: 9,505
Net tonnage: 4,936
Length overall: 545 ft (166.12 m)
Breadth: 58 ft 4 in (17.78 m)
Depth: 33 ft 3 in (10.13 m)
Cargo capacity: 190,000 cu ft in six holds served by 10 hydraulic cranes
Boilers: Coal-fired, three double-ended and four single-ended boilers, 185 psi
Main engines: Twin screw, two sets compound triple-expansion reciprocating engines, 12,000 IHP, 17 knots
Ship's company: 370
Passengers: First class 348, Second class 166

Mongolia *at anchor off Gravesend. She was to fall victim to a mine laid by the German raider* Wolf *off Bombay* (P&O).

Marmora 1903

The third ship of the 'M' Class entered service only three weeks after the *Mongolia*. She was the *Marmora*, and was the first P&O liner to exceed 10,000 gross tons. This time the tender had been won by the Belfast shipbuilders Harland & Wolff, and at £344,084 they had completed her at an extremely competitive price. *Marmora* was launched on April 9 1903, and it is interesting to note that as she was being towed to the engine works at Abercorn Basin, the keel of His Majesty's steam yacht *Enchantress* was being laid on the slip which *Marmora* had just vacated. On November 13 that year she was registered at Belfast and was ready to undertake her trials. One week later on November 20 she was handed over to her owners, being the sixth ship to be completed by Harland & Wolff for the P&O company. She arrived at Tilbury in early December, and on the 17th and 18th of that month was opened to the public.

On New Years Day 1904, commanded by Captain Langbourne, she made her maiden voyage to Bombay, sailing via Marseilles. In March that year she undertook her first voyage to Australia, and it is an interesting fact that she and her coal-fired sisters had to bunker at seven points on a single voyage to that continent. They were London (prior to leaving), Marseilles, Port Said, Aden, Colombo, Fremantle and Sydney. At an average speed of 15 knots *Marmora* consumed 9,000 tons of coal per round voyage, and with the cost of coal in 1904 being approximately 19s 6d per ton, her fuel costs were in the region of £8,775 every voyage.

In October 1907, while homeward bound from Australia, *Marmora* rescued three survivors from the 1,200 ton Cardiff registered cargo vessel *Mervinian*. She had left Swansea for Marseilles on October 2, and foundered two days later in the Bay of Biscay when her cargo shifted in heavy weather. Six people were drowned and the three survivors had been adrift in their open boat for over a week before they were picked up by *Marmora* and landed at Plymouth on her arrival there.

On December 11 1908 *Marmora* left Tilbury carrying the Princess Royal, her husband the Duke of Fife and their two daughters the Princesses Alexandra and Maud on a voyage to Egypt, arriving at Port Said on December 22. It was the first of several winter trips which the family made to Egypt for health reasons, but which were to end unhappily, as we shall see later.

On August 3 1914, only a day before war was declared, *Marmora* was at Tilbury when she was requisitioned by the government for use as an armed merchant cruiser and work began to convert her for this new role. When HMS *Marmora* left London on August 18, she was sailing down the Thames for the last time, bound for Las Palmas where she was to form part of the Cape Verde Islands division of the 10th Cruiser Squadron, whose task was to intercept and check shipping on the Madeira-St Vincent trade route. *Marmora* arrived in Las Palmas on August 30, and later that day sailed for her first patrol. On September 4 she sighted and intercepted the German motor schooner *Rhineland*, and after taking the crew prisoner, *Marmora* opened fire and sank the abandoned ship. Later that month the prisoners were landed at Freetown.

Marmora spent the next four months patrollng between Freetown, the Cape Verde Islands, Canary

Islands and Gibraltar, and continued with this routine until 1917. In early 1915 she was part of a special group, together with the cruiser HMS *Highflyer* and the AMC HMS *Empress of Britain* (Canadian Pacific), formed to search the West African coast for the German auxiliary cruiser *Kronprinz Wilhelm*, which had already sunk 15 Allied merchant ships. However, on April 10 1915, with her provisions exhausted and in serious need of repair the *Kronprinz Wilhelm* sailed into Newport News, Virginia, and internment. Two years later she was seized by the US Navy.

Marmora spent the latter half of 1915 and early part of 1916 patrolling in the Caribbean, using Bird Island as an anchorage and bunkering base. On June 23 1916 she arrived in Liverpool for a three-month refit during which she was thoroughly overhauled and her armament was modernised. It was her first visit to the UK for nearly two years. On September 29 she sailed once again for the Caribbean, where she would spend the rest of the year. By November 1916 the government had apparently tired of continually paying P&O charter rates for *Marmora* and she was compulsorily purchased. P&O disputed the government's right to do this and having won their case they repurchased her in February 1917. By that time *Marmora* was undergoing another refit at Devonport.

She sailed on February 12 to spend the rest of her career escorting convoys from South Africa or South America to the UK. It was whilst escorting a convoy between Dakar and Devonport on November 14 1917, at 3.35 pm, that the periscope of an enemy submarine was sighted 30 yards off the starboard bow. For two hours *Marmora* searched the area and dropped depth charges, but no further signs of the submarine were seen and the convoy arrived safely in Devonport eight days later. For the next five months these convoy escort duties continued without incident and on June 9 1918 she left Rio de Janeiro with a convoy for her last Atlantic crossing.

On July 18 1918 when *Marmora* was docked at Cardiff, her commander, Captain W.E. Woodward RN, received sailing orders from the Vice Admiral, Milford Haven. She was to leave Cardiff on July 22 and proceed to Dakar, arriving there on August 3. At Dakar she was to escort a homeward bound convoy HD45, leaving on August 5. Two days later she was to hand over this convoy to HMS *Almanzora* and proceed to Freetown to escort another homeward bound convoy. So at 5.45 pm on July 22 *Marmora* left Milford Haven and proceeded to Barry Roads, where she took over as escort to a merchant ship SS *Boonah*. At just after 7.00 pm with the destroyers *P66* and *P67* forming an additional escort they sailed for Dakar. *Boonah* took station four cables on the starboard beam and *P66* on the port bow of *Marmora*, whilst *P67* positioned herself off the starboard bow of *Boonah*. By 10.00 pm that evening they ran into dense fog, and as there had been reports of a submarine, at 5.15 am on July 23 the four ships began to zig-zag. By 3.45 pm that day they were in a position 50° 24'N, 8° 48'W, midway between the Scilly Isles and the Old Head of Kinsale, steering on the northwesterly course of a zig-zag when a lookout on the port side saw the wake of two torpedoes about 30 yards from the ship. There was no time to give any warnings as seconds later the first one struck the ship abreast number one gun on the port side between the funnels. Both exploded with devastating effect.

On the bridge Captain Woodward rang down to the engine room 'stop both', and the ship settled 12 ft by the head taking a slight list to starboard. As the ship did not appear in immediate danger of sinking 'slow ahead both' was ordered so as to get away from the vicinity of the submarine. Shortly after this the Engineer Commander reported both stokeholds flooded and the engines were stopped for the last time. As the radio aerial had been carried away in the explosion the signal 'submarine in sight' was hoisted. By 4.15 pm the forward well deck was almost awash and with the ship settling fast the order was given to abandon ship. In his report Captain Woodward states that this command was carried out in perfect order, with excellent discipline being maintained. One boat was ordered to remain alongside to take the last remaining officers away. Captain Woodward described how he went below to the saloon, to see water flooding in. Then when he was satisfied that everyone was clear he and Private F. Marshall, Royal Marines, the last men remaining aboard, left the ship. At 4.46 pm, having heeled right over to starboard, with forecastle under water, and stern high up in the air, HMS *Marmora* righted herself briefly and then sank bow foremost.

Meanwhile the two destroyers which had been circling the ship picked up the survivors and transferred them to *P67* which set course for Milford

Haven. On mustering them it was found that ten men were missing. Three of them were Able Seamen who had been manning number one gun on the forecastle and it was presumed they were killed by the first explosion. The other seven were merchant seamen and were firemen or trimmers, five of whom had been on duty in the after stokehold and were probably killed by the second torpedo. One of the trimmers, who had been off duty, was last seen on a raft by himself and in an exhausted condition and it was presumed he must have been washed off and drowned. An exhaustive search of the area by the USS *Stockton* failed to find any trace of him. The last casualty was Leading Fireman Edward Gallagher who was lost in the forward stokehold, and who, according to his Captain, 'behaved most gallantly, as after the explosion he carried one man up from the foremost stokehold then went down again to bring up more men and in so doing lost his life—a noble act of self sacrifice.'

Technical data

Gross tonnage: 10,509
Net tonnage: 5,244
Length overall: 545 ft (166.11 m)
Breadth: 60 ft (18.28 m)
Depth: 37 ft 3 in (11.35 m)
Cargo capacity: 196,580 cu ft in six holds served by 10 hydraulic cranes
Boilers: Coal-fired, five double-ended and two single-ended boilers, 215 psi
Main engines: Twin screw, two sets compound quadruple-expansion reciprocating engines, 10,500 IHP, 17 knots
Ship's company: 365
Passengers: First class 377, Second class 187

Marmora *on her trials, looking aft along the boat deck* (Harland & Wolff).

Above Marmora, *a view of the ornate woodwork in the first class dining saloon* (Harland & Wolff).

Below Marmora, *a view of the first class smoke room whilst fitting out* (Harland & Wolff).

Above Marmora, *the second class music room* (Harland & Wolff).

Below Marmora *as an armed merchant cruiser during the First World War, note the gun positions on the 'Hurricane' deck and on the forecastle* (Imperial War Museum).

Macedonia 1904

The fourth ship of the 'M' Class to enter service was perhaps the most well known of them all. However, it was not her career with P&O which brought her name into the public eye, but her war service with the Royal Navy.

Once again P&O gave the building contract to Harland & Wolff of Belfast, and *Macedonia* was launched on Thursday July 9 1903. She was registered in Belfast in January 1904, and in the following month on Saturday February 13 1904 she sailed on her maiden voyage to Bombay, calling at Marseilles to pick up overland passengers, before proceeding to Suez. *Macedonia*, like the rest of the class, was a handsome vessel, and like *Marmora* was distinguishable by her tall thin funnels. Following her successful maiden voyage *Macedonia* was placed on the Australian mail service, the whole round voyage taking about 16 weeks. She left for her first Australian sailing on April 29, and on her return she brought back the crew of the P&O liner *Australia* which was wrecked off Melbourne on June 20 that year.

At the end of her second Australian trip, when she arrived at Gravesend on Christmas Eve 1904 in one of London's dense winter fogs, she was in collision with a cargo ship *Christian IX*, which was afterwards involved in another collision with a vessel called the SS *Kirkaldy*. Fortunately *Macedonia* was not damaged, and three weeks later she sailed on her next voyage to Bombay. In 1907 she made an experimental voyage to the Far East, and the following year she set a record for the run between Fremantle and Colombo, of seven days and 20 hours. But the P&O ships were not the only ones setting records. On October 16 1908 *Macedonia* sailed from London bound for Bombay and the Ellerman City Line steamer *City of London* left Liverpool for the same port. The *City of London* arrived at Bombay on the evening of Thursday November 5, while *Macedonia* arrived a few hours later on the Friday morning.

In May 1910 she was fitted with radio equipment and the first message received was the news of the sudden death of King Edward VII. In February 1913 *Macedonia* had one of her Australian voyages extended to Auckland in New Zealand.

In early 1914 the plating under the bridge was raised, as one of the main complaints about her was that she was a very wet ship forward, having practically no flare, that is, the overhanging curve to her bow. In early August 1914 she was in Tilbury and due to sail for Australia on the 21st of that month. However, on the outbreak of war she was requisitioned by the government for use as an armed merchant cruiser. Her conversion was completed in Tilbury Docks in record time. She was commissioned on August 8, and by the evening of the 10th all of her eight 4.7 in guns had been mounted on board. On August 11, she moved from Tilbury Dock to a buoy off Gravesend, and the following day she sailed for St Vincent in the West Indies, calling at Funchal in Madeira on August 17. On September 2 she sailed for South America and her first of many patrols between Pernambuco and Abrolhos Rocks off the coast of Brazil. Fifteen days later on September 17 she rendezvoused with the AMC HMS *Carmania* (formerly the Cunard liner SS *Carmania*), which had been involved in a spirited action off Trinidade Island (Brazil) three days previously with the German auxiliary cruiser *Cap Trafalgar* (formerly a liner belonging to Hamburg—South America Line). *Carmania* had sunk the German vessel, but had been badly damaged herself and *Macedonia* had to escort her to Sierra Leone. Both ships sailed at 5.30 pm on the 17th, and *Macedonia*'s officers on watch were instructed to check *Carmania*'s position every half hour. During the voyage *Macedonia*'s crew collected £61 for the relatives of those killed on *Carmania* during the action. By September 26 both ships had reached Freetown, and at 5.45 pm the same day *Macedonia* sailed once again for Pernambuco, in company with HMS *Orama* (Orient Line). During October she was involved with the cruiser HMS *Bristol* in the search for the German light cruiser *Karlsruhe*.

On November 1 1914, when Admiral Craddock's squadron was defeated at Coronel off Chile, *Macedonia* was patrolling with the *Bristol* off Abrolhos Rocks. During the next few days her crew was kept busy breaking up the wooden fittings and cabins which had caused such dangerous fires in *Carmania*. By early December a British battle fleet was well on its way to the Falkland Islands, in order to hunt down and destroy Admiral Von Spee's German squadron. On December 3 *Macedonia* received orders to accompany the cruisers *Caernarvon* and *Kent* from the Abrolhos Rocks to the Falklands. The elderly battleship *Canopus* was already at Port Stanley, and she had laid a minefield across the entrance to Port William. At 11.30 am on December 6 *Macedonia* and the cruisers sighted the battlecruisers *Invincible* and *Inflexible*. The following day the fleet reached Port Stanley, and Admiral Sturdee decided that before setting out to hunt the Germans they must take the opportunity for coaling and maintenance. *Macedonia* remained on patrol off Cape Pembroke. Unknown to the Admiral the German squadron was less than a day's steaming away from Port Stanley and heading for the islands, intending to raid the radio station and coal stocks at Stanley.

At 2.30 am on the fateful day of December 8 1914, as the German ships got their first sight of the Falkland Islands, *Macedonia* was ordered to anchor in Port William which the ship's log shows her doing at 4.02 am. At 5.15 am a collier made fast alongside *Invincible*, which proceeded to coal ship. At 8.45 am *Macedonia* weighed and proceeded to an anchorage inside the minefield. The next log entry is dramatic: '9.30 am Enemy ships sighted and reported by flagship'. The German squadron had caught the British fleet unprepared, but they failed to take advantage of this and fled south-east at full speed. Looking again at *Macedonia*'s log we see the entry: '10.30 am Fleet proceeded to sea and eastwards.' The Battle of the Falkland Islands does not need retelling here, suffice it to say that four German cruisers were sunk, with only one, the *Dresden* escaping. After the main British fleet had left, only *Macedonia* and *Bristol* remained and, according to *Macedonia*'s log, *Bristol* sailed at 11.05 am.

Once again the next entry is exciting: '11.30 am Three merchant ships reported off Point Pleasant.' (Near Fitzroy and Bluff Cove.) At the time it was thought they may be enemy troop transports. In fact there were two vessels, the *Baden* and *Santa Isobel*, both colliers for the German squadron. *Macedonia* put to sea and both she and *Bristol* were ordered to destroy the transports. At 2.20 pm that day the German ships were sighted and the two British vessels gave chase. An hour later *Bristol* and *Macedonia* ordered the Germans 'to stop or we would fire.' *Macedonia* took off the crew of the *Baden* and *Bristol* the men of *Santa Isobel*. By 5.40 pm all the prisoners were on board *Macedonia*, and both British ships opened fire at short range on the *Baden*, which sank at 7.53 pm. Then at 8.15 pm as *Bristol* left the scene, *Macedonia* had opened fire on the *Santa Isobel*. She sank at 9.30 am after *Macedonia* fired a further eight shots into her. It was 7.00 am the next morning before *Macedonia* was back in Port William, and later that day some of her prisoners were transferred to the *Canopus*. For the next four days she remained at the Falkland Islands, sailing at 3.15 pm on December 14 in company with the merchant ship *Crown of Galicia* for Liverpool. During the voyage the large number of German prisoners on board were kept busy with the upkeep of the ship.

At 11.20 pm on January 13 1915 *Macedonia* made fast in Sandon Dock, Liverpool, where the ship's company were given leave. She remained at Liverpool until February 8, when she sailed once again for the South Atlantic. The rest of 1915 was spent on patrol off the coast of South America, between Abrolhos Rocks and the River Plate area. She spent Christmas and the New Year in Simonstown, but by March 1916 she was on patrol once again off the River Plate. She remained off South America until August 5 1917, when she paid off at Simonstown.

By October 10 that year she had recommissioned and sailed once again for South America where she continued to patrol off the River Plate. On March 20 1918 she left Rio de Janeiro as a convoy escort, and this was to be her role until the end of the war. Most of these convoys were between West Africa and Devonport, and her last wartime voyage commenced from Dakar on October 31 1918. Her log for this trip makes interesting reading. When the First World War ended on November 11 1918, *Macedonia* and her convoy were in a position Longitude 15° 52'N, Latitude 19° 2'W, and at 12.30 am on November 12 the ships in the convoy switched on all navigation lights, for the first time in four years. Happily the lights were going on once again all over Europe. At 8.00 am on November 17 the convoy arrived in Newport in South Wales.

Although the war was over, it was to be almost another three years before *Macedonia* was handed back to P&O. The rest of her service with the government was as a troop transport. Eventually she was reconditioned in the naval dockyard at Portsmouth, and on Thursday September 15 1921 she left for Tilbury and the mail service once again. Her first post-war sailing from London on October 21 that year was to Bombay, and in fact her last ten years of service were spent on the Indian and Far East services. She made only one Australian voyage in 1924. Passengers of this era may remember a brass plaque situated over the first class companionway leading to the saloon. It read, '*Macedonia*, Requisitioned 3rd August 1914 by HM government as armed merchant cruiser. Employed on patrol in South Atlantic, present at Falkland Islands battle, afterwards employed on convoy duty from May 1918 to end of war.' It was a permanent reminder of P&O's first involvement with those lonely islands in the South Atlantic.

In 1931 *Macedonia* was 27 years old and by then much bigger and better ships were about to enter P&O's mail service. She made two voyages to Bombay before returning to Tilbury in September that year. On September 18 1931 she left Tilbury for the last time on a normal passenger voyage, but this time the final destination was the shipbreakers yard in Japan. She left Shanghai on October 27 and a week later was handed over to be scrapped in Japan. The brass plaque from the first class companionway was taken down and kept in P&O's London headquarters, an echo from a bygone era and reminder of one of the most decisive sea battles of the First World War.

Technical data

Gross tonnage: 10,512
Net tonnage: 5,244
Length overall: 545 ft (166.11 m)
Breadth: 60 ft (18.28 m)
Depth: 37 ft 3 in (11.35 m)
Cargo capacity: 196,580 cu ft in six holds served by 10 hydraulic cranes
Boilers: Coal-fired, five double-ended and two single-ended boilers, 215 psi
Main engines: Twin screw, two sets compound quadruple-expansion reciprocating engines, 15,000 IHP, 18 knots
Ship's company: 370
Passengers: First class 377, Second class 187

Macedonia *in the Thames* (P&O).

Mooltan 1905

The fifth ship of the 'M' Class was *Mooltan*, her name being a variation of Multan, a town in the Punjab and now part of Pakistan. She was built by Caird & Co of Greenock at a cost of £314,982, and had a gross tonnage of 9,621. Accommodation was provided for 348 first and 166 second class passengers, and her quadruple expansion engines gave her a speed of 18 knots. Her first class cabins were situated on the main deck amidships, and most of the second class cabins were on the same deck, but further aft. The design and decoration of all the public rooms was by Mr T.E. Callcutt, and the layout was the same as that of the other four ships which had preceded her.

Mooltan was launched at 1.00 pm on Thursday August 3 1905, with no ceremony, and she was registered two months later on October 4. Soon after her first arrival at Tilbury she was opened to the public on the weekend of October 28/29 at a charge of one shilling, all the proceeds going to the Seamen's Hospital at Greenwich. She sailed on her maiden voyage to Bombay on November 3 1905, via Marseilles, Suez and Aden, arriving at Bombay on November 24, just three weeks later. She left Bombay 15 days later and arrived once again in Tilbury on the penultimate day of that year. *Mooltan*'s next voyage was to Australia on January 19 1906, and in fact she replaced the 18-year-old *Oceana* on that route. *Oceana* was one of P&O's celebrated 'Jubilee' Class of the 1880s on the London—Bombay service, but she was lost in 1912 after a collision with a sailing barque. Two years after *Mooltan* made this first sailing to Sydney she carried the elderly Empress Eugenie from Marseilles to Colombo.

The Empress, who was one of history's tragic figures, had been born in May 1826 of a noble but impoverished Spanish family. At the age of 26, in January 1853, she married Napoleon III, Emperor of the French. She was associated with her husband in all his gigantic schemes which kept the world in such a state of unrest. When the Franco-Prussian War broke out in 1870, the Second Empire of Louis Napoleon collapsed, and he and his family were forced to take refuge in England. He died three years later, and in 1879 their only son was killed in the Zulu Wars. Empress Eugenie lived in Farnborough, Hampshire in dignified retirement and she became a close friend of Queen Victoria's. In late 1907 she caught a severe cold in Norway and was advised to spend the winter in a warm climate.

She decided to fulfil a lifelong ambition to visit India and travelling incognito she took the overland train to Marseilles in order to embark in *Mooltan* for the voyage east. *Mooltan* had sailed from Tilbury on January 3 1908 and a week later the Empress boarded her for the trip to Colombo. On January 15 she arrived in Port Said and the Empress Eugenie travelled to Cairo, where she was mistaken for a 'Thomas Cook package tourist', something which greatly amused her. *Mooltan* arrived in Colombo on January 26 1908, and the Empress disembarked and went to the Governor's residence where she was to stay. Unfortunately before she could set out for India she became very ill, and the doctors advised her to return home. By coincidence the first homeward bound mail steamer was *Mooltan*, on her return voyage from Australia to London. Empress Eugenie embarked on March 19 1908, and arrived in Marseilles 16 days later on April 4. Although she lived for another 12 years the Empress never got to India.

In December 1908 *Mooltan* was once again bound for Australia leaving Marseilles at 10.00 am on December 25 with her next stop being Port Said. Two days later as she passed Sicily those on board felt the shock waves from the terrible earthquake on the island which almost destroyed Messina. On June 24 1911 she carried P&O guests to the Coronation Review at Spithead, and she took her place in line 'H' opposite Ryde Pier. The King aboard *Victoria & Albert* inspected the fleet between 2.30 pm and 4.15 pm that day. For the next five years *Mooltan*'s career was without incident, and when war came in August 1914 she was at Tilbury and about to embark passengers for Australia. She left on schedule on August 7, calling at Marseilles a week later. Among her passengers were Lord Kitchener and 45 of his staff who were on their way to Port Said on the first stage of a journey to Russia, where he was to consult with his opposite numbers in that country.

Mooltan continued in P&O's passenger service to Australia, and she made one more sailing in 1914, on November 28. She made three voyages to Sydney in 1915, and the same during 1916. It was whilst she was on her first voyage of that year, in February 1916 while crossing the Bay of Biscay, that she encountered two very suspicious vessels which were almost certainly enemy raiders. Although they were never identified, *Mooltan* was able to outdistance them with her superior speed. In 1917 *Mooltan* made only two sailings from London to Australia, and the second voyage was never completed.

On July 25 1917 *Mooltan* left Malta at 5.00 pm, with the French Messageries Maritimes steamer *Lotus*, and with an escort of two Japanese destroyers the *Ume* and *Kusynoki*. She was homeward bound with mails from

Mooltan *at speed* (P&O).

Australia, and there were 554 passengers and crew on board. The call at Malta was unscheduled and was the result of a naval signal, the four ships being bound for Marseilles. At 7.15 pm the next day, July 26, when the ship was 100 miles south of Sardinia, a torpedo was sighted by lookouts about 800 yards away on the starboard beam. The alarm was sounded, and the helm put hard a starboard, in an effort to comb its tracks. But it was too late, and the torpedo struck the ship a glancing blow on the starboard side about 35 ft abaft the stem, and 15 ft below the water line. The resulting explosion threw up a huge column of green flame, and tore a large hole in the hold. Distress signals were sent out and the engines put into reverse bringing the ship to a standstill. The boats were lowered and all the passengers and some of the crew got away.

The destroyers reacted quickly; one endeavoured to locate and attack the submarine, which was in fact *U-C27*, while the other circled the stricken *Mooltan*. On inspection it was found that the forward part was flooded, and she appeared to be settling by the head. There was no hope of *Mooltan* keeping afloat long, and the commander of the convoy ordered the ship to be abandoned quickly. By 8.15 pm that evening all the survivors were aboard the destroyers, and later some were transferred to the *Lotus* to equalise numbers in each vessel. The next day was an anxious one as the reduced convoy passed through dangerous waters, but they arrived safely in Marseilles at 1.00 am on July 28 1914. Only one member of *Mooltan*'s crew had been killed and P&O agents took care of all the survivors when they landed. The passengers left the port some 12 hours after their arrival on a train for London, along with the special mails which had been rescued.

Mooltan sank at about 10.15 pm on July 26 1917, having been hit by a second torpedo.

Technical data

Gross tonnage: 9.621
Net tonnage: 4,828
Length overall: 520 ft 3 in (158.61 m)
Breadth: 58 ft 4 in (17.78 m)
Depth: 33 ft 3 in (10.13 m)
Cargo capacity: No figures available
Boilers: Coal-fired, four double-ended and two single-ended boilers, 215 psi
Main engines: Twin screw, two sets quadruple-expansion reciprocating engines, 13,000 IHP, 18 knots
Ship's company: 370
Passengers: First class 348, Second class 166

Salsette 1908

In 1908 the P&O Company took possession of one of the most interesting little steamers included in the large building programme which they had in hand. She was the 5,842 gross ton *Salsette*, and many people considered that she was one of the most beautiful ships the company had ever owned. She was designed for the express mail and passenger shuttle which linked Bombay and Aden, connecting with the Australian mail steamers which called at Aden every other week. P&O had taken into account their experience with the smaller steamers *Isis* and *Osiris* which ran a similar express service between Brindisi, Alexandria and Port Said. *Salsette*'s name was taken from an island off Bombay harbour. She was indeed a fine looking vessel, with two yellow funnels and two masts in perfect proportion and reputedly not a single parallel line in her white-painted yacht-like hull. She had accommodation for 100 first and 120 second class passengers but very little cargo capacity as she was essentially a passenger and mail ship.

Salsette was ordered in June 1907 from Cairds of Greenock and she was launched at 12.30 pm on Thursday April 2 1908. Unfortunately the event was overshadowed by a tragic accident in the afternoon before the launch, when a carpenter who was working on the shade deck above the flying bridge overbalanced and fell 70 ft to his death in the yard below. However, the launch went without a hitch as the ship took to the water in fine style and was towed to Scotts' basin for fitting out. After completing her trials on July 2 1908 she was delivered to P&O and she made an initial cruise, with invited guests, to the Bay of Biscay and then to Tilbury. She had cost P&O £210,689 to build.

Before she left Europe for the waters east of Suez, *Salsette* made two cruises from Tilbury. The first was on August 8 1908 to the northern capitals calling at Amsterdam, Christiania, Copenhagen, Kronstadte and Kiel, returning to London just over three weeks later on August 31. The second cruise was for a month, and was advertised as a Dalmatian Cruise. She left London on September 9 that year and called at Gibraltar, Algiers, Corfu, Venice and Sicily. Fares for both cruises started at 35 guineas. The second cruise terminated at Marseilles, and five days later on October 14 she sailed for Bombay. Although there was a slight delay at Suez, she made a record run between Marseilles and Bombay arriving late on October 25, having completed the journey in the record time of 11 days, 21 hours.

Despite her speed and although she was otherwise a reliable ship, *Salsette* was a poor sea boat and tended to roll heavily. During most of her career she carried a large golden cock at her masthead to signify the fact that she was the fastest ship in the fleet. It was obviously well deserved because in 1910 she averaged 18.3 knots across the Indian Ocean between Aden and Bombay, with a time of three days, 19 hours, seven minutes. Many people attributed this to the skills of her Chief Engineer 'Pater' Sinclair who, it was said, could make her do everything but sing.

For six years between 1908 and 1914 she ran an uninterrupted service on the Aden to Bombay shuttle. In Aden when she rendezvoused with the Australia mail steamer it became a matter of pride to load the mails and embark passengers and to sail the moment the last mail-bag was on board. When war came in August 1914 she was between Aden and Bombay, and

Left Salsette *undergoing her trials* (P&O).

the declaration had no immediate effect on her. It was late 1915 before the war disrupted her normal routine and on November 6 1915 she made her first sailing from London to Bombay. Thereafter she took her place on the Indian or Australian mail routes, and it was shortly after she left London bound for Sydney that *Salsette* met her end.

She sailed from London on July 19 1917, bound for Bombay and Sydney, carrying on board a large consignment of money to pay the British garrison in Egypt, as well as passengers. She embarked the Channel pilot at 7.00 pm and got under way once again at 10.30 pm. She passed the Shambles lightship without incident and exchanged signals with a patrol ship. At noon the next day, when she was 15½ miles south-west of Portland Bill she was hit in the starboard side by a torpedo. The Chief Officer had seen the track and shouted a warning, but it was too late. Her Master, who had rushed out of the chart room, heard the explosion and saw boats on the starboard side disintegrate, as a large volume of water crashed down onto the hurricane deck. The engines were stopped, and the order given to abandon ship.

At this stage of the war emergency drills were practised early in the voyage and it was to pay off, for in five minutes all the undamaged boats were away. Number three boat, in the charge of the Second Officer, stood by the doomed *Salsette* for her commander and the handful of men left on board. All the confidential books and codes were dumped in weighted bags, and after ensuring that everyone was away, the commander and his officers left the ship. Just before 1.00 pm, about 50 minutes after she had been hit, *Salsette* sank. 15 members of her crew, 14 of them from the engine room, lost their lives. By then destroyers and other craft were on the scene and the survivors were soon landed at Weymouth. At 6.00 am the next day, July 21 1917, the following telegram was received at the P&O offices

At anchor east of Suez, the golden cock mascot can be seen at her masthead (P&O).

in Leadenhall Street. 'Confidential. Your *Salsette* sunk by submarine in Channel today. Armed trawler reports she has 300 survivors on board. Admiralty.'

Technical data
Gross tonnage: 5,842
Net tonnage: 2,392
Length overall: 440 ft (134.11 m)
Breadth: 53 ft 2 in (16.21 m)
Depth: 28 ft (8.53m)
Cargo capacity: No figures available
Boilers: Coal-fired, four double-ended and two single-ended boilers, 215 psi
Main engines: Twin screw, two sets quadruple-expansion reciprocating engines, 10,000 IHP, 20 knots
Ship's company: No figures available
Passengers: First class 100, Second class 120

Morea 1908

Of the 'M' Class ships built for the P&O Company before the First World War, the 10,890 gross ton *Morea* was generally considered to be the best looking. She could be described as a 'mark three' version of this popular class, and she was built by the Glasgow company Barclay Curle & Co of Whiteinch at a cost of £309,692. It was a credit to the Clyde shipbuilders of those days that the construction of the vessel, from the laying of the keel to her trials on the Clyde, took exactly one year. The keel was laid on November 5 1907, and she was launched just over nine months later on Saturday August 15 1908. The naming ceremony was performed by Mrs Russell Ferguson, wife of the Managing Director of Barclay Curle & Co, and the owners were represented by Mr H.J. Taylor.

It took only 12 weeks to complete her elaborate fittings, and on Tuesday November 3 1908 she began her trials on the Clyde. Sir Thomas Sutherland was on board when she ran a series of speed trials on the Skelmorlie measured mile. During the trials she attained a speed of over 18 knots and on their successful completion the following day, Sir Thomas formally took over the ship on behalf of the P&O Company, and personally broke out the company houseflag at her masthead. After this brief ceremony he had to leave for London, and so a luncheon party on board the next day was presided over by Mr James Gilchrist, the chairman of Barclay Curle & Co, the toast being 'Success to the *Morea*'.

Like the other 'M' Class ships *Morea* had five passenger decks; the boat deck, promenade deck, hurricane deck, spar deck and main deck. The 407 first class passengers were berthed amidships, their cabins being on the promenade, hurricane, spar and main decks. The 200 second class passengers were accommodated aft, most of their cabins being on the main deck. Public rooms for both classes were on the hurricane deck, the first class lounge and music room being right forward, and the first class smoke room being further aft. The second class music room and smoke room were aft of this. Dining saloons for both classes were on the spar deck and separated by the galley and kitchens. The first class saloon was amidships and its main feature was the large open well overhead, which extended through three decks to a large dome of stained glass on the boat deck. *Morea*, like other ships of her era, was coal fired, and powered by two sets of quadruple-expansion reciprocating engines, developing 13,000 IHP

Morea left the Clyde for London on the morning of Friday November 6 1908 and arrived in Tilbury four days later. On Saturday November 21 an open day was held, with the vessel being opened to the public with tickets at one shilling each. All the funds taken were in fact for the benefit of the Passmore-Edwards Cottage Hospital at Tilbury. *Morea* left for her maiden voyage to Australia via Marseilles, Suez and Colombo on Friday December 4 1908. She then had a routine and uneventful few years of service but, although she handled beautifully, she suffered in the early days from excessive creaking and groaning. It took repeated changes of her propellers to remedy the problem, and eventually she became the quietest ship of the class. In 1909 she was fitted with the new 'Marconi system of wireless telegraphy' and in 1911 her route was extended to Auckland. In September 1911 whilst on passage from Ushant to Plymouth, *Morea* came upon the 1,300 ton Ellerman steamer *Perim* lying disabled, her machinery having broken down. The vessel was seaworthy, but her Captain wished to be taken in tow. As *Morea* was preparing to do this the steamer *San Remo* arrived on the scene and offered to take over. So *Morea* was able to continue her voyage to Plymouth and on to Tilbury.

Morea made her last pre-war sailing from London on July 10 1914. At that time, although events at Sarajevo had taken place two weeks previously, there were no thoughts or serious rumours of war. She called at Gibraltar and Marseilles, and by July 23 she had cleared the Suez Canal. Events then moved quickly and three days after she left Colombo for Fremantle war was declared. Those on board heard the news in a radio message received from the Cocos Islands. It made little difference to the ships already at sea, other than cause some excitement among passengers and crew and *Morea* continued her voyage to Sydney fully illuminated. She arrived in the port on August 22 and sailed once again for London on September 7 1914.

Meanwhile in the Indian Ocean, the German light cruiser *Emden*, commanded by the resourceful Captain Karl von Müller, had begun a cruise creating havoc among British shipping there. The *Emden* had left the isolated German base at Tsingtao on August 7 1914. After coaling in the Mariana Islands in the Pacific, she sailed through the Molucca Passage arriving in the Indian Ocean south of Java on August 28. She then embarked on a 70-day cruise during which she captured 23 British vessels and bombarded British ports. On September 10 1914, three days after *Morea* left Sydney for London, *Emden* entered the Bay of Bengal to continue her highly publicised marauding career. Fortunately *Morea* avoided the German ship, and on her arrival in Colombo she was ordered to Bombay to pick up the mails and passengers. The news and rumours about the *Emden* were rife, and at Bombay the Lascar deck crew refused to proceed any further. None of the Lascars ashore could be induced to sign on for the passage to London and so a company of Royal Engineers who had embarked at Colombo were asked to take the seamen's place. An agreement was reached between Captain J.D. Andrews of *Morea*, and the officer commanding the engineers, and soon the sappers were proficient at mooring and unmooring the ship. Groups of passengers turned out at 6.00 am every morning to hose and scrub down the decks and they included several professors who were taking passage at the time. Apparently even the cold mornings of the English Channel did not dampen the enthusiasm of the volunteers and the decks were kept spotless. When the passengers disembarked at Tilbury they received a rousing send-off from *Morea*'s crew.

Morea sailed once again from London for Australia on October 31 1914, and by the time she reached Bombay the menace of the *Emden* was no more, for she had been destroyed by the Australian cruiser HMAS *Sydney* on November 9 in the vicinity of the Cocos Islands. This was *Morea*'s last sailing from London in 1914. In 1915 she made three voyages to Australia, on February 20, May 29 and October 2. After the completion of the last voyage she was requisitioned as an ambulance and troop transport, during which service she carried men of the Australian Expeditionary Force to Europe.

She was released back into P&O service in March 1916, and on March 31 that year she sailed once more for Australia. She made two further sailings during 1916, on August 18 and December 8. But on May 19 1917 the Director of Naval Sea Transport wrote to P&O informing them that *Morea* was once more to be requisitioned, this time as an armed merchant cruiser. It is interesting to note the net rate of hire paid by the government; 21 shillings per gross ton for the first three months, 20 shillings for the following nine months, and 14 shillings for each month there after. The cost of the first three months' hire of *Morea* amounted to £114,345. She was commissioned as an AMC at the Royal Albert Dock on July 5 1917, and she sailed for Plymouth 16 days later on July 21. Her duties from then until the end of the war were solely as a convoy escort. During the remainder of 1917 she escorted nine convoys between Devonport and West Africa, the only untoward incident being a fire in the Captain's cabin on October 13 when she was two days out of Plymouth Sound bound for Freetown. The start of 1918 saw her in Freetown once again, and on January 8 she sailed with a convoy for Devonport. Two weeks later on January 22, just outside Plymouth, lookouts sighted a torpedo and after evasive action she managed to avoid it. In March 1918 she went into refit at Devonport Dockyard, but she was back in service by

April 17, when she left for Dakar with a convoy. She arrived there on April 26 and left four days later as escort to a convoy bound for Rio de Janeiro. She arrived in Rio on May 14 where she was visited by a US Navy Admiral. Her stay in the port lasted until the end of that month, and it must have been *Morea*'s only visit to the continent of America.

She escorted her last convoy from Dakar on September 14 1918 arriving in Devonport at the end of the month. She then went into drydock at the naval dockyard, and she was still there when the First World War ended on November 11 1918. Like other ships requisitioned by the government she needed extensive re-conditioning before she could take her place once again on the passenger services. She left Devonport on December 2 1918 bound for London. She remained berthed at Purfleet until it could be decided where the work could be carried out. It was finally decided to send her to the Clyde and she sailed on December 28 1918 to arrive in Greenock two days later. Work on the ship was badly delayed by industrial troubles, the longest hold up being caused by a joiners' strike. This refit was the responsibility of the Admiralty and the lack of progress with the work was summed up in a notice which some wag put at the foot of her gangway. In neatly painted letters it said, 'HMS *Neversail*. Come on board and draw your pay.' In a more sober vein, when one looks at the state of British shipbuilding today it is a serious indictment. Eventually the government got tired of waiting for the vessel to be completed, and she was handed back to the P&O Line with a lump sum for the company to carry out the necessary work. P&O immediately moved *Morea* to Avonmouth where she was quickly restored to her former luxury and she made her first post-war sailing from London to Sydney on October 18 1919. It was the company's first post-war passenger voyage on its own account.

Morea made her first sailing of 1920 on February 20 to Sydney, with her second sailing on April 24 from Marseilles to Bombay. She made two more voyages that year, one to Australia and one to Bombay. In 1921 she started the year with a trip to Sydney, and spent the rest of the year on the Bombay route. In December 1922 she made her first voyage to the Far East and Japan; like the other 'M' Class ships she was to sail on the secondary service more and more as the years went by. She made her last sailing on May 16 1930, when she left London for Japan to be broken up. It was a normal passenger/cargo voyage, and she called at Marseilles, Suez, Aden, Bombay, Colombo, Penang and Singapore. She left Hong Kong on June 20 and Shanghai a week later. Her final destination was Kobe where she arrived on July 1 1930, to be handed over to Japanese shipbreakers.

Technical data

Gross tonnage: 10,890
Net tonnage: 5,965
Length overall: 562 ft (171.3 m)
Breadth: 61 ft 2 in (18.64 m)
Depth: 33 ft 3in (10.13m)
Cargo capacity: No figures available
Boilers: Coal-fired, four single-ended and four double-ended Scotch boilers, 215 psi
Main engines: Twin screw, two sets quadruple-expansion reciprocating engines, 13,000 IHP, 17 knots
Ship's company: 307
Passengers: First class 407, Second class 200

Above Morea *arrives at Tilbury, assisted by the tug* Sirdar, *a post-1914 view* (P&O).

Left *The classic lines of the 'M' Class are caught in this view of* Morea (P&O).

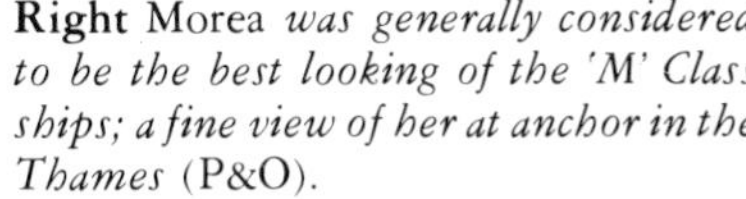

Right Morea *was generally considered to be the best looking of the 'M' Class ships; a fine view of her at anchor in the Thames* (P&O).

Malwa 1908

The seventh ship of the 'M' Class, *Malwa*, was like *Morea* another 'mark three' version of this famous class. Once again P&O went to Caird & Co of Greenock, who built the liner at a cost of £308,455, which was some £27,723 less than it had cost to build *Moldavia* five years earlier. *Malwa* was a ship of 10,883 grt and was originally to have been named *Medina*, until the company learned that this name would be objected to on grounds of duplication and it was in fact another three years before the name could be used. This was the second *Malwa*, the first being a 2,933 ton vessel which entered service in 1873. She had a career of 11 years with P&O, and is probably best remembered as the ship which brought home the body of the explorer David Livingstone.

The new *Malwa* was launched at 11.45 am on Saturday October 10 1908 and it was a rather low key affair with no invitations being issued. Nevertheless, by early morning people from all over the shipbuilding town of Greenock had taken up positions on the Steamboat Quay, West Harbour, and Princess Pier in order to get a view of her as she entered the water. The naming ceremony was gracefully performed by Miss Constance M.J. Caird, youngest daughter of Mr Patrick Caird. The launch went without a hitch, and shortly afterwards four tugs towed her to Scotts' fitting out basin where her engines and machinery were to be installed.

Once again the architectural supervision of the building was carried out by Mr T.E. Colcutt, and perhaps *Malwa* will be best remembered for her first class music saloon with its four panel paintings by Professor Moira. The two larger paintings represented Eastern and Western dancing, and the smaller pair represented Oriental and Occidental music. Another idea which reflected the changing times was that the music saloon was to be available for passengers of both sexes and smoking would be permitted.

By December 19 that year *Malwa* was ready to undertake her trials and, these having been completed successfully, she sailed for Tilbury Dock. She was due to sail on her maiden voyage to Australia on January 29 1909 and two days before this the Chairman and Directors of the P&O company gave a luncheon on board. There were some 300 guests, and Sir Thomas Sutherland presided. It is interesting to note that one of the most prominent guests was Sir James Lyle MacKay, Chairman of the British India shipping company. It was another five years before the two great shipping giants, the P&O and BI companies merged, and Sir James, by then Lord Inchcape, would succeed Sir Thomas Sutherland as the Chairman of the P&O. Even five years before the merger the two great companies had many common interests.

After returning from her maiden voyage *Malwa* made a series of pleasure cruises from Tilbury in conjunction with the company's *Vectis*. The first cruise took her to the Atlantic Isles and the second to the fjords; it was the third cruise during August that year which was most interesting. She sailed on a northern capitals cruise from August 7 to August 30, which took her through the Baltic to the Gulf of Finland and the Russian port of Krondstadt near Leningrad (then called St Petersburg). While she was there a party of Russian naval officers were entertained on board. It is difficult to imagine any present day Soviet naval officers in a similar situation! In September 1909 she resumed her voyages to Australia, then in February 1910 she became the first P&O liner to visit New Zealand, with Lord Kitchener among her passengers. On February 17 she left Auckland for the return voyage with over 100 passengers bound for Australia and England. On July 7 1910, when she was 23 miles out from Colombo en-route for London, *Malwa* was in collision with the 3,627 ton cargo ship SS *Nairn* (Park Steamship Co). Fortunately there were no casualties on either ship and *Malwa* was only slightly damaged, but seven days later the *Nairn* limped into Calcutta with her bows stove in, stem smashed and plates severely damaged. *Malwa*'s next voyage to Australia was on August 26 1910 and she left on schedule from Tilbury.

At the outbreak of the First World War on August 4 1914 *Malwa* was in Adelaide in the final stages of a voyage to Sydney. For the first three years of the war she continued in P&O service, on a much reduced fortnightly mail service to India and Australia. During these years very little was done to gear the shipping industry to wartime conditions, and vessels sailed independently with little or no protection other than their own speed and manoeuvrability. *Malwa* was lucky and she came through without incident. However, in early 1917 she was requisitioned by the government for use as a troop transport, and during that year she had two lucky escapes from submarines.

The first occasion was at 6.45 am on May 12 1917 when *Malwa* was sailing in convoy and a torpedo fired by a U-boat passed close under her stern, missing the rudder by about three feet. Unfortunately a second torpedo from the same submarine sank another ship of the convoy. Later that year on November 30 when *Malwa* was in the Irish Sea, the lookouts sighted the conning tower of a submarine on the port beam. *Malwa* was manoeuvred to bring it astern, and the escort attacked with depth charges. By then the submarine had submerged and it was not known if the attack was successful. A few minutes later *Malwa* collided with what was described by the forward lookout as a 'long dark object'. It seemed that there had been two submarines in company, and that *Malwa* had collided with, and presumably sunk the second of them. As the damage to *Malwa* was not too serious her commander dispersed the crew from boat stations and she continued the voyage.

Most of *Malwa*'s service as a troopship was on

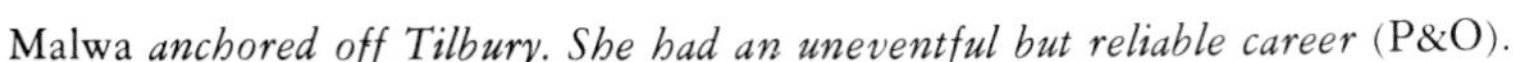

Malwa *anchored off Tilbury. She had an uneventful but reliable career* (P&O).

Mediterranean convoys, and in the latter part of the war this was extended to Istanbul (Constantinople). On September 22 1918, while she was on this service in the Mediterranean, her lookouts spotted the wake of a torpedo, and on receiving the warning, her commander turned the ship to comb its track; with the torpedo running parallel, it glanced off the ship's hull and failed to explode. It was indeed an extremely skillful escape and was P&O's last encounter with the enemy during the war.

When the war ended *Malwa* was released from government service almost immediately and after a thorough refit she returned to P&O service, making her first post-war sailing to India and Australia on September 24 1920. She was one of only four of the 'M' Class ships to survive the war and it soon became clear that she had retained all of her pre-war popularity. For a short time the P&O could only provide a rather patchy service to Australia, but in 1921 with new tonnage coming into service the route was restored to its pre-war normality and *Malwa* was used more and more on the Far East voyages to Shanghai and Japan. In 1926 she called at Southampton to embark passengers, being the first P&O vessel to make a scheduled stop at the port for 40 years. Two years later in 1928 she brought home General Duncan, the 'C-in-C' of the Sanghai Defence Force with his staff. By early 1932 she was 23 years old and in the spring of that year she was sold to Japanese shipbreakers. However, with rumours that tariffs were to be imposed on second-hand ships imported into Japan, delivery was delayed until later that year.

On October 21 1932 *Malwa* left Tilbury on her final voyage which was to take her to the breakers' yards. It was a normal sailing and her passenger lists and cargo holds were full as she left England for the last time. Her voyage was terminated at Kobe, and on December 16 that year she was handed over to the shipbreakers. She had made very little news during her 24 year career, but she had served the company well.

Technical data
Gross tonnage: 10,883
Net tonnage: 5,900
Length overall: 540 ft (164.59 m)
Breadth: 61 ft 2 in (18.64 m)
Depth: 33 ft 3 in (10.13 m)
Cargo capacity: No figures available
Boilers: Coal-fired, four double-ended and four single-ended boilers, 215 psi
Main engines: Twin screw, two sets compound quadruple-expansion reciprocating engines, 15,000 IHP, 17-18 knots
Ship's company: 370
Passengers: First class 400, Second class 200

Malwa *after she was released by the government in 1918* (P&O).

Mantua 1909

On February 20 1909, as *Malwa* was on her maiden voyage, the eighth ship of the 'M' Class was launched at Caird's yard in Greenock. The naming ceremony for the *Mantua* was performed by Miss Bessie Caird, and once again a noon launch took place. When *Mantua* took to the water she left Caird's yards vacant and with no new orders in sight it was thought they might have to close down for a few months, but fortunately this was not necessary. Two months later on April 20 *Mantua* was ready to undertake her trials, having been registered at Greenock five days earlier. She had cost £308,053 to build and was the first P&O liner to have radio equipment fitted when she was built.

As she left the James Watt Dock for an anchorage at the Tail of the Bank prior to running over the measured mile, she was involved in an incident which nearly ended in tragedy. Standing by the great new ship was a small boat with two of Caird's employees ready to pick up a hawser. As the *Mantua* was moved, the small boat appeared to be drawn into her propellers. One of the men panicked and jumped into the water intending to swim away, but in fact he was drawn towards the propellers. A lifebelt from *Mantua* was thrown which he managed to grab, and another small boat then rescued him—none the worse for his immersion.

Mantua arrived in Tilbury from the Clyde on May 8 1909 and on June 4 left for her maiden voyage to Australia. In November 1909 it was announced that in the spring and summer of 1910 she would make a series of four cruises from Tilbury. The first of these was to Lisbon, Tangier, Gibraltar and the Atlantic Isles of Madeira and the Azores, arriving back in London on June 13. The minimum fare for the cruise was 20 guineas. The other three cruises were to the Norwegian fjords and the northern capitals, completing the series on August 29. These summer cruises became an annual event, and it was while she was on a fjords cruise in late July 1914 that her commander was warned of the imminence of war. *Mantua* was in Christiania (now Oslo) when Austria declared war on Serbia and the complicated series of alliances which eventually involved all the great European powers was set in motion. There was a danger that if *Mantua* stayed to complete her cruise she would be trapped in the Skagerrak by the German High Seas Fleet. So a signal was sent urgently recalling her to London where she arrived on August 4 1914, just in time for the declaration of war and to be requisitioned by the Admiralty for service as an armed merchant cruiser with the Royal Navy.

The conversion was completed in nine days, and armed with eight elderly 4.7-in guns she was commissioned under Captain C. Tibbits RN, with her P&O commander Captain F.W. Vibert as his First Lieutenant. Her first duty took her to Archangel on a special mission with the armoured cruiser HMS *Drake*. In March 1915, she joined the Northern Patrol of the 10th Cruiser Squadron and was mainly employed on the patrol line between the Faroes and Iceland. In June that year she intercepted the 10,000 ton Norwegian-America liner *Kristianiafjord*, with 544 passengers on board and despite strong protests from her Captain the Norwegian liner was sent into Stornaway under armed guard. Three months later when *Mantua* was again on patrol she stopped the Swedish ship SS *Avesta*. After an armed guard had been put on board to take her into

Kirkwall, *Mantua* resumed her patrol. A few days later, early in the morning of October 1, a U-boat was sighted on the port bow. The submarine signalled the *Avesta* to stop immediately, and although the armed guard had hidden themselves and the Swedish Captain was prepared to co-operate with the British seamen, there was a German crew member on the ship and a thorough search by the U-boat Captain was likely to result in the capture of the *Mantua*'s men. The situation was becoming very tense as the U boat approached, when smoke appeared to the east. Obviously fearing this was a unit of the 10th Cruiser Squadron, the U-boat steered away to the north-west. 18 hours later *Avesta* arrived in Kirkwall, and *Mantua*'s guard was safe.

It was September 9 1916 when *Mantua* arrived alongside Meadowside Quay in Glasgow, after her final patrol in northern waters. The rest of that month was spent in drydock. On October 19 as she left for Belfast to pay off and to complete her refit, she was involved in a collision with another vessel which resulted in some damage to her port side. However, the following day she arrived at Harland & Wolff's yards at Belfast where she was to remain for five months.

On March 15 1917 she left Belfast for Devonport. She was to spend the rest of the war escorting convoys between that port and the continent of Africa, with just one from South America in 1918.Her hull had been dazzle painted in order to make her less visible at a distance, and to disguise her as a warship. She was one of the first armed merchant cruisers to be painted this way, and it became clear in October 1917 that it was unfortunately only too successful. *Mantua* had left Devonport on October 2 escorting a convoy bound for Dakar. Four days later at 8.20 am on October 6, when she was off the coast of Portugal, a large grey-hulled, three-masted sailing barque was sighted on the port bow. Although there were no guns visible, she was fitted with radio aerials, and *Mantua*'s Captain suspected she might be a German raider working in conjunction with U-boats. In fact she was the French barque *Quilotta* of Dunkirk, and her Captain suspected that *Mantua* was a German raider. It must be remembered that although the German fleet had been cleared from the seas, there was believed to be at least one German raider in the Atlantic working with U-boats. *Mantua*'s main concern was the safety of her convoy, and at 9.20 am she hoisted the international signal EC—'what ship is that'. This signal was ignored and at 10.10 am *Mantua* fired a warning shot to attract attention to the signal. The sailing vessel immediately opened fire from two guns and shortly afterwards hoisted the French ensign. In the exchange of fire between the two ships *Mantua* was hit amidships and four men were wounded, but at 11.12 am the heavier armament of the armed merchant cruiser began to tell and a big explosion was seen in the fore part of the sailing ship and the French ensign came down.

Mantua ceased fire, but a few minutes later two more explosions on the sailing ship were mistaken for more shots being fired at *Mantua* which then recommenced heavy fire with all her guns. At 11.45 am the sailing ship was blazing fiercely and listing heavily to starboard, and ten minutes later she sank. *Mantua* then steamed through the wreckage to search for survivors. At first it seemed there would not be any, but fortunately one of her officers spotted a boat load of 29 crewmen some distance away who were picked up at 12.45 am. It was then discovered what a tragic mistake had been made. A subsequent court of enquiry placed the blame equally with both ships, but it is difficult not to sympathise with *Mantua*'s Captain faced with such a dilemma. His two concerns were the safety of the convoy and of his own ship. His signals went unanswered and the *Quilotta* had opened fire after the warning shot. Had he failed to reply to her fire while endeavouring to obtain assurance of her nationality, she could certainly have disabled his ship; if she had indeed been a raider he may well have even lost his ship and some of those in the convoy. One must also admire the bravery of the French Captain who withstood the heavy fire of the armed merchant cruiser for nearly an hour. Five days later *Mantua* arrived safely in Dakar with her convoy, and disembarked the survivors of the unfortunate *Quilotta*.

After one more round voyage to Freetown as convoy escort, *Mantua* docked in Liverpool on Boxing Day 1917. Then on New Years Day 1918 she went into drydock at Birkenhead, and was there for the rest of the month. When she sailed again in February she was bound once more for West Africa, and convoy escort duties. On most of her return voyages from Freetown to the UK she carried cargoes of gold bullion. In May that year she also made a round trip to Rio de Janeiro as part of a convoy escort. She made her final wartime sailing from Devonport on November 9 1918, two days before the armistice. Six days later she arrived in Gibraltar where she embarked the survivors of the battleship HMS *Britannia*, which had been torpedoed by a U-boat off Cape Trafalgar on the same day that *Mantua* had sailed. She arrived back in Devonport for the last time on November 20, and ten days later she sailed for Gravesend where she remained for the next month. At 11.39 am on January 3 1919, she left on her final voyage under the white ensign bound for Vickers Armstrong's shipyards at Barrow-in-Furness where she was to be reconditioned as a passenger liner. She tied up alongside the quay at Barrow at 3.38 pm on January 5 and on the 21st of that month the white ensign lowered for the last time, she was handed back to her owners.

On January 3 1920 she made her first sailing to Australia, via Bombay and Colombo. She made seven round voyages to Australia before being transferred to the Far East route to Shanghai and Japan. During one of these voyages in late 1924 her Captain died while the ship was at Port Said, on the outward leg of the journey. As it happened another P&O Captain was on the passenger list going east, so he was appointed to the command and brought the ship home in January 1925.

By 1935 *Mantua* was 26 years old and she was outdated technically. New tonnage had been introduced on the Far East route and although *Mantua* was in excellent condition and fit for many more years of service, it was the policy of P&O to sell for breaking up when a ship was falling below the speed and other standards required. On August 9 1935, commanded by Captain Jack Legg and with a full passenger list, she sailed from Tilbury for the last time. This time her voyage was to terminate at Shanghai, for in July she had been sold to shipbreakers in that city for £32,000. It was a condition of the sale that she was not to be re-sold or employed but was to be broken up. She could have raised a higher price had she been sold for further employment, but it was not in P&O's or the nation's interests to encourage cheap foreign competition against British shipping. She arrived at Port Said on August 21, and at Penang on September 5, before reaching her final destination, Shanghai, on September 15 1935. Six days later, on September 21, she was handed over to the shipbreakers. She was the last survivor of a bygone era, and of one of P&O's most famous class of mail liners.

The last survivor of a bygone era, the Mantua *of 1908* (P&O).

A familiar sight before the Tilbury Landing Stage was opened, Mantua *anchored off Gravesend* (P&O).

Technical data

Gross tonnage: 10,946
Net tonnage: 5,980
Length overall: 540 ft (164.59 m)
Breadth: 61 ft 2 in (18.64 m)
Depth: 33 ft 3 in (10.13 m)
Cargo capacity: No figures available
Boilers: Coal-fired, four double-ended and four single-ended boilers, 215 psi
Main engines: Twin screw, two sets compound quadruple-expansion reciprocating engines, 15,000 IHP, 18 knots
Ship's company: 375
Passengers: First class 400, Second class 200

Maloja 1911

In 1909 P&O placed orders for the final two ships of the 'M' Class; they were to be 12,000 tonners and would represent the ultimate in the development of the class. They were to be named *Maloja* and *Medina* respectively, but unfortunately their careers were all too brief. The contract for the first of them the *Maloja*, was won by Harland & Wolff of Belfast and she was built by them at a cost of £328,202. She was launched on Saturday December 17 1910 and she was peculiar among P&O ships in having a Swiss name, taken from the town of Maloggia near St Moritz. Accommodation was provided for 450 first class and 220 second class passengers. Her quadruple-expansion engines gave her a maximum speed of 19 knots, and she could hold $17\frac{1}{4}$ for long periods. Her first class dining saloon, on the spar deck, stretched the full width of the ship and was decorated in English oak to contrast with the smoking room, which was in Austrian oak. She had a substantial refrigerated cargo capacity because she was, like the other ships of the class, designed for the service to Australia. She was delivered to P&O on August 15 1911, but it was to be another six months before she sailed on her intended route. Her maiden voyage was a 19-day cruise to Tenerife, Madeira and Lisbon, with fares starting at 16 guineas.

In April 1911, while *Maloja* was fitting out at Belfast, it was announced that her sister *Medina* would carry King George V and Queen Mary to India. Soon after this P&O announced that *Maloja* would make a special visit to India carrying distinguished guests and passengers for the Delhi Durbar in late 1911. Fares for the return voyage to Bombay had been advertised from 75 to 120 guineas, and initially a good proportion of her berths had been booked. She arrived back in London from her maiden voyage on October 12 to prepare for her sailing to India. However, as the sailing day got closer the hotel accommodation charges in Delhi were announced, and they were so exorbitant that many intending passengers cancelled their bookings.

Maloja sailed from Tilbury on November 7 1911, four days before *Medina* left Portsmouth with the King and Queen. At 8.00 am on November 11 she passed Gibraltar, arriving at Marseilles two days later where the overland passengers joined her. By 8.00 pm on November 19 she had cleared the Suez Canal, and after one more stop at Aden she arrived in Bombay at 7.00 am on November 28, four days before *Medina*. A month later, on December 29 she left Bombay for Tilbury on the return voyage, calling at Aden, Port Said, Marseilles, Gibraltar and Plymouth, arriving back in London on Saturday January 20 1912. It had been a voyage which had been given plenty of publicity but commercially it was a failure. The large numbers of cancellations had effectively destroyed any profits that might have been made.

It was February 9 1912 before *Maloja* left London for her first voyage to Australia, calling at Marseilles a week later. Like the other ships of her class she received a great welcome on her arrival in Sydney, and over the next two years she became popular with many travellers to that continent. She made her last peacetime sailing from Tilbury on June 24 1914 and when war was declared in August she had just left Brindisi in Southern Italy bound for Suez, then on to India and Australia. She arrived back in London in late October 1914, and it soon became clear that she was to stay on P&O's reduced passenger service. She made her next sailing from London to Australia on November 14 1914. The voyage was advertised in the press, just as before the war, and *Maloja* sailed alone. But then these were the early days before the Germans unleashed their unrestricted submarine warfare on Allied shipping. For 18 months after war broke out she continued to sail on her passenger and cargo voyages for P&O, and perhaps the only indication of anything unusual was her defensive armament, and the fact that more and more of her passengers were on government service.

Maloja made her last sailing from London on Saturday February 26 1916, commanded by Captain C.E. Irving RNR. She had 121 passengers aboard, which included 40 women and 18 children, as well as 335 crew members. She was carrying mail for Egypt, and destinations east of Suez. Many more passengers and most of her letter mail were to be embarked at Marseilles, where she was due on March 3. By 10.30 am on Sunday February 27 *Maloja* was steaming down the Channel and was between Dover and Folkestone, two miles south-west of Dover Pier. As a safety precaution her boats had been swung out and were ready for lowering. All the passengers had been advised to carry their lifebelts, and there is no doubt that these two factors helped to save a lot of lives. Suddenly she hit a mine and there was a terrific explosion alongside the tourist saloon aft. Sadly some passengers, including children, were killed by this explosion and the ship herself was severely damaged. Captain Irving ordered the engines to be put full astern in an effort to take the way off the ship and passengers and crew were got into the lifeboats within minutes. But the engine room flooded rapidly and the engines could not be stopped, the boats could not be lowered safely and many were washed away as she moved astern at eight or ten knots with a 75 degree list. She foundered in about 20 minutes with the loss of 122 lives.

One passenger, Mrs L.E. Gregory of Lee Green, London recalled that she and another lady passenger were walking along the deck when the explosion occurred and the force of it threw them both down. Mrs Gregory was badly shaken, but managed to crawl to her saloon cabin and get a lifebelt. A friend seeing her in difficulty helped her to put it on, and there is no doubt that it saved her life because she could not swim. She and her friend climbed into a lifeboat, but it got so overcrowded that they decided to jump into the sea and take a chance. After about 15 minutes they were picked up, exhausted, by a rescue boat. Another passenger recalled that as the engines were put astern it soon became clear that they could not be stopped, and that Captain Irving then attempted to beach his ship, but she sank too quickly. He also spoke of the crew's admirable calmness and discipline, and thought that if the engines could have been stopped in time, then all those who survived the explosion would have been rescued.

Captain W.D. Shepherd of the Canadian cargo ship *Empress of Fort William*, which was bound for Dunkirk with a cargo of coal, described how he tried to reach the *Maloja* but failed, for his ship was also blown up by a mine. When off Dover he saw the liner well down by the stern, apparently trying to make for the shore. He gave orders to his engine room to give all possible speed and for the mate to get all the boats ready for the rescue of *Maloja*'s survivors. Captain Shepherd recalled seeing the liner with a severe list and almost lying on her side. Many people were actually standing on the side of the vessel, and the scene put him

in mind of those famous photographs which were taken of the German battleship *Blücher*, when she turned turtle and sank. Captain Shepherd was himself a keen amateur photographer and as his ship went to the rescue of *Maloja*'s passengers he took several photographs of the scene. He saw at least eight of the liner's boats which could not be launched owing to the list and one boat which was lying end on to the liner full of people with many others waiting to get in. Unfortunately his mercy dash was cut short because at this point his own ship struck a mine, and Captain Shepherd and his crew were fighting for their own lives as the *Empress of Fort William* sank rapidly. Happily Captain Shepherd and his crew were saved, but his historic photographs of the end of a great liner were lost.

Being so close to Dover the tragedy of the *Maloja* had been witnessed by many people in that port, and it was not long before a flotilla of small ships came to the rescue of the struggling survivors. Soon the Lord Warden hotel in Dover was filling up with passengers, who only hours before were looking forward to their voyage to India. The surviving crew members were mustered at the Sailors Home. The saddest scene was in Dover's Market Hall where the bodies of those drowned were laid out.

Captain Irving, who had only left the ship as she rolled over, and then spent nearly an hour in the water before being picked up, praised the efficiency of his crew and the calmness of his passengers. It was a tragic end to a fine ship. The wreck of the *Maloja* lay undisturbed for 48 years, but in 1964 it was considered to be a hazard to shipping and was blown up.

Technical data
Gross tonnage: 12,431
Net tonnage: 6,078
Length overall: 550 ft 5 in (167.79 m)
Breadth: 62 ft 9 in (19.17 m)
Depth: 34 ft 3 in (10.49 m)
Cargo capacity: No figures available
Boilers: Coal-fired, four double-ended and four single-ended boilers, 215 psi
Main engines: Twin screw, two sets compound quadruple expansion reciprocating engines, 15,000 IHP, 17¼ knots
Ship's company: 375
Passengers: First Class 450, Second Class 220

Left *Stern view of* Maloja *whilst under construction at Belfast. Her name was taken from the Swiss town of Maloggia* (Harland & Wolff).

Right *A first class single berth cabin,* Maloja *1911* (Harland & Wolff).

Left *A bow view of* Maloja *shortly before she was launched* (Harland & Wolff).

Above right *Almost completed, the first class dining saloon, the large open well can be seen in the centre of the room* (Harland & Wolff).

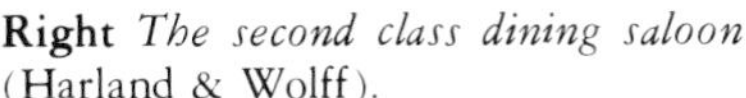

Right *The second class dining saloon* (Harland & Wolff).

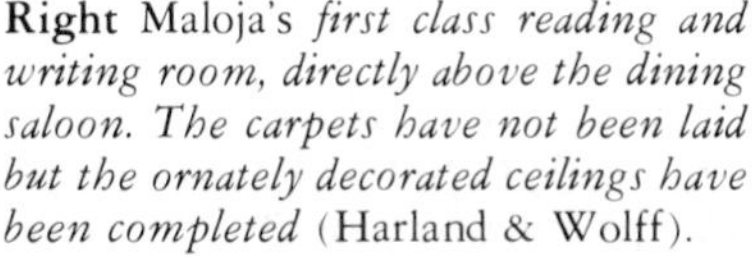

Right Maloja's *first class reading and writing room, directly above the dining saloon. The carpets have not been laid but the ornately decorated ceilings have been completed* (Harland & Wolff).

Above Maloja*'s second class library* (Harland & Wolff).

Below *The first class smoke room,* Maloja (Harland & Wolff).

Medina 1911

The last ship of the 'M' Class was the *Medina* and like her sister *Maloja* her career lasted less than ten years. She was built at a cost of £332,377 by Caird & Co of Greenock and was launched on Tuesday March 14 1911. The naming ceremony was performed by Lady Alice Shaw-Stewart, the daughter of the Marquis of Bath and the wife of Sir Hugh Shaw-Stewart, a local dignitary. This time the event was given plenty of publicity. In fact the *Daily Mirror* of March 16 ran a whole page of photographs of the launch and was the only national newspaper to announce that *Medina* had been chosen to convey King George V and Queen Mary on their voyage to India for the Delhi Durbar. This announcement was denied by both P&O officials and Mr Patrick Caird, who assured the *Mirror*'s reporter that his company would complete the *Medina* to P&O's specifications. Nevertheless, on April 26 that year it was confirmed that *Medina* would carry the King and Queen to India later in the year. Like the *Ophir* in the royal tour of 1901 she was to be commissioned into the Royal Navy and her crew would be mainly naval personnel.

As the *Medina* was being fitted out at Greenock, the arrangements for the royal journey were being made. In June 1911 it was announced that Rear Admiral Sir Colin R. Keppel would fly his flag in *Medina*, which would be commanded by Captain A.E.M. Chatfield RN (later Lord Chatfield). By September that year the ship was ready to sail for Southampton for the final fitting out of the royal suites. She was a handsome looking vessel painted in white livery with a double band of royal blue and gold, and buff funnels. As the King had a definite flag etiquette laid down for him whenever he went to sea, it was necessary to mount a third mast immediately in front of the fore funnel, and this extra mast was borrowed from the P&O steamer *Nankin*, which was under construction at Caird's yard.

On September 27 1911, *Medina* arrived in Southampton, where Sir Thomas Sutherland disembarked after travelling in her from Plymouth. Now the furnishing of the royal suites began. The largest of the royal apartments was the drawing room, which would normally have been the first class music saloon forward on the hurricane deck. The dominant colour theme in this room was light blue, the windows being curtained and the chairs and settees upholstered in silk of this shade, which went admirably with the light oak panelling. The carpet was of a simple trellis pattern in light shades of grey. A considerable quantity of the furniture was brought over from the Royal Yacht. Immediately below this room was the dining saloon, which was partly lit through an oval aperture in the deck of the drawing room. A long table ran down the centre of the room with three round tables on either side of it, and the carpet was a plain royal blue Wilton. Just forward of the dining room on the starboard side, were the Queen's private apartments consisting of sitting room, bedroom, dressing room, and bathroom. The four corresponding rooms on the port side were the King's. The Admiral and most of the royal staff were accommodated on the hurricane deck aft.

By October 10 *Medina* was at Portsmouth where she was commissioned as HMS *Medina*, and later that month she sailed for her full power trials in the Channel. All the engineer officers were P&O men, but the firemen and greasers were navy stokers. Like the other ships of the class *Medina* was a twin screw vessel powered by two sets of reciprocating engines developing 15,000 IHP, which gave her a service speed of 16½ knots, although on her six-hour full-power trial she attained 18½ knots.

As she lay at South Railway Jetty in Portsmouth dockyard, her bows were plainly visible from the harbour railway station and thousands of sightseers flocked to see her. Those lucky enough to be in Portsmouth on Saturday November 4 may have seen Her Majesty Queen Mary visit the ship as she spent three hours on board that afternoon. A week later at noon on November 11 1911, a dull and misty day, the King and Queen boarded the *Medina* for a family luncheon on board prior to their departure. The ship sailed at 3.00 pm, half an hour late. Undeterred by the pouring rain thousands of people turned out to see her off, and Southsea beach was a sea of miniature Union flags and black umbrellas. The procession of ships was led by the Trinity yacht *Irene*, followed by *Medina* flying the Admiralty flag on the fore, the Royal Standard on the main, and the Union flag at the mizzen. Astern of her, and carrying the Lords of the Admiralty came the steam yacht *Enchantress*. As *Medina* passed the crowded beach at Southsea and dipped her ensign in response to the yacht club's salute, the escorting cruisers waiting abreast of Clarence Pier got under way and joined the procession. It must have been a splendid sight for those who were able to witness it.

The first few days of the voyage were extremely uncomfortable for the royal passengers, and the unsettled weather showed why many P&O passengers chose to join the ships at Marseilles. Once she was east of Gibraltar the weather improved and by November 28 the *Medina* arrived off the barren rocks of Aden. Six days later at 1.55 pm on Saturday December 2 1911 she arrived in Bombay and anchored some distance from the Apollo Bunder. The King and Queen disembarked for their journey to Delhi and to the Durbar, which of course was as important in British India as the Coronation was in the UK. On January 10 1912, with all the pomp and ceremony over, the King and Queen once again boarded *Medina* in Bombay and set sail for Portsmouth. At Port Said a luncheon was held on board for the Khedive of Egypt and Lord Kitchener but at Malta the ship had to be drydocked after her propellers had fouled the moorings of her buoy. There was an enthusiastic welcome in Gibraltar, whose citizens are always pleased to see their monarch. The programme of festivities was somewhat curtailed owing to the death the previous day of the Duke of Fife. In December 1911 the Princess Royal, her husband the Duke, and their two daughters had been on their way to Egypt on the P&O liner *Delhi*, when the vessel was wrecked on the coast of Morocco. His subsequent immersion was believed to have caused the Duke to catch a chill which developed into pleurisy and led to his death on January 29 1912.

The royal tour ended at Portsmouth on February 5 1912, and so did *Medina*'s highly publicised service with the Royal Navy. She then returned to Caird's at Greenock to be refitted for P&O service. Her rather incongruous looking third mast was removed and her hull and funnels were painted black. She sailed from Tilbury on her maiden voyage for P&O, bound for Australia, on June 28 1912 and with her entry into service P&O's ten 'M' Class vessels provided a completely homogeneous fleet on the fortnightly mail run.

Captain G.G. Randell, a well known P&O officer who later became a dock superintendent, tells a story of a rather unusual passenger carried by *Medina* during 1913. He was billed as the fattest man in the world and apparently weighed 53 stones; he was on his way from Tilbury to Adelaide to be the star turn in a travelling show. Two second class cabins had to be dismantled and converted into one and the unfortunate individual, who was rather a recluse, had a portion of deck screened off for his use. On arrival in Australia his agent wanted him hoisted carefully ashore by one of the ship's cranes, but he was so frightened at this idea that a specially reinforced gangway was provided. This is just one example of the wide variety of passenger carried by P&O!

Medina's peacetime career with P&O lasted just two years, and on July 20 1914, a week before Austria-Hungary declared war on Serbia, she sailed from Fremantle for Colombo arriving there on August 1. Three weeks later she was back in London, and like her sister *Maloja* she was to stay in P&O's service. Her next voyage to Australia was on September 19 1914, sailing on her own as she would for the two and a half years of the war that she served.

On February 1 1917 the Germans unleashed their unrestricted submarine warfare on Allied shipping, sinking any kind of vessel without warning. Two months later on April 28 1917 *Medina* was returning to London from Bombay. She had made her usual call at Plymouth to disembark mail and some passengers, leaving at 4.00 pm that day. She was due to dock at Tilbury in the early hours of the following day, but at 5.30 pm on the 28th she was about 15 miles east of Start Point in Devon, when she passed the Royal Navy destroyer HMS *Spitfire*. Less than half an hour later she was torpedoed by the German submarine *U-31*. *Medina*'s quartermaster had spotted the torpedo but there was not enough time to manoeuvre the ship and the torpedo exploded on the starboard side aft, blowing up the after part of the hurricane deck and the starboard engine room, killing the Fourth Engineer and four firemen. As his ship appeared to be settling rapidly, Captain H.S. Bradshaw ordered all the boats away, and this was carried out very efficiently. Captain Bradshaw left the ship at 6.45 pm but remained close by in his boat until *Medina* sank half an hour later. One witness, Midshipman F. Poole RNR, was on HMS *Spitfire* and had the first dog watch on *Spitfire*'s bridge. He recalls passing *Medina* at 5.30 pm and 20 minutes later glancing in her direction to see that she had made an unusually large swing to the south, not in accordance with her zig-zag diagram. She appeared to be slowing down and he called the Captain; just as he arrived a message came through from *Medina* saying she had been torpedoed. *Spitfire* headed towards her at full speed, and on arrival Midshipman Poole recalls she was a little down by the stern.

Fortunately it was flat calm so there were no problems in launching lifeboats and these were soon towed into Dartmouth and Brixham by the small craft which had appeared on the scene. Midshipman Poole remembers that they zigzagged around the stricken *Medina* for half an hour fully expecting her to sink at any moment. Meanwhile another destroyer HMS *Laurel* had arrived and prepared to take *Medina* in tow and head for Plymouth as it appeared she might not sink after all. Midshipman Poole remembers that as this was happening *Medina*'s commander was standing in a boat nearby sadly watching his ship. Just as a man was about to board *Medina* to make fast the towrope, there was a muffled explosion on board as her boilers blew up. Then in the words of Midshipman Poole: 'A few minutes later her bow rose slowly to a sharp angle for about a third of her length then stopped. She seemed to be hesitating as if protesting at her ignominious end, then quietly but gracefully slid beneath the waves—nothing was left of her but a few odd pieces of flotsam to mark the last resting place of a gallant lady.'

Technical data
Gross tonnage: 12,358
Net tonnage: 6,879
Length overall: 550 ft 5 in (167.79 m)
Breadth: 62 ft 4 in (19.01 m)
Depth: 34 ft 5 in (10.49 m)
Cargo capacity: No figures available
Boilers: Coal-fired, four double-ended and four single-ended boilers, 215 psi
Main engines: Twin screw, two sets compound quadruple-expansion reciprocating engines, 15,000 IHP, $17\frac{1}{4}$ knots
Ship's company: 375
Passengers: First class 450, Second class 220

Daily Mirror *March 16 1911, the launching of* Medina. *This was the first indication that she was to be used as a royal yacht* (Syndication International).

MARCH 16, 1911 Page 9

Launch of the Medina in Which the King Will Make His Voyage to India

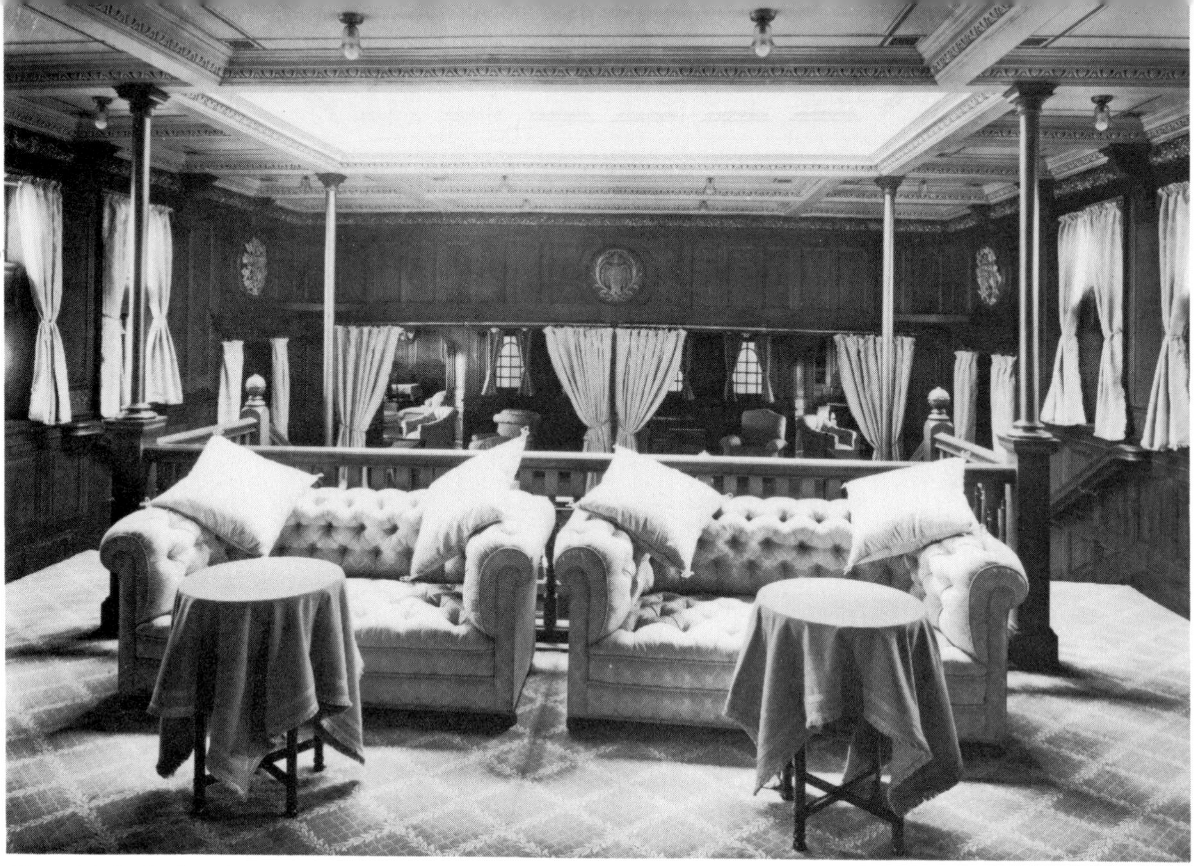

Above Medina's *first class music room as the royal drawing room* (P&O).

Below Medina *in white livery with buff funnels, and her third mast borrowed from the* Nankin (P&O).

Above *The first class dining saloon,* Medina (P&O).

Below Medina *in P&O livery* (P&O).

The Branch Line Steamers 1911-1914

The background to the 'B' Class ships, the first of which entered service towards the end of 1911, was very different from any other liners of the P&O. They were the last vessels to wear the funnel colours of the Blue Anchor Line, a company which had been founded in 1869 by the Danish born shipowner, Wilhelm Lund. Perhaps the Blue Anchor Line was better known in Australia than the UK, because their ships mainly carried emigrants from England to that continent via South Africa.

In July 1909 the company's latest and largest ship the 9,000 ton *Waratah* disappeared without trace on a voyage between Durban and Capetown. 92 passengers and 119 crew members were lost in what became one of the greatest unsolved mysteries of the sea. There is no doubt that Blue Anchor Line's business suffered as a result of this catastrophe and P&O, who had been looking for an entry into the route to Australia via the Cape, purchased the five vessels which made up the Blue Anchor fleet along with the goodwill of the company for £275,000. P&O called their new service the Branch Line, and it was managed separately from all their other passenger operations, mainly because the ships carried all white crews to comply with South African regulations. The fleet which P&O took over was a rather varied collection of ships and they set about planning five replacement vessels. In September 1910 they invited tenders for the first two steamers for their Branch Line.

Caird & Co of Greenock won the contract for all five ships. They were all rather heavy looking ships of just over 11,000 tons, schooner rigged with two masts and an elliptical stern, and one upright funnel. Some of the old Blue Anchor vessels had carried first class passengers and third class emigrants, but on January 11 1911 P&O announced that in future the branch service steamers would convey only 'one class' of passenger to Australia at fares ranging from £16 to £25, and the new class of ship would be arranged on these lines. So in effect the 'B' Class were to be emigrant/cargo ships with accommodation aimed at a 'higher quality' of passenger. All the 'B' Class ships were able to carry 1,100 passengers, of whom 350 travelled in permanent berths, the remainder being accommodated in temporary quarters which could be dismantled for the homeward voyage and then used as cargo space. There was a dining saloon, together with a smoking room, verandah and a music room for the use of the passengers. All five ships started their careers with the Blue Anchor Line funnel markings; a black funnel with a white band and a diagonal chained anchor in blue. But in 1914 they were given plain black funnels in line with other P&O vessels.

All the 'B' Class ships were named after Australian settlements, and the first of them *Ballarat* was launched on September 23 1911 by Mrs F.C. Allen, wife of the manager of P&O's Branch Line. The new ship had cost P&O £176,109 to build and she entered service on November 1 that year, making her maiden sailing to Australia. Two months later on January 24 1912, the second ship of the class *Beltana* was launched. Her first few months were dogged by bad luck, for while fitting out she broke adrift from her moorings and suffered considerable damage before she could be secured again. Nevertheless, she was still completed on time, being registered on April 25 and delivered to P&O in early

May. Despite the efforts of the builders her maiden sailing which had been scheduled for June 13, was delayed by a transport workers, strike and it was July 9 1912 before she sailed from London. Later that year, on October 27 the third ship of the class *Benalla* was launched. She entered service in March 1913, which was also the year that saw the launchings of the last two Branch Line steamers, the *Berrima* on September 13, and the *Borda* on December 17. It was March 1914 before all five ships were on the Australian run, and they then provided a three-weekly, 14 knot service for the emigrant passengers to Australia—at the time a very prosperous business for shipowners. But after only five months the First World War brought it to a halt for the next five years.

Four of the class were immediately taken up as troopships, a use for which they were ideally suited. *Berrima* was taken up in Australia as an armed merchant cruiser, but two months later in October 1914 she too was converted to a troop transport which seemed a sensible decision in view of her speed. From September 1914 to January 1915 the *Benalla* transported troops of the Australian Expeditionary Force to Europe, but then she was handed back to P&O who were struggling to keep up a skeleton service. It was whilst she was on a P&O voyage from London to Sydney in July 1915 with 800 emigrants on board that she suffered a serious fire. She left Table Bay, Cape Town on July 16 and three days later, 800 miles from Durban, the fire was discovered in number two hold. The New Zealand Shipping Company's *Otaki* went to her aid, but *Benalla* had to put in to Durban where the fire was extinguished with the assistance of the local fire brigade. It was a week before she was able to resume her voyage once more. Later that year she was again taken up by the government for trooping. On December 3 1915 while she was on a voyage in the Mediterranean with 2,500 troops on board, she went to the aid of the BI vessel *Torilla* which was being shelled by a U-boat. *Benalla* opened up with her 4.7-in gun and drove the enemy submarine off; she then stood by until dark when *Torilla* could continue in safety. In fact she was escorted by warships to Port Said, where she was fitted with more effective armament.

Some months later on April 11 1916 the *Berrima* was proceeding to Port Said from Malta with nearly 2,000 troops and a huge quantity of ammunition and explosives on board. At 4.55 pm that day a submarine was sighted on the surface about five miles away on the starboard quarter, and it submerged shortly after the sighting. It was a tense time for everyone as *Berrima* increased her speed but much to the relief of all those on board there was no attack and they arrived safely in Port Said. On reporting the sighting to the Admiralty *Berrima*'s Captain must have been relieved to learn that it was the British submarine *E 21* proceeding to Malta from the Levant. However, in early 1917 *Berrima* was involved in a far less harmless incident which she was very lucky to survive.

On the afternoon of February 18 1917 she left Plymouth bound for London and a few hours later 50 miles west of Portland Bill, she was struck by a torpedo or mine on the port side of number four hold, abaft the engine room. Four men were killed by the explosion, the engines were stopped, distress signals sent out, and the crew were ordered to abandon ship. Only the Captain, Chief Officer, Second Engineer, five seamen and the baker remained on board. About an hour later the crew were picked up by the destroyer HMS *Forester*, and soon afterwards the men remaining on board *Berrima* were ordered away. With the water level in the engine room rising, and the ship's stern down by 35 ft, it was thought that she might founder at any time. However, in the early hours of the following morning she was still afloat, and upon the arrival of a tug eight men went back on board to secure a hawser. The tug then began the long tow into Portland; it was touch and go, for *Berrima* was settling lower in the water as the hours went by, but by 6.30 pm on February 19 she had arrived safely in Portland harbour. It was not long before salvage pumps were at work and *Berrima* survived to put to sea again.

Ballarat, however, was not so lucky. On April 25 1917 she was homeward bound from Australia carrying 1,400 troops of the Australian Imperial Forces, mainly reinforcements for the 2nd & 4th Australian Brigades in France. She was about 24 miles south-west of Wolf Rock at the entrance to the English Channel, the destroyer HMS *Phoenix* escorting her and with 50 men posted as lookouts. The Australian troops had arranged various events to celebrate Anzac Day, which were to commence at 2.30 pm that day with a thanksgiving service. Just after 2.00 pm the men were beginning to muster for the occasion when, despite all the lookouts, a

Ballarat *when she first entered service, with the Blue Anchor Line funnel colours* (P&O).

torpedo fired by the German submarine *U-32* exploded on the starboard side aft, smashing her starboard screw and bending the port shaft. The watertight bulkhead between the shaft tunnel to the engine room was seriously damaged and the main engines were soon under water. After hearing the engineer's report, the commander gave the order to abandon ship, and the troops who had all been mustered took to the boats and rafts. *Ballarat* was low in the water when naval vessels prepared to come alongside to take off the last of the Australian troops. It was thought that the ship might sink at any moment, but there was no sign of any panic amongst the soldiers who, in the words of their commanding officer, 'stood on the *Ballarat* in the last parade, their straight lines of eager, cheery faces, and the quiet steadiness of the officers. Nowhere was there the slightest sign of panic or haste.' In the event everyone was taken off the ship by HMS *Lookout* and a naval drifter, and landed safely. *Ballarat* did not sink immediately and was taken in tow but she finally sank at 4.30 am the following day only seven miles off the Lizard. Some days later King George V praised the 'admirable discipline and fearless spirit' of the Australian soldiers on the *Ballarat*. It is interesting to note that in December that year Lord Inchcape personally negotiated compensation of £420,000 from the Treasury for the loss of the ship.

In October 1917 the remaining four 'B' Class ships were taken over under the government's Liner Requisition Scheme. At last British shipping was being organised for wartime conditions, and all British liners were requisitioned. The owners received hire at government rates, and the profits derived from private freight carried at market rates went to the government and not to the shipowners. *Benalla* and *Beltana* were mainly employed on the transatlantic route carrying munitions and supplies.

All four ships survived the war, and in early 1920 returned to commercial service with, and in, P&O colours. Soon after her return to service on February 1 1920, *Berrima* was on her way home from Australia with 300 pasengers when she ran aground on the shingle sand near Margate. Two tugs failed to refloat her that day, but the following day five tugs and a destroyer managed to free her on the high tide. She was then able to complete her voyage. On May 13 1921, it was *Benalla*'s turn to be involved in a more serious mishap. She was steaming down the Channel, having left London the previous day with 1,150 emigrants bound for Australia, when she was struck amidships in thick fog by the oil tanker *Patella*. She was about seven miles from Eastbourne at the time, and although neither ship was seriously damaged, it was thought advisable to beach *Benalla* in Pevensey Bay. The fog was so thick that the lifeboats launched from Newhaven and Eastbourne were unable to locate her for seven or eight hours. Fortunately their services were not required. *Benalla*'s passengers were served breakfast at 7.00 am, and a few hours later the tender *Lady Brassey* started to disembark them and land them at Dover. The *Benalla* was damaged on the port side abaft the bridge and number four hold was flooded. She was refloated on the evening tide, at about the same time that the first of her passengers were arriving back in London, where a variety of vehicles were pressed into service to get them into hotels to await another ship. At 8.00 am on May 15 *Benalla* put in to Southampton before returning to London where she was docked and repaired.

Later in 1921 *Berrima* was in the news once again when she carried 50 Barnardo boys from London to Sydney were they were met on October 25 by the State Governor. They were all given a tweed suit and a bank account with a deposit of £1, and one hopes that their dreams of a new world and new life were realised.

By now a new class of Branch Line steamers had joined the fleet and by the late 1920s the earlier vessels were nearing the end of their useful lives. In 1927 *Benalla* transported the first consignment of steel for the construction of Sydney Harbour Bridge, which was to begin in October 1928. Also that year *Beltana* was involved in two collisions. The first one was in June 1927 when a small British ship the *Clyde* collided with her in Sydney Harbour, but the damage to both vessels was only slight. The next incident occurred at 3.00 pm on August 30 as she was proceeding down the Thames outward bound on a voyage to Australia, when she collided with the steamer *Torrington* and had to be beached. It was not long, however, before she was in service once again, and in 1928 she brought over the crews of the Australian cruisers *Canberra* and *Australia* which had recently been completed on the *Clyde*. In May 1929 she helped to search for the missing Danish ship *Kobenhavn* in the Indian Ocean, alas without success. It was one of her last voyages, for she spent the greater part of 1929 laid up off Southend, although she did make one return voyage to Australia via Suez, the Cape route being abandoned that year.

The first of the four sisters to be sold was *Beltana*. In March 1930 she went to a Japanese company who planned to rebuild her for the whaling trade, but these plans came to nothing and she was broken up three years later. In July 1930 *Berrima* was sold to Japanese shipbreakers, followed in August that year by *Borda*. She had in fact been laid up since 1928 when the Branch Line service began to decline. Finally, in September 1930 *Benalla* was also sold to Japanese breakers, being handed over in January 1931. These ships were the last link with Lund's Blue Anchor Line, and there must be many Australians who still remember them.

Technical data

Gross tonnage: 11,120 (*Ballarat*), 11,168 (*Beltana*), 11,118 (*Benalla*), 11,137 (*Berrima*), 11,118 (*Borda*)
Net tonnage: 6,890 (*Ballarat*), 6,975 (*Beltana*), 6,988 (*Benalla*), 7,037 (*Berrima*), 7,036 (*Borda*)
Length overall: 560 ft (170.6 m)
Breadth: 62 ft (18.89 m)
Depth: 41 ft (12.49 m)
Cargo capacity: No figures available
Boilers: Coal-fired, two double-ended and two single-ended boilers, 215 psi
Main engines: Twin screw, two sets quadruple-expansion engines, 9,000 IHP, 14 knots
Ship's company: No figures available
Passengers: Third class 1,100

The second of the 'B' Class ships Beltana (P&O).

Left *The rather heavy lines of the 'B' Class show clearly in this view of* Benalla *at anchor* (P&O).

Right Berrima *the fourth ship of the Branch Line steamers* (WSPL).

Right Beltana, *the first of the four surviving sisters to be sold* (WSPL).

Right *The* Benalla *was sold to Japanese shipbreakers in September 1930. She was the last link with Lund's Blue Anchor Line* (WSPL).

The 'K' Class 1914-1915

The first decade of the 20th century had brought an increased demand for the P&O secondary services to the Far East and to meet it a new class of six ships, all of around 9,000 tons, entered service in 1914 and 1915. They were all named after towns or districts in central Asia. None of them had a long career with the company, mainly due to the fact that technical improvements during the 1920s soon left them outdated. They were twin screw ships powered by quadruple-expansion engines, which gave them a speed of 14 knots. They had accommodation for just under 150 passengers and substantial cargo space.

The first three ships of the class entered service before the outbreak of war in 1914, and they were all built by Cammell Lairds of Birkenhead, being the first vessels built by that company for P&O since 1859. With modernised yards they were able to compete for larger contracts with more favourably placed builders. The keels for the first two were laid on November 20 and 27 1912 being named *Khiva* and *Khyber* respectively. *Khiva*, which was named after a Russian province now part of Soviet Central Asia, was launched on September 19 1913. She was named by Mrs G.C. Henning, wife of the P&O Captain who was in Birkenhead supervising the building of the three ships on behalf of his company. Two months later on November 29 the *Khyber* was launched; she was named by the Mayoress of Birkenhead, Mrs J. Moon. It was rather a difficult launch as there was a wrecked steamer, the *Rissa*, almost in her path, but with the skilful use of drag chains she was swung clear of the obstruction.

Khiva sailed from Birkenhead on January 6 1914, and was delivered to P&O the next day, well before the contract date. She had cost £197,658 to build and made her maiden voyage to the Far East on January 24 that year. On March 14 1914, the third ship of the class was launched. She was originally to have been named *Kandahar*, but this was changed to *Karmala* while she was being built, the name being taken from a town in Maharashtra state in southern India. Her sponsor was Mrs F. Ritchie, the wife of a P&O Director who was also a guest at the ceremony. A few days later *Khyber* completed her trials, and like *Khiva* she was finished months ahead of schedule, being handed over on March 17. She had cost £196,346 to build and made her maiden voyage to China and Japan on April 22 1914. The third ship of the class and the last one to enter service before the war, *Karmala*, was delivered to the company on June 22 1914, and sailed on her maiden voyage from London to Bombay on August 1 1914, only three days before war was declared. On arrival in India she was immediately taken up for service as the headquarters ship for an expeditionary force which was destined for German East Africa.

Meanwhile on September 24 1914 the fourth ship of the 'K' Class was launched. She was the last of the six to be built by Cammell Lairds at Birkenhead, and she was the very last to enter service, her completion being delayed owing to the war. Originally she was to have been named *Khorassan*, but this was changed to *Kalyan*, a town near Bombay in India. The next two ships were named *Kashgar* and *Kashmir*, the former after a city in Chinese Turkestan (now named Kashi), the latter after the state in north-west India. Both were built at Greenock by Caird & Co, and fitting out was completed very quickly. The *Kashgar* was launched on

November 13 1914, and delivered to P&O the following month on December 15. *Kashmir* was launched on February 16 1915 and handed over on April 2 the same year. Finally the much delayed *Kalyan*, which had been requisitioned for trooping while fitting out, was completed on April 28 1915.

After the outbreak of war *Khiva* and *Khyber* remained on P&O service. The former had just managed to complete two round voyages to Japan and she sailed on her third voyage to India on October 28 1914. On the day war was declared *Khyber* had arrived in Suez on the return leg of her maiden voyage. After returning to London she sailed once again to the Far East on September 5 1914. During the first two years of the war they made voyages to India, the Far East and to Australia where the secondary tonnage was used to offset war losses and ships taken up by the government. On October 16 1914, *Karmala*, which had been fitted out as a troopship, sailed from Bombay carrying two brigades of Indian troops in a convoy which included four British India liners. *Karmala* was the headquarters ship for the Indian Expeditionary Force B and her immediate destination was Mombasa before going on to German East Africa, now Tanzania. There the troops were to be landed about one and a half miles from Tanga, with the objective of capturing the town. The landing went ahead as planned on November 3 1914, but unexpected opposition was met on the outskirts of the town. Eventually the operation was called off and the troops had to re-embark on the transports, which themselves were under heavy fire. *Karmala* was the first P&O ship to be involved in action and to come under fire, but she would not be the last.

In early 1915 *Karmala* was returned to P&O, joining *Khiva* and *Khyber* on the Far East route and in November that year she sailed to Australia. When *Kashgar* and *Kashmir* entered service they too joined the Far East and Australia route.

1915 was quite an eventful year for the 'K' Class ships. In April when *Kalyan* entered service as a troopship, she went straight out to the Mediterranean where she took part in the Gallipoli campaign. While going close in to the beach at Suvla Bay to land troops and two batteries of guns, she was hit by shore fire, the shell going straight down the funnel. Fortunately damage was localised but it could have been a catastrophe because she was heavily loaded with artillery ammunition. On August 6 *Kyber* had just returned to Tilbury from Australia when a fire was discovered in her bunkers. The precious cargo was quickly unloaded and thousands of tons of water were pumped aboard. The fire smouldered for a long time but never got out of control and again damage was only slight. Later in the year on November 9, *Kashgar* was in the eastern Mediterranean bound for the Far East, when lookouts spotted the periscope of a submarine on the port quarter. *Kashgar* opened fire with her defensive armament and the U-boat disappeared, only to reappear on the starboard quarter shortly afterwards. A second shot was fired and the submarine gave up its chase. Although *Kashgar* did not score a hit, those well aimed shots certainly saved her.

1916 was an uneventful year for all six ships of the class, but 1917 was definitely not. In March *Karmala* was in the Mediterranean when she was attacked by a U-boat using both torpedoes and guns. Once again the submarine was beaten off by accurate fire from the merchantman's gunners. In April *Khyber* was homeward bound from Suez when she lost one of her propellers and had to put back into Port Said. In the spring and summer of that year the five ships which were still running for P&O were requisitioned by the government. *Khyber* and *Karmala* were mainly employed in the North Atlantic ferrying badly-needed foodstuffs eastwards and steaming west in ballast. *Kashgar*, *Khiva* and *Kashmir* were employed on Mediterranean trooping duties, and it was during this time that the latter two were involved in incidents with submarines. The first occasion occurred in March 1917 when *Khiva* was off Sicily and only prompt manoeuvring saved the ship as the torpedo passed close to the stern. The second incident, on June 8, involved *Kashmir* when she was on passage between Messina and Alexandria with over 2,000 troops on board. Only fast action by HMS *Nemesis*, one of the escorts, saved her from the U-boat which had been following the liner for some time. The third encounter with a submarine that year was on July 16, again in the Mediterranean. *Khiva* was 50 miles south-west of Sicily when once again a torpedo was spotted heading towards her. For the second time in the space of a few months the ship was manoeuvred well and the torpedo passed only 15 yards astern.

As the war dragged into its fourth year there were another eventful 12 months ahead for the ships of the 'K' Class. Early in the year *Karmala* had a lucky escape; while loaded with cargo in severe weather, she was controlling a convoy from the USA to England when her steering gear broke down. It was only by the skill of her officers that she avoided a collision. In August that year *Kalyan* was converted into a hospital ship for service at Archangel where Allied forces had landed to assist the 'White Russians' in their campaign against the Bolsheviks. When the conversion was completed *Kalyan* looked a strange sight; with all her weather decks plated up one member of her crew commented that she looked more like an aircraft carrier than a merchant vessel. The whole ship was given extra insulation and steam heating and 800 beds were fitted for casualties. With her all-English crew of 200 she arrived in the River Dvina and berthed at a quay close to the cathedral in Archangel just before the ice closed in and made the city unapproachable by sea. Once this had happened a trench had to be dug through the ice around the ship so that the hull was not strained by the pressure. The crew got on well with the local population who were very kind and hospitable. Bunkering was extremely difficult in temperatures ranging between 30 and 40 degrees below zero. Coal was brought across the river on horse drawn sledges.

When the thaw came in the spring of 1919 *Kalyan* made several trips between Archangel and Leith, before leaving altogether in September 1919 when Allied intervention in the Russian civil war ended. Meanwhile on October 6 1918 *Kashmir*, which was now on the North Atlantic carrying supplies and US troops, was involved in a tragic accident. She was part of a convoy which had come across the Atlantic bound for the Clyde. They had come into the North Channel by the coast of Northern Ireland and so were not far from the safety of the port. But at about 9.00 am, in foul weather with severe gales, *Kashmir*'s steering failed and she veered off course colliding with the Orient liner *Otranto*, badly damaging her on her port side amidships. She foundered with the losss of 431 lives, 335 of them being US troops and the remainder crew members. There were no casualties on *Kashmir* and although she suffered considerable damage to her bows, she was able to make the Clyde safely where she disembarked her troops and went into dock for repairs.

When the war ended the six 'K' Class ships continued in government service. *Khyber* left the North Atlantic to take up Expeditionary Force service, ferrying British ex-POWs home and returning Belgian refugees from England to Antwerp. On January 13 1919 she was on her way to Hull with 1,300 wounded repatriated POWs, when she ran aground off the Norfolk coast. Her passengers, who were naturally all eager to get home, were landed and taken to a camp at Ripon. The following day *Khyber* was refloated and was soon back in service. *Karmala* was employed repatriating Australian troops from Europe whilst *Kashmir*, which had been speedily repaired on the Clyde, was allocated to cross-Channel trooping duties. At first the Ministry of Shipping had given notice that she would be handed back to P&O in December 1918, but then changed this plan and it was decided she would ferry troops between Le Havre and Southampton. She made her first trooping voyage from Le Havre on January 7 1919 and was due to make her second trip a few days later. However, her commander informed the Ministry that in his opinion it was not safe to take his ship into Le Havre. He thought that with her length of 500 ft, with her boats permanently outboard and with the ship in ballast she presented a lot of top hamper to the strong winds. In his view with the restricted area of the port and the strong currents, the two harbour tugs were not strong enough to cope with his ship.

He was to be proved right, for on January 9 1919, when leaving the Wharf at Le Havre all the blades were stripped from her port propeller. She was able to continue her run to Southampton where she was laid up for 17 days for repairs. A few weeks later in March she was returned to P&O, and made her first post-war voyage to Australia via the Cape before resuming her intended route to the Far East. In January 1919 *Khiva* was handed back to P&O and she made her first post-war voyage to Bombay and the Far East, leaving London on January 16. *Khyber* resumed her P&O service in September 1919, after being used to repatriate Australian troops and made her first voyage to Bombay, as did *Kashgar* in October 1919. In December that year the last two of the six sisters *Karmala* and *Kalyan* were back in commercial service with P&O, with the latter undertaking her maiden voyage for the company.

The years of peace which followed the end of the war

were not without incident for the 'K' Class ships. On April 22 1920 when *Khiva* was in Singapore on her way home from Yokohama, fire broke out in one of her holds. Although it burned for some hours, it was brought under control at noon the next day, having destroyed 500 tons of camphor and cotton. A few months later in July 1920 *Kalyan* was involved in a collision with the ex-P&O troopship *Himalaya*; little damage was done and both ships resumed their voyages. In January 1921 *Khiva*, which had not been reconditioned since the war was docked in London for the work to be done when it was held up by a joiners' strike, so she was moved to Portsmouth Dockyard where the refit was completed. She returned to service in the autumn of that year. In November 1922 while *Khyber* was alongside in Marseilles, she was badly damaged when a nearby shed full of copra caught fire. She was given a thorough overhaul in Falmouth in 1924, but two years later she spent some time laid up at Southend.

In January 1927 *Karmala* was chartered by the government for use as a troop transport. There had been disturbances in Shanghai, and to protect the British concession the government sent troops to form the 'Shanghai Defence Force'. *Karmala*'s passenger sailing to the Far East scheduled for February 10 was cancelled, and she sailed for Hong Kong on January 29 carrying troops of the Border Regiment and the Middlesex Regiment, who formed the 13th Infantry Brigade. She also had on board armoured cars and their crews from the Royal Tank Corps. *Karmala* and the other troopships arrived in Hong Kong on March 3.

In November 1928 *Kashgar* was involved in a series of collisions at Dunkirk. First she collided with the quay, then hit and sank a floating dock, and finally collided with a French steamer *Nicole Shioffino*. However, she sailed on schedule the following month for the Far East. A year later on February 11 1929 *Kashmir*, which had returned from the Far East to discharge cargo in European ports, was grounded in the River Scheldt near Kruisschars after a collision with the small Belgian coaster *Leopold De Wael*. *Kashmir* had been outward bound from Antwerp and the Belgian ship was on her way in to the city when the collision occurred. *Kashmir* was badly damaged aft and had to undergo temporary repairs before being refloated two days later with the assistance of no less than ten tugs. She then went into dock at Antwerp for further repairs, which kept her out of service until June 26 that year.

In March 1929 *Khiva* was on her way out of Shanghai, when she went to the aid of the German liner SS *Giessen* which had broken in half on Button Rock, 110 miles from the city. She rescued the crew of the wrecked ship and some months later the German government showed its appreciation by rewarding *Khiva*'s Captain and crew.

By 1930 there was more new tonnage on the stocks intended for the Far East route and although the 'K' Class ships were less than 20 years old, being slow coal-burners, their days were numbered. *Khiva* left London for her final passenger voyage on December 20 1930. She arrived safely in Japan, and left Otaru in the north of the country in mid February carrying only cargo. Five days later there was a serious fire in her second class accommodation, the main deck being completely gutted. She was forced to put into Dairen (now Lüda) in China where temporary repairs were made. She arrived back in London on April 14 1931 and was sold to Japanese breakers for £15,500 in May. She left London on her delivery voyage on September 6 that year and was handed over at the end of November. *Khyber* sailed on her final voyage from London loaded only with cargo on October 24 1931, and was handed over to Japanese shipbreakers in December that year. She had been sold for £16,250. *Karmala* lasted until 1932, leaving London on May 6 for her final cargo voyage. Once again she had been sold to Japanese scrappers, being handed over on July 5 that year. *Kashgar*'s final cargo voyage was not without incident. She left King George V Dock on the evening of January 30 1932, and at 12.28 am the following day she collided with the German ship *Han Maersk*.

Neither ship was seriously damaged, but as *Kashgar* was making water in number two hold she put into Southampton where she received temporary repairs. She left Southampton to resume her final voyage on February 2 and arrived in Kobe on March 26 1932 to be handed over to the shipbreakers T. Okushoji. *Kashmir* made her final cargo voyage from London on June 3 1932 and was handed over on July 31 1932, having been sold for £14,400 to the same shipbreaking firm as *Kashgar*. *Kalyan* which had been in P&O service for only ten years, left London on December 4 1931 and was handed over on February 12 1932 to the Japanese shipbreakers to whom she had been sold for £16,750.

The six sister-ships of the 'K' Class had had short but eventful careers with P&O, and there is no doubt that the First World War prevented them from showing their true value to the company.

Technical data

Gross tonnage: 9,135 (*Khiva*), 9,114 (*Khyber*), 8,983 (*Karmala*), 8,840 (*Kashgar*), 8,960 (*Kashmir*), 8,987 (*Kalyan*)
Net tonnage: 5,590 (*Khiva*), 5,674 (*Khyber*), 5,680 (*Karmala*, *Kalyan*), 5,551 (*Kashgar*, *Kashmir*)
Length overall: 480 ft 6 in (146.46 m)
Breadth: 58 ft 2 in (17.73 m)
Depth: 37 ft 7 in (11.46 m)
Cargo capacity: No figures available
Boilers: All ships coal-fired, fitted with two single-ended and two double-ended boilers, 215 psi
Main engines: All ships twin screw, two sets quadruple-expansion engines
IHP: 7,000 (*Khiva*, *Khyber*, *Kashmir*), 9,000 (*Karmala*, *Kashgar*, *Kalyan*)
Speed: 14 knots (*Khiva*, *Khyber*, *Kashmir*), 15 knots (*Karmala*, *Kashgar*, *Kalyan*)
Ship's company: No figures available
Passengers: First class 80 (*Khiva*, *Khyber*, *Karmala*), 79 (*Kashgar*, *Kalyan*), 78 (*Kashmir*), Second class 68

Left *The first of the class,* Khiva *is launched at Birkenhead* (Cammell Laird).

Above right Karmala *is launched at Birkenhead, the wreck of the* Risa, *which was such a hazard when* Khyber *was launched, can be seen to the left of* Karmala (Cammell Laird).

Below right Karmala *being towed to the fitting out basin* (Cammell Laird).

Below Khyber, *the second 'K' Class ship* (Laurence Dunn collection).

"THE KARMALA"
IN THE BASIN

Above *June 22 1914,* Karmala *leaves Cammell Laird's yard at Birkenhead on her delivery to* P&O (Cammell Laird).

Below *One of the Greenock-built 'K' Class vessels, the* Kashmir (Laurence Dunn collection).

Kaisar i Hind 1914

As the last of the 'M' Class ships joined the P&O fleet in 1911, it was decided to build a similar vessel for the London-Bombay mail service. The order was placed with Caird & Co of Greenock in August 1912, and in the following month it was announced that she would be named *Kaisar i Hind*. The name, which meant 'Empress of India', was chosen in honour of the royal visit to the Indian Durbar six months previously. The new ship would be the second in the company to bear the name, the first being a vessel built in 1878 which had a career of 19 years. The second *Kaisar* was a ship of 11,430 gross tons, and her accommodation was an improvement on all previous vessels; in particular her first class cabins were mainly single berth, and the provision of an electric fan in each cabin ended an old grievance with regular P&O passengers. In addition the smoking room was more spacious and extended through the entire width of the liner.

She was a twin screw ship powered by quadruple-expansion engines which developed 14,000 IHP and gave her a speed of 18½ knots, which was faster than any other P&O ship and which was to save her from submarines on several occasions. She was a remarkably good looking ship, schooner rigged with a straight stem, elliptical stern, and two perfectly proportioned funnels. Her outline was later somewhat marred by the addition of a top gallant forecastle, but this improved her seaworthiness as she had been very wet forward prior to this modification. Her limited cargo space earned her the reputation of being pretty but not profitable.

The launch was scheduled to take place on Saturday June 27 1914, but owing to the low tide it was postponed. The following day conditions were better and the launch took place at 3.00 pm, the naming ceremony being performed by Miss Edith Cole. Very little publicity was given to the event by the press, most newspapers being full of other sensational news. In a distant capital, Sarajevo in Bosnia (now Yugoslavia) the Austro-Hungarian heir presumptive, the Archduke Francis Ferdinand, and his consort had been assassinated on the same Sunday that *Kaisar* took to the water! At midnight on August 4 1914 when war was declared, *Kaisar i Hind* was in the James Watt dock at Greenock fitting out. This was completed very rapidly, and on September 30 that year she started her trials on the Clyde, having cost P&O £363,176 to build. Five days later she arrived in Tilbury to prepare for her maiden voyage to Bombay which was scheduled for October 24 1914.

She left London on time, commanded by Captain Charles D. Bennett RNR. Sailing alone and unescorted, she set a new record for the voyage between Plymouth and Bombay of 17 days 20 hours 52 minutes. For the next 18 months the *Kaisar* ran on P&O's reduced service to Bombay without incident. This changed at 7.20 am on March 23 1916 when she had her first encounter with a U-boat. She was midway between Crete and Malta at the time with Lord Chelmsford, the Viceroy of India, his family and staff on board, when a torpedo was seen approaching from starboard. Fortunately it passed harmlessly astern and Captain Bennett sent out radio warnings, but two hours later the submarine sank another merchant vessel. The second attack on the *Kaisar* occurred some 15 months later when she was homeward bound from Bombay, and in the Atlantic about 100 miles west of Casablanca. At 8.00 am on June 17 1917 a torpedo was seen approaching but once again *Kaisar* was handled skilfully and the torpedo passed 12 ft astern. A month later at 5.20 am on July 17 she was outward bound to Bombay, and 120 miles south-west of the Scilly Isles when a torpedo was seen travelling towards her on the port beam. Once again evasive action was taken, and this time the torpedo missed the stern by only six feet. It is fortunate that this was one of the last torpedo attacks on her, for the margins of safety were diminishing each time! It seems that the U-boat commanders were unaware of *Kaisar*'s extra turn of speed and did not make allowances for it when firing their deadly torpedoes.

In October 1917 she was taken up by the government under the Liner Requisition Scheme and she spent the rest of the war as a troop transport, sailing mainly in Mediterranean convoys between Marseilles, Taranto and Alexandria. On one occasion she was chartered to the French government and was packed with coloured French troops whose hygiene standards left a lot to be desired. It was after this voyage that a number of suspicious illnesses broke out on board, so she was sent to Southampton where she was thoroughly cleaned and fumigated. She had her last encounter with the enemy on April 22 1918, seven months before the end of the war. She was in the Mediterranean with over 3,000 troops and 500 crew members on board, and this time the torpedo struck the ship in a most vulnerable spot. For some unknown reason it failed to explode. Had it done so a hole would have been blown in the engine room and stokehold. When she docked soon after this incident it was found that the torpedo had dented her hull plates, and for many years after the war these damaged plates were painted bright green in contrast to the red of the underwater hull. By now she had earned the very appropriate nickname 'Lucky *Kaisar*', a name she kept to the end of her career.

After the armistice in November 1918 *Kaisar i Hind* remained on government service, repatriating Australian troops and carrying British regiments between the UK and India. However, by October 1919, although she was on government charter more and more berths were being placed at the disposal of the P&O company. When she sailed from London for Bombay on October 10 1919, she had on board 1,900 troops and 240 cabin passengers. The government allotted these berths to P&O at such short notice that 'pier head jumps' became quite common, with vacant cabins being booked only hours before she sailed and with so many people awaiting ships for India there was no problem filling them. In fact the captured Hamburg America liner *König Friedrich August* made several voyages between London and Bombay for P&O during 1920 in an attempt to clear the long waiting lists of would-be passengers. It was during 1920 that *Kaisar* was finally released by the government and was able to sail on her first peacetime voyages for her company.

In 1921 she was chartered to Cunard for an Atlantic crossing. Like P&O, Cunard had lost a lot of tonnage during the war, and although they had ordered 13 new ships, three of which were to be delivered in 1921, they had long queues of passengers waiting to sail to the United States. *Kaisar* left Tilbury for Bombay on March 11 1921, arriving back in London on May 7 that year. Three days earlier she had been advertised in the Cunard sailings list for the first time as leaving Southampton for New York on June 8 1921. She left Tilbury for Southampton on June 4 renamed *Emperor of India* for Cunard, although the translation was in error as *Kaisar* means 'Empress'. She sailed from Southampton on schedule and went directly to New York, arriving there on June 17. She was then chartered to the American Tourist Agency for a cruise across the Atlantic to Scandinavia, leaving New York on June 25 and calling at St John's Newfoundland, Reykjavik, Trondheim, Bergen, Leith, Amsterdam and finally at Tilbury. The cruise was not very successful as *Kaisar* had been designed for the tropics and had no heating and she was dogged throughout the voyage by thick fog. The trip was further marred by an explosion in the stokehold which killed three Indian firemen and badly scalded four engineers. Perhaps one of the most disappointed people on the cruise was a girl stowaway who slipped on board in St John's thinking the ship was bound for New York, but found herself on a much longer journey. The cruise ended at Tilbury on July 26 1921, and after a thorough overhaul *Kaisar* sailed on her first P&O voyage to Bombay on October 14. She remained on this service for the best part of her career.

In June 1922 *Kaisar* was due to make P&O's first call at Tangier for eight years and a large number of French passengers from that city had booked for a passage to

Marseilles. Unfortunately the severe weather at the time and lack of port facilities caused the cancellation of this visit, leaving her intending passengers stranded. But this was only a minor hiccup and for the next eight years she sailed on the Bombay service without incident. In 1930 she was once again in the news when on May 22, five days after leaving Bombay for London, she lost her port propeller. Her speed was reduced to 13½ knots and when she arrived at Port Said on May 26 divers went down to survey the damage. It was found that the shaft had broken inside the tube, but fortunately there was no other damage. She was able to proceed on her voyage and arrived in London on June 9 where repairs could be carried out. In the following year, on November 1 1931, *Kaisar* made her routine call at Malta when she was outward bound to Bombay. While she was in Grand Harbour strong winds blew up causing her to drag her anchor and to collide with the Italian ship *Citta Di Trieste*, sinking several wooden lighters as well.

After the introduction of the *Viceroy of India* on the Bombay route in 1929, *Kaisar* was used on the Far East service as well as to India. She was a popular ship with both passengers and crew, particularly in the second class where one of her smoking room stewards, Charley Ward, had refused promotion time and time again so that he could stay with the ship. A P&O Marine Superintendent who travelled home from the Mediterranean in *Kaisar* a year or so before she was broken up, recalled the outstanding comfort which the liner provided and above all the excellent food, which he considered to be very tasty. He attributed this to the coal burning galley, which gave the food a good smoky flavour. But by the late 1930s, although she was only 24 years old she was hopelessly outdated particularly with respect to the coal-burning boilers.

Kaisar made her final round voyage from London to Japan on January 14 1938, with Sir Archibald and Lady Clark-Kerr among her first class passengers; he was travelling to Hong Kong to take up his appointment as the British ambassador to China. The liner arrived in Singapore in time for the opening of the much vaunted naval base on February 14. At the end of the month she reached Kobe, leaving on March 10 for her return voyage to London. On April 21 she called at Plymouth and many observers were surprised to see her flying a 72 ft paying off pennant from her mainmast. The pennant, which had been made by the crew, had a miniature P&O houseflag in the hoist and beyond it a red St George's Cross running for about half the length, the rest being plain white bunting. *Kaisar* was the first merchant vessel to fly a paying off pennant in Plymouth, as it was a tradition usually only observed by the ships of the Royal Navy. She arrived at King George V Dock in London early on the morning of Friday April 22 for the last time, where her master Captain L.Edwards was presented with the pennant and her Baggage Master Mr. C. Osborne bade farewell to the ship in which he had served since her launch. She had been sold to Hughes Bolkow & Co of Blyth for £28,500, and she was delivered seven days later on April 29 1938.

The Kaisar i Hind. *She was nicknamed 'lucky Kaisar' owing to the number of near misses she received from enemy torpedoes* (P&O).

She had been a popular ship and had she stayed in service for another 18 months she could have provided a useful service in the Second World War. But perhaps the luck which stayed with her between 1914 and 1918 might not have held and the scrap steel from her hull must have been invaluable to the expanding armaments industry of 1938-39.

Technical Data
Gross tonnage: 11,430
Net tonnage: 5,989
Length overall: 520 ft (158.49 m)
Breadth: 61 ft 2in (18.64 m)
Depth: 33 ft 1in (10.08 m)
Cargo capacity: No figures available
Boilers: Coal-fired, four double-ended and four single-ended boilers, 215 psi
Main engines: Twin screw, two sets inverted quadruple-expansion reciprocating engines, 14,000 IHP, 18½ knots
Ship's company: No figures available
Passengers: First class 315, Second class 333

Above *Built for the London — Bombay service,* Kaisar i Hind *was used on the Far East route towards the end of her career* (P&O).

Below Kaisar *arrives at King George V Dock in London on Friday April 22 1938, flying her paying off pennant.* (P&O).

Naldera and *Narkunda* 1920

When the First World War ended in November 1918, the P&O fleet was sadly depleted and the years which followed saw a massive rebuilding programme. The first two new mail steamers to be completed after the war were the *Naldera* and *Narkunda*, and their entry into service in 1920 was a milestone in the company's history. They were the first two ships to exceed 16,000 gross tons, and they were the first P&O vessels with three funnels and cruiser sterns. Both ships had been ordered six years previously in the last months of Sir Thomas Sutherland's chairmanship, for in August 1914 the two great shipping companies, the P&O and BI lines merged and Sir Thomas retired in favour of Lord Inchcape who was to lead the company over the next 17 years.

Naldera was ordered in November 1913 from Caird & Co of Greenock. She was the 83rd vessel and the biggest but also the last built by Cairds for P&O, for Caird & Co were subsequently taken over by Harland & Wolff. The second ship *Narkunda* was ordered in early 1914 with the contract going to Harland & Wolff in Belfast. When the war came, work on the two ships was suspended for three years and the hulls lay idle on the stocks. In 1917 they were taken over by the government, who seemed to have no clear idea of what to do with them. One thing was important; the slipways were needed, so both ships had to be brought to the launch stage. *Naldera* was launched on December 29 1917, and *Narkunda* followed on April 25 1918. In the months which followed, government indecision dogged *Naldera*; the first idea was that she should be an auxiliary cruiser and so her original profile of two masts and three funnels was altered to one mast and two low funnels. Then it was decided that she should be a fast cargo ship, but before this came about further orders were given to complete her as a troopship. She was in fact completed for this role in May 1918, but before she went into service it was decided to use her as a hospital ship, and finally as a seaplane carrier. It was said that in the space of a few months she had been everything but a submarine!

When the war ended *Naldera* and *Narkunda* were handed back to P&O with permission for the company to make what they could of the two ships. In the case of *Naldera* it must have been a difficult task, but just over a year later, on March 25 1920, she left Greenock for London, followed five days later by *Narkunda*. They were a splendid sight with their three tall funnels, but there were subtle differences in their design, one of which was a range of cabins on *Narkunda*'s promenade deck forward of the bridge, which were very popular despite the athwartships bunks. She was readily distinguishable by a short top gallant forecastle which *Naldera* did not have. Both ships had accommodation for 673 passengers, 426 of these being first class. They were coal burning ships, and their quadruple-expansion engines gave them a speed of 17½ knots. One of the most splendid public rooms was *Narkunda*'s first class dining saloon, the walls of which were painted to give the appearance of old ivory. Round the oval well, which rose from the centre of the saloon, was a gaily painted frieze by Professor Gerald Moira, which, when illuminated by lights hidden below in the cornice moulding, presented a blaze of gorgeous colour.

Naldera sailed on her maiden voyage to Sydney on April 10 1920 while *Narkunda*'s maiden voyage to

Bombay was two weeks later on April 24. Both ships arrived back in London in June that year, and thereafter they sailed to Australia via Marseilles and Colombo. On the evening of July 29 1921 *Naldera* was leaving Bombay for Sydney, when she collided with the *Clan Lamont* which was at anchor. *Naldera* suffered damage to her bows and put back into Bombay for repairs which took two days. By the summer of 1922 *Naldera*'s voyages to Australia were being advertised by Thomas Cook as 'round the world tours'. The first of these voyages was on November 3 that year, returning in May 1923, with fares at £1,400 per person and the number of applicants limited to eight. In December 1923 during one of *Narkunda*'s voyages to Australia, jewellery worth £2,000 was stolen from a passenger's cabin, and despite searches of the vessel by police at Colombo, Fremantle and Melbourne it was never traced. On October 2 1924 *Naldera* had just returned from Bombay and was docking at Tilbury, when a small cargo vessel the *Scotstoun Head* collided with her causing some damage to the port side amidships. However, she was able to sail once again for Bombay two weeks later on October 17.

In 1927 *Narkunda* was converted to burn oil, a factor which was to prolong her career, whereas *Naldera* carried on as a coal-burner. By now both ships were sailing to the Far East as well as Australia. In July 1930 while *Naldera* was homeward bound between Fremantle and Colombo, she ran into severe weather. The heavy gales broke off gooseneck ventilators which caused flooding in number two hold, and hundreds of tons of meat cargo were spoiled and had to be jettisoned. Four years later in October 1934, while on a voyage to Bombay *Naldera* ran aground in the Suez Canal. She was refloated 24 hours later, after reducing her cargo. In 1937 she was in the news once again when, on January 16 while docking at Southampton to embark passengers and cargo for the Far East, she damaged her starboard propeller, resulting in a delay of 36 hours during which she had a replacement fitted. Although she was still only 17 years old *Naldera* was nearing the end of her career. Her final two voyages were to Kobe in Japan. The first trip was completed in early May 1938. She left London again two weeks later on May 20 for her final passenger sailing. On August 12 she left Kobe for London. After leaving Port Said, she called at Malta, Marseilles, Gibraltar and Plymouth, docking alongside the Tilbury Landing Stage at 7.30 am on Friday September 23 1938.

But instead of going straight to the breakers yard, she got caught up in the humiliation of the Munich agreement which gained her a few weeks' reprieve. At the time Neville Chamberlain,the Prime Minister, and the French Prime Minister, Edouard Daladier, were negotiating with Hitler and Mussolini over the future of Czechoslovakia. The order of the day was appeasement and on September 29 vital border areas of that country were handed over to Hitler. Certain regions of that unfortunate country were to be given the chance of holding a plebiscite to decide whether they wanted to join Hitler's Reich and it had been agreed that a force of 2,000 members of the 'British Legion Volunteer Police' would travel to Czechoslovakia to supervise the operation. To transport them across the North Sea the government chartered the *Naldera*, and by early October they were embarked ready for the voyage.

But Hitler was not going to let democracy stand in his way and on October 10 he made a particularly inflammatory speech declaring that the British Legion was neither wanted nor needed, and so in the spirit of appeasement it was left to Germany to decide the new borders with Czechoslovakia. By October 17 the 'British Legion' force had been stood down and dispersed, and *Naldera* was then sold to Messrs P & W McLellan of Glasgow for £36,000. She left Tilbury for the breaking up yard at Bo'ness in the Firth of Forth on Saturday November 19 1938.

Meanwhile *Narkunda* continued the P&O service to the Far East and Australia. She left London for Sydney on June 23 1939 on her last peacetime voyage, arriving in Colombo on the morning of July 16. As preparations were under way for her to enter harbour, smoke was seen coming from her number six cargo hatch. While this was being dealt with by the Second Officer, there was a huge explosion and the hatch cover was blown into the air. It had been caused by a build up of gas from fermentation in the cargo, although in the tense summer of 1939 there were rumours that it was a bomb. Four members of the crew were killed and 23 were injured. The structural damage was negligible, but 350 tons of cargo destined for Australia were damaged. After a delay of two days a certificate of seaworthiness was given, and she arrived in Sydney on August 3.

When war was declared on September 3 1939,

Narkunda was in the Indian Ocean homeward bound and three days out from Colombo. The voyage to London was completed on schedule and she made two more passenger trips to Shanghai via Marseilles, Suez, Bombay and Singapore, arriving back in Southampton on May 31 1940. She had been unable to disembark the overland passengers at Marseilles owing to the political situation, and after passing Gibraltar she was fired at by an unknown vessel which attempted to pursue her, but *Narkunda* shook her off as she headed home at full speed. The waters of Europe were becoming very dangerous indeed. She made only one more full passenger voyage, which was from Southampton to Hong Kong via Cape Town, returning by the same route to Liverpool on October 28 1940. When she sailed again two weeks later she was carrying a mixed complement of fare paying passengers and troops on a voyage via Cape Town to Penang, arriving back in Liverpool on April 14 1941. After this she was used solely for carrying troops, with the exception of two special trips.

In the summer of 1941 she took part in troop landing exercises at Inverary and Scapa Flow, followed by a period in drydock at Liverpool. After a short return voyage between the Clyde and Freetown, she sailed to the Far East on November 13 1941 calling at Freetown, Durban and Addu-Atoll in the Indian Ocean. By this time Japan had entered the war on the side of the Axis powers, and the British army in Malaya was in retreat. In January 1942, a month before Singapore fell, *Narkunda* went into Keppel Harbour to evacuate women and children from the island, returning to the Clyde on May 22 that year. In late June and July she made a short trooping voyage to Gibraltar, and on July 30 1942 she left the Clyde for Suez sailing via the Cape. However, when she arrived in Durban it was announced that she was to call at Lourenco Marques in Mozambique to repatriate British diplomats who had been exchanged for Japanese diplomats held by the Allies.

Four huge Union Jacks and the word 'DIPLOMATS' in lettering 10ft high were painted on the hull. Among the passengers were Sir Robert Craigie the British Ambassador in Tokyo, and Sir Josiah Crosby the ambassador in Thailand. The voyage back to Liverpool was memorable as the whole ship was floodlit each night, which was very different from the darkened ship everyone was used to. *Narkunda* and the liner *El-Nil*,

Naldera, *the first liner to be commissioned under the post-1914–18 building programme* (P&O).

which had assisted with the repatriation, arrived in Liverpool on October 9. From there she sailed to the Clyde to prepare for a trooping voyage as part of the North African invasion force.

Narkunda left the Clyde and the UK for the last time on November 1 1942 in a follow up convoy for 'Operation Torch', the joint American/British landings in Algeria, designed to cut off the Axis forces in North Africa. On November 12 she arrived in Algiers, and after disembarking some of her troops she left for Bougie the following day, arriving there at 7.30 am on November 14. All day she disembarked troops and stores, and at 4.00 pm she sailed for home. It seemed she might be safe, but between 4.58 pm and 5.20 pm she was subjected to continuous heavy air attacks. A stick of bombs fell close to the port side and the explosions caused severe underwater damage. Almost immediately *Narkunda* developed a heavy list to port; by 6.30 pm the ship had been abandoned and at 6.42 pm she sank by the stern. The survivors were picked up by HMS *Cadmus*; 31 of her crew members had been killed and the remainder were later repatriated to the UK by *Stratheden* and *Ormonde*.

With the *Viceroy of India* and *Cathay* having been lost three days earlier, *Narkunda* became the third P&O liner to be lost during the North African landings.

Technical data
Gross tonnage: 16,088 (*Naldera*), 16,118 (*Narkunda*)
Net tonnage: 8,936 (*Naldera*), 9,424 (*Narkunda*)
Length overall: 600 ft (182.88 m) 581 ft 5 in (177.22 m)
Breadth: 62 ft. 2 in (20.47 m) (*Naldera*), 69 ft 5 in (21.16 m) (*Narkunda*)
Depth: 49 ft 2 in (14.99 m) (*Naldera*), 49 ft 4 in (15.03 m) (*Narkunda*)
Cargo capacity: No figures available
Boilers: Coal-fired, four double-ended and four single-ended boilers, 215 psi. *Narkunda* converted for oil burning in 1927
Main engines: Twin screw, two sets of quadruple-expansion reciprocating engines; 18,000 IHP, 17½ knots (*Naldera*), 15,300 IHP, 16 knots (*Narkunda*)
Ship's company: 462
Passengers: First class 426, Second class 274

Narkunda *enters the water at Belfast, she is ready to be dazzle painted for one of the many roles envisaged for her during the First World War* (Harland & Wolff).

Above Narkunda *is towed to the fitting out basin. She was launched to clear the slipway for badly needed tonnage to replace war losses* (Harland & Wolff).

Below *March 1920, six years after her keel was laid,* Narkunda *undergoes her trials* (Harland & Wolff).

Below Narkunda *underway during the trials' period* (Harland & Wolff).

Left *A first class two-bedded cabin in* Narkunda (P&O).

Below left Narkunda*'s first class dining saloon, showing the splendid frieze painted by Professor Gerald Moira* (P&O).

Right *The first class music room,* Narkunda (P&O)

Above *The lower bridge deck,* Narkunda (P&O).

Below Narkunda *was the third P&O liner to be lost in the North African landings during the Second World War* (P&O).

The Branch Line Steamers 1921-1923

Of all the P&O liners launched between the two world wars, the 'B' Class ships which were built for the Branch Line were the least successful, and only 15 years after the first ship was delivered, the last one went to the breaker's yard. Like their predecessors, the Branch Line ships of 1911, the 'B' Class of the 1920s were extremely heavy and clumsy looking ships, with straight stems, elliptical sterns and one upright funnel. All five vessels were ordered during the First World War, but their construction did not begin until it was over. They had a gross tonnage of just over 13,000, and with their quadruple-expansion engines, developing 9,500 IHP, they had a service speed of 13½ knots. They had accommodation for nearly 500 third class passengers in permanent cabins, and over 700 in temporary berths. These were structures set up as dormitories for the voyage between London and Australia, and removed for the homeward journey to make room for cargo. Harland & Wolff built four of them at their Greenock yard; the other, *Baradine,* was built at Belfast.

The first of the quintet to enter service was *Baradine* on September 21 1921, when she left on her maiden voyage to Sydney. Four months later she was followed by *Ballarat* which sailed on January 27 1922, and the third ship *Balranald* made her maiden voyage on April 5 1922. The fourth of the sisters *Bendigo* sailed for the first time in the summer of 1922, on August 9, but it was March 30 1923 before the final ship of the class *Barrabool*, made her debut. All five ships sailed via Cape Town, and to comply with the regulations there they carried all-white crews. The 'B' Class ships offered a fortnightly service, and the improved conditions were popular with both emigrants and other passengers who were unable to afford the luxury of the mail steamers.

Soon after the last of the five ships entered service, *Baradine* ran into slight trouble. She was outward bound in early September 1923, when fire broke out in her reserve coal bunker, number three hold. Fortunately it was extinguished after the hold was flooded. Four months later on January 16 1924, *Bendigo*, which had just arrived home from Australia, collided with the coaster *Corcrag* in the Thames off Erith. Although *Bendigo* suffered only slight damage, the smaller ship was severely damaged to her port quarter and she was beached. In August 1925 *Balranald*, which had just left Cape Town outward bound to Sydney, struck a submerged object with some force and severely damaged her port propeller, which delayed her arrival in Australia. A few weeks later on October 1 1925 *Baradine*, which was about to leave for Sydney, was in collision with the LMS ferry *Catherine* off Gravesend. *Baradine* was undamaged but the *Catherine* was badly damaged to her stern and she then collided with Tilbury Pier and damaged her bow.

By 1926 it became clear that the emigrant trade was collapsing, and the demand for third class berths was drastically reduced. In early 1929 the Branch Line route via Cape Town was abandoned, and the five ships were withdrawn during the year for a thorough overhaul. The first to be docked was *Baradine*, and the work was carried out at Falmouth. During the refit her boilers were converted to burn oil fuel, and she was equipped with Bauer-Wach exhaust turbines. Her accommodation was greatly improved, the temporary berths being removed completely and the cabin accommodation altered to cater for 586 one class passengers.

Baradine left Falmouth on March 30 1929 for London, after completing her trials off the Cornish coast. During the trials she more than fulfilled the expectations of her engineers, when she averaged 16½ knots and at times attained 17 knots in seven runs over the measured mile. During the voyage up-Channel to London she maintained an average speed of 16 knots. She made her first voyage from London to Australia via Suez on April 12 1929 carrying both passengers and the mails. During 1929 the other four ships of the class were given identical refits, and they were completed in September that year when *Barrabool* left for Sydney. All five ships took their place on the mail service to Australia via Suez, carrying their passengers at third class rates, but with much improved conditions. A lot of attention had been given to catering, the dining saloons were improved and a late dinner served. For their entertainment passengers had cinema facilities, and gramophone music for dancing on deck. Once the ships were into warmer waters large canvas swimming pools were rigged on deck. It seemed that the 'B' Class ships had been given a new lease of life, but in fact seven years later they would all be scrapped.

Bendigo's first voyage after her refit was on July 5 1929, and by the end of the voyage a month later she had received some world-wide publicity. The 'B' Class ships still carried a large number of passengers under the assisted passage scheme run by the Australian government. When she sailed on July 5 she had on board 401 passengers, 206 of these being emigrants on assisted passage. Also on board was Mr Collingwood Hughes, an ex-Member of Parliament with his wife, and on the passenger list he was described as a 'publicity director'. When the ship arrived in Fremantle, Mr Hughes gave a press conference at which he strongly criticised the standard of emigrant going to Australia. He was particularly scathing in his remarks to the press, describing many of the young male emigrants as 'street corner loafers', and some of the children as mentally weak. His remarks immediately became headlines in the Australian and British press, and the media maintained that Britain was looking to Australia to solve her unemployment problem. Mr Hughes' accusations were immediately denied by *Bendigo*'s Captain and Welfare Officer, but the press, sensing a story, would not let it go and an official enquiry was ordered. Meanwhile on board *Bendigo*, which had sailed for Adelaide, there were a lot of justifiably indignant passengers who bitterly resented his remarks and he was surrounded by an angry crowd. Eventually Mr Hughes and his wife were isolated in their cabin under guard, from where he wrote an apology and retracted his remarks. However, once he was safely ashore he again reiterated his allegations about the standard of emigrant on board *Bendigo*. Fortunately the official enquiry stated that the selection of emigrants was sufficiently thorough and vindicated procedures and *Bendigo*'s Captain who had denied the accuracy of Mr Hughes' remarks. Unfortunately the incident and the resulting publicity did not do the 'B' Class ships any good.

On Saturday May 17 1930, *Balranald* arrived in London from Australia, and was the first large passenger steamer to use the new landing stage at Tilbury, which had been opened the day before by the Prime Minister Ramsey MacDonald. Later that year on December 17 *Barrabool*, which was homeward bound from Australia, arrived at Port Said with a damaged tailshaft. However, after a survey she was allowed to proceed at reduced speed. On Friday November 18 1932 *Baradine*, lying in King George V drydock, suffered a fire in one of her holds. The local fire brigade attended and after a few hours it was extinguished. She was able to sail for Australia according to schedule a week later on November 25.

By late 1934 the popularity and the demand for passages on the 'B' Class ships had declined, and in early 1935 the company was forced to reduce the frequency of the service. Despite this the ships continued to lose money, and *Ballarat* was the first ship to be sold. She made her last voyage in December 1934 from Liverpool to Brisbane. She was delayed at Colombo for nine days from January 16 to January 24 1935, with damage to her starboard propeller shaft. She left Australia in late February 1935 arriving home in April. After a short lay up she was sold on May 27 that year to Thomas W. Ward for £23,500, to be broken up at Briton Ferry in South Wales. During her service she had carried 33,000 new Australians to their chosen country. However, *Ballarat*'s story was not over, for on August 18 1935, while she was in the breakers yard at Briton Ferry, fire started in her number one hold. It blazed for a week before it was brought under control, and demolition could begin in earnest.

The four remaining 'B' Class ships were withdrawn in quick succession, the first to go being *Bendigo*. She made her last sailing to Australia on February 14 1936 and on her arrival back in London in early May she too was sold to Thomas W. Ward, this time for £26,000 and to be broken up at Barrow. She arrived there on Saturday May 9 1936—up to that time the largest ship to be broken up in the port. Both *Balranald* and *Baradine* were sold to scrappers in June 1936, the former on June 2 to Douglas & Ramsey of Troon in Ayrshire, and the latter on June 30 to W.H. Arnott Young at Dulmuir. *Barrabool* was the last to go. She made her final sailing to Australia in April 1936 and her return voyage was delayed slightly when she was held up in Colombo with engine trouble. To avoid any delay to the mails they were transferred to *Ranpura*. *Barrabool* arrived in London in July and was sold to shipbreakers at Bo'ness, Firth of Forth. The five sister-ships had had short careers. Had they been laid up for three years they would have proved invaluable as transports during the Second World War.

Technical data

Gross tonnage: 13,144 (*Baradine*), 13,033 (*Ballarat*), 13,039 (*Balranald*, *Bendigo*), 13,148 (*Barrabool*)
Net tonnage: 7,990 (*Baradine*), 7,950 (*Ballarat*), 7,938 (*Balranald*), 7,939 (*Bendigo*), 7,996 (*Barrabool*)
Length overall: 519 ft 9 in (158.42m)
Breadth: 64 ft 5 in (19.63 m)
Depth: 42 ft (12.8m)
Cargo capacity: No figures available
Boilers: Coal-fired, two double-ended and three single-ended boilers, 215 psi; Converted for oil burning in 1929
Main engines: Twin screw, two sets quadruple-expansion reciprocating engines, 9,500 IHP, 13½ knots; Bauer-Wach exhaust turbines fitted 1929, 16 knots
Ships' company: 288
Passengers: Third class 491, temporary berths 743; 1929 Third class 586

The finishing touches being put to Baradine *as she lies alongside the fitting out berth* (Harland & Wolff).

BARADINE

Left Baradine *on the stocks at Harland & Wolff's Belfast Yard* (Harland & Wolff).

Right Baradine *shortly before she left for her trials* (Harland & Wolff).

Right Baradine *leaving Belfast in September 1921* (Harland & Wolff).

Right Baradine,—*the 'B' Class of the 1920s were extremely heavy and clumsy looking ships* (Harland & Wolff).

Above Ballarat. *She met an ignominious end in a Briton Ferry scrapyard in August 1935, when she was gutted by fire.* (P&O).

Below Bendigo. *She made the world headlines in July 1929, when an ex-Member of Parliament complained about the standard of emigrant on board* (P&O).

Above Balranald, *the third ship of the class to enter service* (P&O).

Below Barrabool, *like the rest of her class, was converted to oil fuel in 1929, and fitted with Bauer-Wach exhaust turbines. This increased their service speed from* 13½ *to* 16 *knots.* (P&O).

Moldavia 1922

The *Moldavia* was the first ship of post-war (1914-1918) design to join the fleet in the rebuilding programme and although her straight stem and counter stern gave her a rather dated appearance, down below in the engine room her double reduction geared turbines were a great technical advance. In fact she was the first P&O liner to be so fitted. She had a short career of 15 years, but she will probably be remembered by many people who cruised in her during the 1930s.

Moldavia was built by Cammell Laird & Co of Birkenhead, and she was constructed of the finest warship steel plates left over after the First World War. She was a twin screw coal burning ship with a speed of 16 knots. The liner was built for the Australian service, and at 16,436 gross tons was the largest vessel to be put on that route, although her passenger capacity of 214 first and 180 second class passengers was well below the numbers which could be carried by *Naldera* or *Narkunda*. The first class music and smoking rooms along with a verandah cafe were arranged on the promenade deck, while the second class music and smoking rooms were on the shade deck aft. The passenger cabins were arranged on the 'Inchcape' plan, each having access to its own porthole for outside light and air; inside cabins were designed with a narrow passage to the ship's side.

The launch was on Saturday October 1 1921, and fitting out took the best part of a year. Nevertheless by Tuesday September 19 1922 she was ready for her trials in the Mersey. Later that day she was handed over to P&O and immediately sailed for London calling at Avonmouth on the way. On October 13 1922 she sailed from London on her maiden voyage to Australia, arriving to a great welcome in Sydney on November 28.

During 1923 she continued to sail to Australia and on December 26 that year she arrived in Fremantle on the last part of a voyage from London. Just before she left the port fire broke out in her number three hold which contained a cargo of fibre loaded in Colombo. The First Officer who went to investigate it was almost suffocated and as it was getting out of control the local fire brigade was called. They had to flood the hold which meant the cargo in there and a large quantity of passengers' heavy luggage was ruined, but the hull itself was undamaged. *Moldavia* left Australia once again in February 1924 and arrived in Colombo on the 20th of that month where she embarked the group chairman Lord Inchcape and his wife for the voyage to London, arriving back there at 11.00 am on March 14 that year.

For the next seven years she continued on the service between London and Australia. In 1928 a second (dummy) funnel was added to counter criticism to her design. However, it did nothing to solve the problem, because although it made her look bigger it also seemed to unbalance her appearance by being too far aft. At the same time her boilers were converted to burn fuel oil instead of coal. Two years later, in April 1930 her second class accommodation was redesignated third class but in March 1931, with the impending entry of the *Strathnaver* and *Strathaird* onto the Sydney route, P&O announced that *Moldavia* would be converted to 'one class tourist', and provide monthly sailings to Australia, along with *Mongolia* (1923) which was also to be converted. *Moldavia* left London on March 13 1931 and made her last voyage as a two-class ship to

Bombay, returning to Tilbury on April 29 to undergo her conversion. This was completed at the end of August that year, and she made her first voyage as a one class ship on September 4, bound for Sydney.

Many people will probably remember the last six years of her career for during this time in the summer months she cruised from the UK to European, Mediterranean and Atlantic ports. It was while she was on one of these cruises during 1935 that her port turbine broke down on July 21 after leaving Monte Carlo. Two days later she put into Gibraltar, where repairs were effected by the naval dockyard and it was July 31 before she arrived back in Tilbury, her lucky passengers having several extra days on their cruise. Two years later, on September 17 1937 she made her final voyage to Sydney, arriving back in London at 5.00 am on Christmas Eve that year. For the next four months she was laid up at Tilbury, and on April 18 1938 she was sold to John Cashmore Ltd for breaking up, being handed over where she lay.

Hers was the briefest career of all the P&O liners of the period between the wars, and had she been kept on for another 18 months there is no doubt she could have given good service as a transport.

Technical data
Gross tonnage: 16,436
Net tonnage: 10,133
Length overall: 552 ft 5 in (168.38 m)
Breadth: 71 ft 7 in (21.82 m)
Depth: 38 ft 5 in (11.71 m)
Cargo capacity: No figures available
Boilers: Coal-fired, three double-ended and four single-ended boilers, 215 psi; converted to oil burning 1928
Main engines: Twin screw, two sets Parsons double reduction geared turbines, 13,250 IHP, 16 knots
Ship's company: 337
Passengers: First class 222, Second class 175; 1931 converted 'one class tourist' 840 passengers

An interesting view of Moldavia, *obviously signed by Lord and Lady Inchcape after their voyage home from Colombo* (P&O).

Above Moldavia, *after the addition of a dummy second funnel in 1928* (P&O).

Left *The main lounge of* Moldavia *when cruising as a one class ship* (author's collection).

Right Moldavia, *the smoking room when a 'one class tourist' ship* (author's collection).

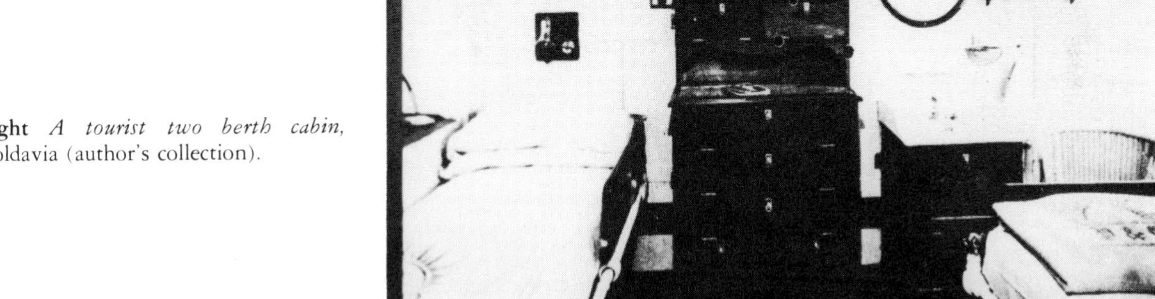

Right *A tourist two berth cabin,* Moldavia (author's collection).

Right *The forward dining saloon of* Moldavia — *this used to be the first class saloon* (author's collection).

Mongolia 1923

Whereas the *Moldavia* had the shortest career of any P&O liner designed between the wars, the *Mongolia* which followed her had the longest. She lasted for 42 years but only 15 of these were with the P&O, and she was one of the few liners which was sold outside the group for further trading. Like *Moldavia* she was an intermediate liner designed to cater for emigrants to Australia who wanted something more than the Branch Line vessels, but who could not afford the expense of the primary mail steamers. She was very similar in appearance to *Moldavia*, but with her larger single funnel she gave the impression of being a much more powerful ship.

Mongolia was built at the Walker-on-Tyne yard of Sir W.G. Armstrong Whitworth & Co Ltd and was launched on Thursday August 24 1922. The naming ceremony was performed by Miss Elsie MacKay, the youngest daughter of Lord Inchcape. The liner was completed in April 1923 at a cost of £1,000,000, having taken four years to build because of intermittent labour troubles. She was fitted with Parsons double reduction geared turbines to drive two propeller shafts and the main engines developed 13,000 IHP which gave her a service speed of 16 knots. She had accommodation for 230 first and 180 second class passengers. On Thursday April 26 1923 she ran a series of trials on a measured mile off the Tyne, and afterwards left for a short cruise in the North Sea. She steamed north as far as the Inchcape Rock before turning round and making for Tilbury to prepare for her maiden sailing to Australia on Friday May 11 1923. She arrived in Sydney on June 25.

Five years after she entered service her coal-fired boilers were converted for oil burning and two years later in January 1930, as in *Moldavia*, her second class accommodation was redesignated third class. This coincided with the demise of the original Branch Line steamers, and Mr H.B.G. Larkin, the general manager of the Branch service, said that he hoped the decrease in emigrant passengers would be balanced by an increase in tourists. But the passengers of the 1930s demanded something better than third class, and so in early 1931 *Mongolia* was converted to 'one class tourist' with accommodation for 840 passengers. She made her first sailing to Australia in this new guise on April 17 1931, with fares at £39 for a single ticket and £70 return.

On September 28 1931 it was reported in the press that *Mongolia* had run aground in the river at Brisbane, but this was soon contradicted by P&O who made it clear she had anchored in the river for repairs and adjustments to her steering gear. Two years later on July 16 1933 she did run aground, this time in European waters. The accident happened while she was entering the port of Copenhagen and she lost her anchor, as a result of which she did not stop in time and a small oil tanker *British Venture* collided with her. *Mongolia* then struck the breakwater and ran aground. Fortunately there was little damage and she was soon refloated, returning to London on July 21. On November 13 1936, when *Mongolia* arrived at Tilbury from Australia, she was met by several ambulances. She had passed through severe gales off Ushant, and this had resulted in 17 people being injured. The heavy seas had in fact smashed in a porthole, and two stewardesses had been cut by flying glass. One of the stewards had been flung off his feet by the heavy seas, breaking his arm. Two weeks later *Mongolia* sailed again for Brisbane, and on December 3 she was involved in a collision with the Spanish cargo vessel *Villa De Madrid* at Marseilles. High winds had blown the two ships together, and part of *Mongolia*'s deck rails were carried away, but luckily no-one was hurt.

1937 was to be *Mongolia*'s last full year of service with P&O, and in the early hours of November 27 that year, when homeward bound from Australia, she was in collision with the Cory collier *Corfleet*, in thick fog off the Nore lightship. The damage to *Mongolia*'s bows was severe, and the collier was holed amidships. Later that day when *Mongolia* docked at Tilbury, many of her passengers were still unaware of the collision. It was her last sailing for P&O, and she was laid up for the next six months. The future did not look good, particularly when *Moldavia* went to the breakers yard in April 1938, but fortunately for *Mongolia* there was a reprieve. She was to be chartered to the New Zealand Shipping Company, a subsidiary of P&O, on a long term basis and she was given a thorough refit. She was painted in their colours of wholly white superstructure and yellow funnel, and her tourist accommodation was altered to cater for 772 passengers. She was renamed *Rimutaka*, replacing the old *Ruahine* on the London to Wellington route via Panama.

She sailed on the first voyage under her new identity on December 8 1938, calling at Curacao, Panama and Auckland but she had only nine months of peacetime service and her second round voyage from London at the end of April 1939 was her last before the war. She arrived back in London on August 1 1939, and sailed once more on the 17th of that month. She was in the Pacific, only two days out from Panama when war was declared, but they were relatively safe waters and she arrived in Wellington without incident. *Rimutaka* was taken up by the Ministry of War Transport, but for much of the war she remained on the route to New Zealand via Panama. Her large cargo capacity was invaluable during the war years, and she also carried personnel to various destinations. In the spring of 1943 she carried troops to relieve the garrison on St Helena, and during 1944 she called at New York and embarked passengers for Australia and New Zealand. In December that year she carried the Duke and Duchess of Gloucester to Sydney where the Duke was to take up his appointment as Governor General of Australia. This time she sailed via the Mediterranean, calling at

Mongolia *as she entered service with P&O.* (P&O).

Malta on Christmas Day, and arriving in Sydney on January 29 1945.

When the war ended *Rimutaka* continued her service between London and New Zealand, and in July 1947 while bound for Wellington, she made a mercy dash to Pitcairn Island where a ten-year-old girl was reported to be ill with tetanus. She was in fact Helena Young, a descendant of the famous *Bounty* mutineer Edward Young. Sadly, despite unremitting care the child died. *Rimutaka*'s post-war career with the New Zealand Shipping Company lasted only four years, and in October 1949, with the entry of new tonnage onto the route, she made her final voyage from London to Wellington.

In January 1950 she was bought by a Panamanian company, the Compania de Navegacion Incres. She was renamed *Europa* and in July 1950 she started a service between New York and Antwerp, but this lasted only 15 months and in October 1951 she underwent a major refit at Genoa to prepare her for service as a cruise-ship. In January 1952 renamed *Nassau* she started her new career cruising in the Caribbean, and she became well known and popular in the United States. In October 1961, although she was 38 years old her owners sold her to a Mexican company, the Natumex Line, and she became Mexico's only cruise liner. Her new owners brought her across to the Clyde for an extensive refit in the Fairfield yard. When she emerged two months later renamed *Acapulco* she was hardly recognisable, her superstructure having been extended

Below *Crossing the line ceremony on board* Mongolia *in the 1930s* (author's collection).

Above right *The New Zealand Shipping Company's* Rimutaka. (P&O).

Below right *Still easily recognisable as the former* Mongolia, *the* Nassau *of the Compania de Navegacion Incres* (A. Duncan).

When she emerged from her Clyde refit in December 1961 renamed Acapulco *she was hardly recognisable, her superstructure having been extended forward and her funnel tapered* (A. Duncan).

forward and her funnel tapered. In December 1961 she sailed to New York intending to embark passengers for a cruise to Los Angeles, but in New York the US Coast Guard declared her to be below the required safety standards and the cruise was cancelled. During 1962 she was used as a floating hotel at Seattle for the World's Fair and in May 1963 she was laid up at Manzanillo in Mexico. She lay there for 18 months before being sold in October 1964 to Japanese shipbreakers, and two months later she arrived at Osaka under tow. She was over 41 years old and she had sailed under four flags and five names, a remarkable career for a ship which P&O had not considered a great success.

Technical data
Gross tonnage: 16,385
Net tonnage: 10,333
Length overall: 551 ft; 7 in (168.12m)
Breadth: 72 ft (21.95 m)
Depth: 38 ft 6 in (11.73 m)
Cargo capacity: 499,982 cu ft (14, 158 cu m)
Boilers: Coal-fired, three double-ended and four single-ended boilers, 215 psi. 1928 converted for oil burning
Main engines: Twin screw, two sets Parsons double reduction geared turbines, 13,250 IHP, 16 knots
Ship's company: 337
Passengers: First class 222, Second class 175; 1931 converted 'one class tourist' 840 passengers

Mooltan and *Maloja* 1923

Of all the P&O liners built in the 1920s the *Mooltan* and *Maloja* were perhaps the best known and most popular ships. They were ordered from Harland & Wolff in Belfast and they completed the first phase of P&O's rebuilding programme after the 1914–1918 war. It was the first time that any of the company's ships had exceeded 20,000 gross tons, but surprisingly, despite the fact that P&O had fitted their two previous ships *Moldavia* and *Mongolia* with geared turbines, both *Mooltan* and *Maloja* were driven by quadruple-expansion reciprocating engines. The company had sacrificed speed for reliability for with 13,300 IHP their twin screws could achieve only 16 knots.

They were provided with over 622,000 cu ft of cargo space in seven holds. However, their small rudders made handling difficult and this capacity was not always fully utilised due to the tight mail schedules not allowing adequate time in port, which was a particular problem in their early years. For passengers there were no problems as they were handsome ships and with their lofty superstructure, broad decks and big oval funnels they were great favourites. Both ships were noted for their steadiness at sea, and their solid comfort aboard. They had accommodation for 327 first class and 329 second class passengers.

The first of the two sisters to leave the stocks was *Mooltan,* being launched on Thursday February 15 1923. There was no ceremony, but the owners were represented by their Superintendent Engineer. Two months later on Thursday April 19 *Maloja* took to the water, being christened by Miss Elsie Mackay at a full ceremony. By September 22 *Mooltan* had completed her trials and left Belfast Lough for Tilbury with a party of distinguished guests on board which included Lord Pirrie, the Chairman of Harland & Wolff, Lord Inchcape and Sir Donald Maclean, father of the arch traitor of the 1950s. *Mooltan* sailed on her maiden voyage to Bombay on October 5 and arrived there three weeks later on the day that *Maloja* left Belfast for Tilbury with her sponsor Elsie Mackay on board, accompanied by her father. *Maloja* left Tilbury on her maiden voyage, which was also to Bombay, on November 2 1923. The two ships met for the first time, in the Red Sea on November 16, as *Mooltan* was homeward bound. After their initial Bombay voyages both ships were put on to the Sydney route.

In November the following year *Maloja* was involved in a dockworkers' strike in Australia which delayed her departure, and when she did sail she left behind 6,000 tons of cargo. In March 1925 she ran aground in Adelaide, but was refloated after discharging some of her cargo. In February 1931 when she was a few hours out of Bombay bound for London, a fire was discovered in number seven hold. It was soon extinguished after the hold was flooded, but most of the cargo was lost. In January 1933 she was in the news again, when in severe weather she put in to Gibraltar Bay to load cargo from a lighter. In the process she lost one anchor, 45 fathoms of chain, and the lighter carrying the cargo was washed ashore. By the time the Second World War came both ships had been in service for over 15 years and they were extremely popular liners on the route to Australia.

Mooltan left Sydney for London on July 21 1939 on her last peacetime voyage before the outbreak of war, arriving in Tilbury at the end of August. Meanwhile

Maloja left London on August 18 1939 for Brisbane, and she was actually in Aden when war was declared. Both ships had been earmarked by the government as armed merchant cruisers and *Mooltan*, whose next voyage to Australia was cancelled, was sent back to her builder's yards at Belfast for conversion. *Maloja,* which had arrived in Bombay on September 7, was handed over to the government the following day and work began immediately on her conversion. Both vessels were armed with eight 6-in guns, and two 3-in high-angle anti-aircraft guns. Their after dummy funnels were removed, but when problems occurred with the engine room ventilation they were replaced in shortened form. *Mooltan* was commissioned at Belfast on October 10 1939, and later that month she sailed for London where she remained until mid January 1940 when she was allocated to the South Atlantic station being based at Freetown. *Maloja* commissioned in December 1939 and she sailed home and up to the cold waters between the Faroes and Iceland, where she joined the Northern Patrol in January 1940.

Two months later at 10.00 am on March 12 *Maloja* intercepted the 7,400 ton German cargo ship *La Coruna* south of Iceland in a position 44£ 28′N, 13£ 00′W, and steering east. When challenged she gave her name as the Japanese *Taki Maru*; *Maloja's* Captain suspected she was German but he was unable to send over a boarding party because of the foul weather. When the snowstorm cleared and she was ordered to heave to, it became clear she was being scuttled as fires broke out forward and aft. Her crew of ten officers and 50 men managed to get off a signal warning German ships of an AMC south-east of Iceland before being picked up by *Maloja*; she then finished off the *La Coruna* with

A good view of Mooltan's *cruiser stern — the small rudder made handling rather difficult* (Harland & Wolff).

gunfire. At the end of May 1940, with most of northern France in German hands and the BEF being evacuated from Dunkirk, *Maloja* was placed at the disposal of the Commander-in-Chief Western Atlantic. After patrolling off the Spanish port of Vigo in the first two weeks of June she joined the Sierra Leone escort force. On July 31 when *Mooltan* was on passage from Plymouth to Freetown, she was attacked three times by German aircraft in the Western Approaches and damaged by some near misses—as a result of which she was ordered to Liverpool for repairs.

In January 1941 it was decided to convert *Mooltan* into a troopship, and she was sent to Tilbury where part of this work was carried out. At the end of May she was sent up to the Clyde where the conversion was completed. In September 1941 it was decided to convert *Maloja* as well, and a few weeks later in October she put into Southampton for the work to be done.

Both ships took part in the north African landings at the end of 1942, and in 1943 *Maloja* followed the army's advance up Italy. At the end of the war in Europe in May 1945, both vessels continued to carry troops to Bombay and Colombo. After the Japanese surrender they both repatriated POWs and civilian internees from the Far East, and in 1947 they were released by the government and handed over to P&O. *Mooltan* was sent to her builder's yard in Belfast for reconditioning, and *Maloja* was refitted by R & H Green & Silley Weir at Tilbury. The two ships had their dummy second funnels restored but retained their black hulls. Instead of returning to the normal passenger run both ships were remodelled largely for the transport of emigrants to Australia, being able to carry 1,030 passengers in 'one class tourist' berths. In April 1947 the Australian government had started the assisted passage scheme, and there were long waiting lists of people wanting to leave austerity-hit Britain to start new lives.

Maloja returned to service on June 10 1948 and was followed by *Mooltan* two months later on August 26. Most of their outward traffic was Ministry of Transport emigrant work. Just over a year after she started her new role, in April 1949, there was an outbreak of smallpox onboard *Mooltan* and six people died of the disease. In August 1950 *Maloja* was chartered to the Dutch government for the homeward voyage to Europe and she assisted with the evacuation of Dutch civilians who had been expelled from the newly independent state of Indonesia. It did not interfere with her normal trade, for the emigrant carriers were rarely fully booked for the voyage home.

By 1954 there had been a decline in the numbers of assisted passage emigrants, and consequently there was a decline in government sponsored tonnage. *Mooltan* made her last voyage from Brisbane to London on November 18 1953, and 5,000 of her 'old friends' came to Hamilton Wharf to see her off. She got a rousing farewell from each port along the route, and she arrived in Tilbury on January 7 1954. Her passengers dispersed, and her Asian crew joined the brand new *Arcadia* which was preparing for her maiden voyage to Australia. 13 days later on January 20 *Mooltan* left Tilbury for the last time. She had been sold to the British Iron & Steel Corporation and was to be broken up at Faslane. As she left the Thames, tugs, ferry boats and other small vessels sounded their sirens and a small crowd gathered to wave good-bye. She arrived in the Clyde on January 22 and at the Tail of the Bank she was taken over by three tugs for the last stage of her voyage to the breakers yard. *Maloja* completed her last voyage in the company's service when she reached Tilbury on February 19 1954, like *Mooltan* having had a wonderful reception at her ports of call. She too was sold to the British Iron & Steel Corporation and was delivered at Inverkeithing on April 2 that year to be broken up. So ended a 30-year chapter in the history of the P&O Company.

Technical data

Gross tonnage: 20,846 (*Mooltan*), 20,837 (*Maloja*)
Net tonnage: 12,835 (*Mooltan*), 12,829 (*Maloja*)
Length overall: 600 ft (182.8 m)
Breadth: 73 ft (22.24 m)
Depth: 44 ft (13.4 m)
Cargo capacity: 622,800 cu ft in seven holds
Boilers: Oil-fired, six double-ended and two single-ended boilers, 215 psi
Main engines: Twin screw, two sets quadruple-expansion reciprocating engines, 13,300 IHP, 16 knots; 1929, *Mooltan* fitted with exhaust-driven turbines and electric motors geared to the propeller shafts, 16,000 IHP, 17 knots; 1930, *Maloja* fitted with Bauer-Wach exhaust turbines, 16,000 IHP, 17 knots
Ship's company: 422 (*Mooltan*), 423 (*Maloja*)
Passengers: First class 327, Second class 329; August 26 1948, 1,030 one class (*Mooltan*); June 10 1948, 1,030 one class (*Maloja*)

Left Mooltan *on the stocks shortly before she was launched in February 1923* (Harland & Wolff).

Above Mooltan *being towed to the fitting out berth* (Harland & Wolff).

Below *September 1923,* Mooltan *on her trials in Belfast Lough* (Harland & Wolff).

Left *The second class lounge on board* Maloja (P&O).

Below Mooltan *as an armed merchant cruiser* (P&O).

Right *August 1948,* Mooltan *has just completed her refit after being handed back to P&O* (Harland & Wolff).

Below right Maloja *as she appeared after the Second World War* (P&O).

MOOLTAN

Above Mooltan *as she appeared after the Second World War* (P&O).

Below *An excellent aerial view of* Mooltan *and Tilbury Landing Stage in the early 1950s* (Skyfotos Ltd).

Razmak 1925

Without doubt the *Razmak* of 1925 occupies a special place in the affections of many people in New Zealand, for this Clyde-built liner spent most of her long career far away in the waters of the Pacific Ocean. She was designed by P&O for the Aden–Bombay shuttle service, as a successor to the *Salsette* lost during the First World War. *Razmak* was a handsome ship of 10,602 gross tons, being schooner rigged with two funnels and a counter stern. Her twin screws were driven by quadruple expansion engines, with low pressure double reduction geared Bauer-Wach turbines, developing 12,000 IHP and giving her a speed of 18 knots. She carried 284 passengers, half of them being first class, and a crew of 262.

The order for *Razmak* went to Harland & Wolff Ltd who built her at their Greenock yard (formerly Cairds). She was launched on Thursday October 16 1924, the naming ceremony being performed by Viscountess Inchcape, the wife of the P&O Chairman. The name *Razmak* was taken from the garrison town in Waziristan on the North West Frontier of India (now part of Pakistan), which was developed by General Lord Rawlinson in 1922, and the General himself was a guest at the launching ceremony. Soon after the launch *Razmak* was towed from the Clyde to Harland & Wolff's Belfast yards in order to have the propelling machinery installed. Four months later on February 26 1925 she ran her trials in Belfast Lough and was taken over on behalf of P&O by Mr Frank Ritchie, a Joint Managing Director of the company.

Razmak made her maiden voyage from London to Bombay on March 13 1925, sailing via Marseilles and Suez. Her return voyage was to Marseilles, leaving Bombay at 5.00 pm on Friday April 10 1925. Among her passengers was Lord Reading, the Governor General of India, who was returning to the UK for political discussions with the government. The passage was completed in record time with *Razmak* arriving in Marseilles early on Wednesday April 22. Later that year when she was in the Indian Ocean bound for Bombay, she received a signal from a French gunboat the *Alerte* requesting water for her boilers. A rendezvous was arranged and in the early hours of November 25 *Razmak* went alongside the warship and transferred 20 tons of fresh water, before casting off and making for Bombay at full speed. *Razmak*'s five years of service with P&O was spent mainly running between Marseilles and Bombay, but occasionally returning to London. By 1930 it became clear that the new ships on the Australian service were able to call at Bombay without disrupting their mail contract schedules and the Bombay shuttle service was becoming superfluous.

It seemed possible that *Razmak* might have been broken up during the 1930s, when fate intervened. In August 1917 the Union Steamship Company of New Zealand had joined the P&O group by the latter's acquisition of the USS Co's shares. One of the company's main passenger routes was between New Zealand and San Francisco across the Pacific Ocean. In August 1930 the company suffered a severe loss when their 7,585-ton ship *Tahiti* sank 460 miles south-west of Raratonga while en route from San Francisco to Wellington. She had lost her starboard propeller and had flooded rapidly through the propeller shaft. Fortunately there were no casualties, but the USS Co lost a valuable ship. As it happened the *Razmak* had returned to London from Bombay on July 18 that year, before being temporarily laid up. It was an obvious answer to the USS Co's problem and it was decided to transfer *Razmak* to them to replace the *Tahiti.*

Razmak left London on October 3 1930 on her final voyage for P&O. She sailed via Gibraltar, Marseilles, Suez, Bombay and Colombo, arriving in Wellington in mid November where she was given a refit and renamed *Monowai.* Her passenger accommodation was changed to cater for 483 third class passengers, fittings for the conversion being taken from the old USS Co ship *Mararoa,* which had been laid up in Wellington for three years. Externally her hull was painted in the company's bronze green, with white upperworks, although the ventilators were left in the familiar P&O buff. Her funnels were painted red with black tops and she looked splendid in her new colours. Captain A.T. Toten of the lost liner *Tahiti* was appointed to her command, and *Monowai* left Wellington on December 2 1930 for her first voyage to San Francisco sailing via Tahiti and Raratonga, arriving there 17 days later on December 19. She soon became very popular, and in January 1931 she broke the trans-Tasman record. In September 1932 she broke her own record by three hours and five minutes, the journey from Wellington to Sydney taking exactly 67 hours at an average speed of 18.25 knots.

She was advertised under Union Royal Mail Line and during 1932 she made five round voyages between Wellington and San Francisco. By the end of that year the Matson Line had put two large liners on the route, and with this formidable competition the *Monowai* was withdrawn from that service and placed on the Tasman service between Wellington, Auckland, Sydney and Melbourne. In September 1933 she also made one voyage between Sydney and Vancouver. *Monowai* had difficulty filling her passenger and cargo accommodation, and in February 1935 it was decided to cancel her call at Melbourne as an economy measure. In January 1936, when she was on her last Tasman voyage before being laid up, she made a dash to Lord Howe Island to rescue a sick woman, who was rushed to hospital when the liner docked in Auckland on January 27. Happily the patient made a good recovery, but for *Monowai* it appeared that yet again she might be destined for the breakers yard.

However, in May 1939 she was put back into service once more, and in the few remaining months before war broke out she made two round voyages across the Pacific between Sydney and Vancouver. She left Sydney for the first voyage on May 11 1939, arriving back there on July 1. Five days later she sailed again calling at Auckland, Honolulu, Victoria and Vancouver, returning by the same route. She arrived back in Sydney on August 26 1939, and that is where she was when war was declared eight days later.

Monowai was requisitioned by the New Zealand government on October 21 1939 and work began to refit her as an armed merchant cruiser at Devonport, Auckland. Then followed a period of indecision. On February 11 1940 work on her was halted and not resumed until June 23 that year when it was definitely decided to complete her as an AMC. She was commissioned into the RNZN on August 30 1940, and for the next 16 months she carried out patrol and convoy escort duties between Australia, New Zealand and Fiji. With the entry of Japan into the war in December 1941 the Pacific became a very dangerous ocean, and on January 2 she left Auckland in company with HMNZS *Leander* escorting the transport *Rangatira* with reinforcements for Fiji. When they were only a few miles from Suva there were two heavy explosions on the port quarter. At first it was thought *Monowai* had been attacked by an aircraft and a submarine, but it was later believed to be two torpedoes fired by a submarine exploding at the end of the breakwater at Suva. During 1942 she continued to patrol and escort convoys in the Pacific, but gradually her use in the role was superseded by the ever increasing numbers of US Navy ships. In December 1942 it was decided to convert her to a landing ship (infantry) and so in April 1943 she left Auckland for the UK sailing via Panama. She paid off at Liverpool on June 18 1943 where the conversion work was to be carried out.

It was January 1944 before the work was completed and in February that year she made a trooping voyage to Port Said and Italy, returning via Sicily with troops and bullion. She was now a very different looking ship with her mainmast and hydraulic cranes removed and 20 landing craft slung from davits on both sides of the hull.

At the end of April she was in the Solent with the ever growing number of vessels preparing for the 'D Day' landings. She left Cowes Roads on the evening of

June 5 1944, and was the largest ship of a veritable armada as they headed for Normandy. She anchored seven miles off the coast at dawn on June 6 and disembarkation began at 6.15 am. One witness, the ship's surgeon, recalls the mass of shipping all around, with warships forming a complete half circle round the horizon firing continual broadsides inland as the men were landed. Some hours later a few of *Monowai*'s landing craft returned, but only six of the original 20 survived, the remainder being blown up by mines off the beaches. After embarking about a dozen casulaties *Monowai* returned to Southampton, and between then and March 1945 she made 45 crossings to France with troops. The only damage she suffered was caused by high winds on the night of January 18/19 when she was alongside a pontoon pier at Cherbourg, but fortunately it was only superficial. On April 22 1945 she sailed from Plymouth for Odessa with 1,610 released Soviet prisoners of war. There were five ships in the convoy and they carried nearly 10,000 released Russian prisoners in all. What sort of a welcome they received in Stalin's Russia is not recorded.

Monowai then returned to Marseilles with 1,600 released French prisoners. She made two more voyages between Odessa and Marseilles before leaving for Colombo to prepare for operations against Japan and the landings in Malaya. The sudden surrender of Japan in August 1945 made the landings unnecessary, and on September 13 she formed part of the third convoy to enter Singapore after the reoccupation. She then embarked 650 service personnel and 199 civilians who had been prisoners of the Japanese, some of whom had not seen home for 11 years. She arrived in Liverpool on October 8 1945 and the people there gave her a great welcome. The next ten months were occupied with trooping duties between the UK, Italy, North Africa

After her launch Razmak *was towed from the Clyde to Belfast to have her propelling machinery fitted* (John Clarkson).

and India, and then in August 1946 she arrived in Sydney where she was released by the government and was able to undergo her re-conversion to a passenger liner.

It had been decided to put *Monowai* back on to the Tasman run, because the six-year old 13,000-ton *Awatea* had been sunk during the North African landings. The refit, which was carried out by Mort's Dock & Engineering Co, was dogged by industrial troubles and it was December 20 1948 before she completed her sea trials and was ready to resume service. On January 19 1949 she sailed on her first Wellington–Sydney run, and at first she was able to maintain a fortnightly schedule between the two countries. However, in 1951 this was broken when she was held up from April to July in Wellington by a dock-workers' strike. By the late 1950s air travel had begun to take away potential passengers and it was getting more and more difficult to fill the berths. In May 1959 she suffered a serious fire in her boiler room, and a year later on Thursday May 19 1960 she made her final sailing from Auckland across the Tasman Sea. She was to be withdrawn from service and offered for sale; she was well past her prime and there could be only one fate for her—the breakers yard. But there was strong opposition in New Zealand where she was such a well-loved ship. She left for a Pacific cruise on June 2 1960, and this really was her last passenger voyage, for she was purchased by the Hong Kong breakers, the Far East Metal Industry Company for £165,000.

There was a last minute attempt by the shipbreaking company to extend the *Monowai*'s career for another year as a passenger liner, but this was refused by the USS Co. She was brought across from New Zealand to Hong Kong in September 1960 by Captain S.M. Barling. On Tuesday September 13 1960 she was taken in tow for her last short trip across Kowloon Bay to the Ngautaukok breaking yards near the airport. She had had a long career of 35 years, most of these in New Zealand where the public were sorry to see her go.

Technical data
Gross tonnage: 10,602
Net tonnage: 4,900
Length overall: 519 ft (158.19 m)
Breadth: 63 ft 2 in (19.25 m)
Depth: 34 ft (10.36 m)
Cargo capacity: No figures available
Boilers: Oil-fired, four double-ended and two single-ended boilers, 215 psi
Main engines: Twin screw, two sets quadruple-expansion reciprocating engines, with low pressure double-reduction geared Bauer-Wach turbines, 12,000 IHP, 18 knots
Ship's company: 262
Passengers: First class 142, Second class 142

Razmak *as she appeared when she entered service with P&O* (P&O).

Above Monowai *as an LSI(L) during World War Two. Her LCAs were normally double banked along each side. Her after armament of one 4-in and two 12-pounder anti-aircraft guns can be clearly seen* (Imperial War Museum).

Below Monowai *enters Sydney Harbour after the Second World War* (author's collection).

The 'C' Class 1925

1925 saw the entry into service of three medium sized vessels for the Australian service. They were constructed at the start of the second phase of a post-1918 building programme and all were ordered at the end of 1923. Each of the ships had a gross tonnage of just over 15,000, and they were built in Glasgow; the first two *Cathay* and *Comorin* by Barclay Curle & Co Ltd, and the third *Chitral* by Alexander Stephen & Sons. Although they were primarily designed for the London-Sydney run, it was intended that they be interchangeable for use on the Far East route, where they were frequently seen after 1930.

Cathay and *Comorin* were both launched on October 31 1924, the former from Barclay's West Yard by Lady Inchcape and the latter from the Clydeholm Yard by Mrs Alexander Shaw, wife of the P&O Deputy Managing Director and the eldest daughter of Lord Inchcape. *Chitral* was launched three months later by Miss Elsie Mackay, who was also responsible for the interior design of *Cathay*'s passenger accommodation. They were good looking ships with two masts, two funnels and cruiser sterns. They had accommodation for 203 first and 103 second class passengers, with a cargo capacity of over 450,000 cu ft in six holds. Their one drawback was that they lacked the reserves of speed required by the mail steamers, but once again P&O had forfeited speed for absolute reliability and had fitted them with quadruple-expansion reciprocating engines which gave them a speed of 16 knots.

Cathay was the first of the two to be handed over and she arrived in Tilbury on March 24 1925 in preparation for her maiden voyage to Sydney three days later. *Comorin* was completed in the following month and made her maiden voyage on April 24. It was mid June before *Chitral* arrived in London on completion of her trials, and she sailed on her maiden voyage to Australia on July 3 1925. All three ships ran to Australia for the first three years, making calls at Marseilles, Suez, Aden, Colombo, then on to Fremantle, Sydney and Brisbane. During one of *Cathay*'s early voyages home from Australia in a gale, fuel oil leaked from an oil bunker contaminating a cargo of meat. A lengthy lawsuit followed and several years later P&O won the case, the blame being put on the builders.

On March 12 1930 when *Comorin* was at Colombo and homeward bound, fire broke out in her number two and three holds. It originated in a cargo of wool and fibre and burned fiercely all that day, causing some damage to the first class dining saloon which was immediately above. There were 204 passengers aboard who were landed as a safety precaution. At one stage the vessel had a list of 30 degrees as the crew and fire brigades fought to get the blaze under control. By the evening of the 13th the fire had been extinguished. After temporary repairs *Comorin* was able to sail three days later though without her first class passengers whose accommodation had been quite badly damaged. All the cargo in the two holds was destroyed, as was a great proportion of the Australian mails. She arrived in London on April 7 1930, and spent the next month in dock undergoing repairs. She did not sail again until May 9 when she left for Bombay and Japan. During 1930 *Comorin* and *Chitral* were fitted with low pressure exhaust turbines, which boosted their speed to 17 knots. However, despite having the same handicap *Cathay* was never modified in the same way.

On November 17 1933 *Cathay* left London bound for Brisbane, carrying the Christmas mail for Australia. By December 15 she was a few hours behind schedule and was trying to make up the lost time when, in the Indian Ocean between Colombo and Fremantle (5°'51'S, 90°'38'E), she lost her port propeller. She continued the voyage on one engine, but by the time she reached Fremantle she was three days late and the mails for the eastern states did not arrive until the New Year. *Cathay* then had to wait in Sydney until *Strathnaver* brought out a replacement propeller. In June 1933 *Chitral* had a rather unusual cargo for her voyage to Shanghai, when she shipped the 'Insect' Class gunboat HMS *Sandpiper* to China for service on the Yangtse. The gunboat had been constructed at Southampton, then dismantled and packed into crates for the voyage. In July 1934 it was the turn of *Comorin* to have propeller trouble when homeward bound from Brisbane in the Red Sea she lost a blade from her port propeller. However, after a survey at Port Said it was decided she could proceed and there was no delay.

Over the next five years the 'C' Class ships plied between London, Australia and the Far East. One of the passengers aboard *Comorin* in late 1938, travelling to Australia, was the novelist H.G. Wells. Unfortunately he was not impressed by her, and he wrote a very disparaging article entitled 'SS *Pukka Sahib*' in the *News Chronicle* of February 13 1939. In the last remaining months of peace in 1939 they were on their last peacetime voyages. On July 12 *Chitral* left Yokohama for London, and nine days later *Comorin* left London for Brisbane; *Cathay* left London on August 4 1939 also bound for Brisbane. It had been intended that they would be converted to armed merchant cruisers in time of war, and all three ships started the war in this role. *Chitral* arrived in London on August 25, and less than two weeks later she was at her builders in Glasgow where the conversion took place. *Cathay* and *Comorin* were both east of Suez when war broke out and *Cathay*'s voyage was terminated at Bombay where she was taken into the dockyard for conversion. *Comorin*, meanwhile, was in Australia and on her return to the UK she too was refitted for war. All three ships lost their rear dummy funnels, and were armed with eight 6-in guns and two 3-in anti-aircraft guns.

Cathay started her naval career with the East Indies fleet and spent the first year of the war on patrol and escort duties in the Indian Ocean. In January 1940 the Admiralty allocated *Comorin* to the South Atlantic station based at Simonstown, but in April that year she moved to the Bermuda—Halifax escort force. In September and October 1940 she was refitted on the Tyne, and in January 1941 she joined the Freetown escort force. She sailed on her final voyage from the Clyde on April 4 1941, bound for Freetown. Along with the destroyer *Lincoln* she was to provide the escort for the merchant ships *Glenartney, Boreas* and *Assiniboine*. They were routed well out into the Atlantic and at 2.00 pm on April 6, in a position 54° 34'N, 21° 20'W, fire broke out in *Comorin*'s engine room. The fire took hold quickly and at 6.20 pm *Lincoln* sent out distress signals. One ship which was not far away was the destroyer HMS *Broke*, which arrived on the scene at 8.10 pm that evening.

There was a heavy sea with waves of 50 to 60 ft and the scene was described by Sir Peter Scott, who was a Lieutenant on board the *Broke*. He recalls seeing *Comorin* lying beam on to the seas with thick black smoke belching from her funnel, an ominous red glow coming from it and clouds of smoke streaming from her lee side. All the boats and rafts were away and the survivors from these had been picked up by *Lincoln* and *Glenartney*, but there were many crewmen still on board *Comorin* who had congregated aft away from the fire. HMS *Lincoln* was operating a Carley float ferry service, but this was far too slow. *Broke*'s captain, Commander Scholfield, decided to take his ship alongside *Comorin*, thus allowing a handful of men to jump on each run. *Broke*'s fo'c'sle was covered with padding and her port side packed with fenders. She then made repeated runs alongside *Comorin*, allowing only seconds for the crew to jump aboard to safety. *Broke* sustained severe damage herself, but by the early hours of the morning everyone was clear of *Comorin*; 450 survivors, all but 20 of those on board, had been rescued by the three ships. HMS *Lincoln* had 121 survivors on board, the *Glenartney* had 104, and the remainder, including Captain J.I. Hallet RN, *Comorin*'s commander, were on board HMS *Broke*. By 5.00 am on April 7 *Comorin* was ablaze from stem to stern. She was then sunk by gunfire from HMS *Lincoln*, disappearing bows first at noon that day. Perhaps the best and most detailed account of this dramatic rescue is in Sir Peter Scott's book, *The Eye of the Wind*, which I would recommend to readers.

Meanwhile, in January 1941 *Cathay* was transferred from the Indian to the Atlantic Ocean, and most of that year was spent escorting convoys. On September 9 1941 the Admiralty decided that she should be converted to a troop transport by the US Navy, and she left the UK on October 5 that year for the Navy Yard at Brooklyn, where the work was carried out by the Bethlehem Steel Corporation. She sailed again for the Clyde at the start of May 1942 and for the next five months she carried troops to South Africa, the Middle East and India. On October 23 1942 she embarked troops in the Clyde to take part in the 'Torch' landings in North Africa. She sailed three days later in the same convoy as *Viceroy of India*. After landing some troops and stores at Algiers, where she came under heavy air attack, she left for Bougie to land the main body of troops in an operation codenamed 'Perpetual'. She arrived at the anchorage outside Bougie at 9.30 am on November 11. The landings were unopposed, the French garrison commander agreeing that port facilities and the airfield could be used.

That afternoon while disembarkation was taking place, the ships in the anchorage were subjected to bombing by German aircraft, and at 5.00 pm an extremely heavy attack developed. The aircraft carrier *Argus* and the monitor *Roberts* were damaged. *Cathay* sustained at least two direct hits, one of which failed to explode, but three bombs which fell close to the engine and boiler rooms on the starboard side caused serious damage. The ship was abandoned, but it was intended that she be reboarded that night if she was still afloat. At 10.00 pm that day a delayed action bomb in the galley exploded, and the fire burned fiercely all night. At 7.00 am the following morning an ammunition explosion blew off the stern and three hours later she sank on her starboard side, completely gutted. Her crew were taken on board the BI ship *Karanja*, but she too was bombed and badly damaged. The crews of both ships were repatriated on board *Strathnaver*.

The sole survivor of the 'C' Class *Chitral* started her war service in October 1939 on the Northern Patrol, and it was not long before she saw her first action. On October 14 she was 'working up' at Scapa Flow when HMS *Royal Oak* was torpedoed and on November 20 while on patrol between Iceland and the Faroes, she intercepted the German ship *Bertha Fisser* off the south-east coast of Iceland. The German vessel had the name *Ada* and her port of registry, Bergen, painted on the hull. As there was no ship of that name *Chitral* gave chase and fired warning shots. The crew of the German vessel scuttled her and abandoned ship and *Chitral* sank her with gunfire. The action was close to the village of Hoefn and the inhabitants witnessed it all; in fact the noise from *Chitral*'s guns shattered windows in the village. That night the derelict *Bertha Fisser* ran ashore on some rocks and broke up. The German crew were taken prisoner and they gave the news that the German battlecruisers *Scharnhorst* and *Gneisenau* were approaching. However, *Chitral* had only indirect contact with them when she rescued 11 survivors from the *Rawalpindi* on November 24, returning to Glasgow with them and her prisoners.

In February 1940 she went to Liverpool for a long refit which kept her out of action until August that year, when she returned to the Northern Patrol. In the following month she assisted with 'Operation Rivet', the transporting of troops to Iceland. In all she made three trooping voyages between the Clyde and Reykjavik. No sooner had she finished these trips when, on November 11, she was ordered to proceed south into the Atlantic to search for survivors of *Admiral Scheer*'s attack on convoy *HX 84*, which included HMS *Jervis Bay*. She spent the New Year patrolling the Denmark Strait with the cruiser HMS *Manchester*, in case the *Admiral Scheer* should try to get back to Germany.

In March 1941 she was transferred to the Halifax escort force, and after a refit in California in October that year she returned to the Clyde and then to the East Indies station. The remainder of her naval career was spent east of Suez. In December 1943 it was decided to convert her to a troopship, and in April 1944 she went to Baltimore where the conversion took place. Her second funnel and mainmast were restored, but her grey livery remained. Dormitories crammed with tiers of 'Standee' bunks were built in what had been first class cabin accommodation, and the music room and lounge became recreation areas. *Chitral*'s role as a troopship lasted for three years, during which time she brought servicemen home to be demobilized, repatriated Italian prisoners of war and Polish troops and also helped to evacuate the British army from India. In the summer of 1947 she received some publicity over conditions on board, but this was a storm in a teacup and a few weeks later she was released by the government. She was reconditioned at the Royal Albert Dock in London where her former black livery was restored and she was fitted out to carry 740 emigrants on each voyage to Australia, under charter to the Ministry of Transport. She made her first voyage in this role on December 30 1948, and in 1950 she assisted with the evacuation of Dutch nationals from Indonesia.

By now *Chitral* was well past her prime, and it became obvious that as soon as the numbers of settlers requiring berths to Australia dropped, her days would be numbered. She made her last voyage from Australia in February 1953, and suffered engine trouble on passage. This was overcome by the efforts of the engineers, and she arrived in London on March 21. She was sold to the British Iron & Steel Corporation for £167,500, and she arrived in the Clyde on April 1 1953, being handed over to the shipbreakers at Dalmuir the following day. The ship's bell was presented to The Mall School at Twickenham in Middlesex, which had been linked with her through the British Ship Adoption Society. The bell still hangs outside the classrooms and it is in regular use, summoning the students to lessons and indicating break times.

Technical data
Gross tonnage: 15,103 *(Cathay)*, 15,115 *(Comorin)*, 15,248 *(Chitral)*
Net tonnage: 8,740 *(Cathay)*, 8,736 *(Comorin)*, 8,805 *(Chitral)*
Length overall: 546 ft 11 in (166.69m) *(Cathay, Comorin)*, 547 ft (166.72 m) *(Chitral)*
Breadth: 70 ft (21.33 m)
Depth: 46 ft (14.02 m)
Cargo capacity: 452,390 cu ft in six holds
Boilers: Oil-fired, four single-ended and three double-ended boilers, 215 psi
Main engines: Twin screw, two sets quadruple-expansion reciprocating engines, 13,437 IHP, 16 knots; 1930, *Comorin* and *Chitral* fitted with low pressure exhaust turbines, 17 knots
Ship's company: 278
Passengers: First Class 203, Second class 103; December 30 1948, *Chitral* converted for 740 'one class tourist' passengers

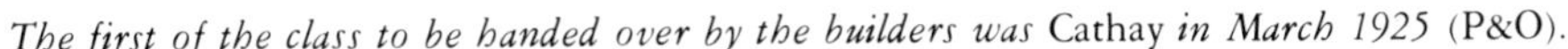

The first of the class to be handed over by the builders was Cathay *in March 1925* (P&O).

Above Comorin *made her maiden voyage in April 1925* (P&O).

Below *It was mid-June 1925 before* Chitral *arrived in London on completion of her trials, and she sailed on her maiden voyage to Australia on July 3 1925* (P&O).

Above Chitral *in her role as an armed merchant cruiser during the Second World War* (P&O).

Below *August 1947*, Chitral *on her last voyage as a troopship enters Grand Harbour, Malta. 19 days later she began her refit before returning to P&Os service once more* (Michael Cassar).

A post-war two berth cabin in Chitral (P&O).

A post-war dormitory cabin on board Chitral (P&O).

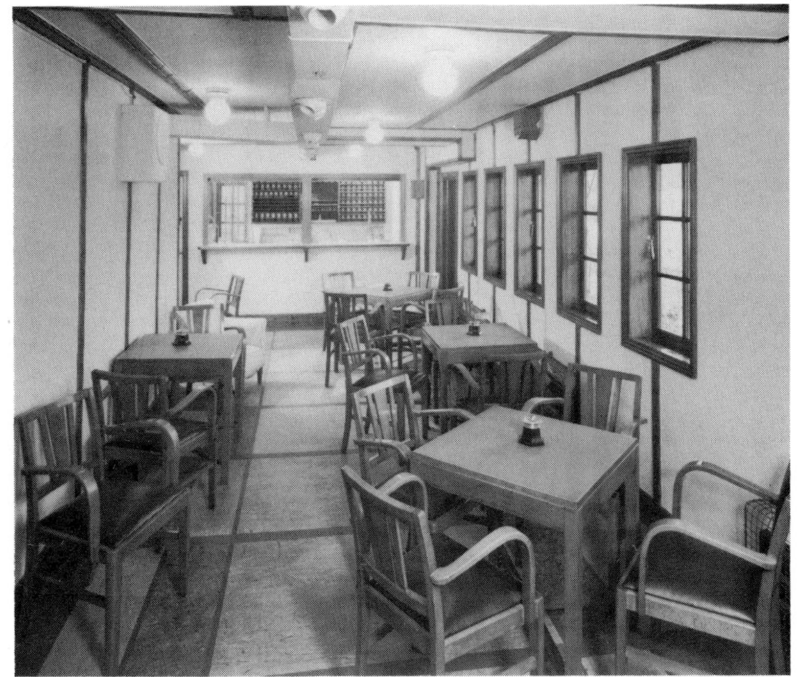

A bar on board Chitral, *after her post-war refit* (P&O).

The smoke room on board the post-war Chitral (P&O).

Above *The after dining saloon on* Chitral *as many emigrants to Australia in the early 1950s will remember it* (P&O).

Below *A fine photograph of* Chitral *in the Channel, homeward bound from Australia in the 1950s* (Skyfotos Ltd).

The 'R' Class 1925

In 1923 the keels were laid for the last class of vessels in the post-war rebuilding programme. They were the four 'R' Class ships, all named after areas or cities of India, and designed in fact for the London to Bombay mail service. Two of the class, *Ranpura* and *Ranchi*, were built by R & W Hawthorne Leslie on the Tyne, and the other two, *Rawalpindi* and *Rajputana*, by Harland and Wolff at their Greenock yard. The first of the four to be launched was *Ranpura*, and she took to the water on September 13 1924. Her sponsor was Mrs C.E. Straker, the wife of the Chairman of Hawthorne Leslie's. Surprisingly there were no P&O representatives present. Just over four months later on January 26 1925 the *Ranchi* was launched; she was named by Lady Addis, wife of Sir Charles Stewart Addis, a Director of the P&O Company.

Exactly two months later on March 26 the first of the Harland and Wolff sisters was launched. *Rawalpindi* was the most famous of the four ships and she was sponsored by Lady Birkenhead, wife of the first earl who was the Lord High Chancellor from 1919 to 1922. Finally on Friday August 7 1925 the last ship of the quartet took to the water; she was the *Rajputana*. The four ships were all delivered to P&O during 1925, in the same order as they were launched, *Ranpura* on April 8, *Ranchi* on July 29, *Rawalpindi* on September 3 and *Rajputana* on December 30. Shortly after *Ranchi* was delivered she sailed south to the Solent and anchored off Cowes at the start of 'Cowes Week'. Viscount Inchcape had invited a large number of guests on board, and the ship made a cruise round the Isle of Wight. In fact for the three days she was there she attracted as much attention as the royal yacht.

The four ships each had a gross tonnage of 16,000 and, like the 'C' Class vessels before them, they were fitted with reciprocating engines to provide, according to P&O, absolute reliability. This seems a strange reason, because by that time geared turbines were proving to be just as reliable. They had a service speed of 17 knots, but they lacked the reserves of speed really needed by the mail steamer. The accommodation for just over 300 first class and 280 second class passengers was situated on 'A' to 'D' decks, with the first class public rooms being situated amidships and the second class further aft on 'A' and 'B' decks. The layout of the public rooms was very similar in all four ships with the first class lounge, music room and smoke room on 'A' deck. The second class lounge and smoke room were on 'B' deck aft, and dining saloons for both classes were on 'C' deck. Much of the decor in the public rooms was designed by Miss Elsie Mackay, the youngest daughter of Viscount Inchcape.

By January 1926 all four ships were in service between Tilbury and Bombay. They also took their turn with cruising duties and turned out to be very popular vessels in this role, due mainly to their handiness whilst manoeuvering in restricted waters. In May 1929 *Ranpura* made one round voyage to Australia, the first part of the trip being her normal route to Bombay and from there she sailed on to Melbourne and Sydney. She was the only one of the 'R' Class ships to visit Australia before the Second World War. In the following year *Ranchi* was fitted with Bauer-Wach exhaust turbines by the London company Green & Silley Weir. She was the only one of the class thus modified, and so her efficiency was improved.

In the early 1930s the Bombay call was incorporated into the Australian and Far East routes and as the need for a separate service had gone, the four 'R' Class ships were put onto the Far East service to China and Japan. During 1935 and the early part of 1936 the Chinese government had loaned many priceless art treasures for an art exhibition at Burlington House in London. When the exhibition was over the treasures were loaded onto *Ranpura* for the journey back to Shanghai. A Royal Navy destroyer was assigned as *Ranpura*'s escort, which indicates how important the British government considered the cargo to be. On April 6 1936, whilst *Ranpura* was entering Gibraltar with her treasure, she went aground. Her passengers were ferried ashore, and when eventually the ship was refloated, divers went down to inspect the hull. Fortunately there was no damage and with the cargo still intact, she was able to resume the voyage, albeit minus some passengers.

The year 1937 saw the start in earnest of hostilities between China and Japan, with an aggressive Japanese nation determined to invade and occupy as much of China as was possible. It was inevitable that the 'R' Class ships would be caught up in this undeclared war. In the summer of that year several thousand British nationals were evacuated from Shanghai during fighting around the city. *Rajputana* was one of six liners which assisted the evacuation from Woosung to Hong Kong. Two months later in early September, *Ranpura* was in Hong Kong when the colony was hit by one of its worst typhoons. Fortunately she had moved out to a safe anchorage and she rode out the storm but 30 vessels were driven ashore, the two largest being the Italian liner *Conte Verde* and the Japanese *Asama Maru*. On September 16 1937 *Rawalpindi* was shadowed by a Japanese destroyer just outside Hong Kong while homeward bound from Japan. So menacing was the warship that the *Rawalpindi*'s Captain stopped his ship. The destroyer came close and demanded to know *Rawalpindi*'s destination, and after receiving the reply 'Hong Kong' it departed.

Just over 18 months later in May 1939, *Ranpura* was involved in a far more serious incident four miles outside Hong Kong. She was about to enter the port when a Japanese cruiser fired blank shots and stopped her, even though she was only one mile outside Hong Kong's three mile limit. The Japanese sent a boarding party of three officers and a signalman and announced their intention of examining the ship's papers. Fortunately *Ranpura* managed to get a signal off to Hong Kong and the destroyer *Duchess* arrived on the scene. Strong protests were made to the Japanese authorities, who replied that they had the right to stop any vessel on the high seas to verify her identity. There was very little Britain could do about such incidents, as her position both militarily and politically was very weak, and appeasement was taking its toll on the nation's status in world events.

In the following months the situation in Europe deteriorated, and by August that year the first steps were taken to convert the 'R' Class ships to their wartime role of armed merchant cruisers. The first of them to be requisitioned was *Rawalpindi*. She was taken over on August 24 1939 and converted in the Royal Albert Dock in London. Three days later *Ranchi* and *Ranpura* received warning telegrams. *Ranpura* was in Aden at the time and she was ordered to Calcutta. *Ranchi* was also east of Suez and she was ordered to Bombay for conversion. *Rajputana* was in Yokohama and she was directed to proceed to Esquimalt on Vancouver Island in Canada. All four vessels had their after funnel, a dummy, removed, and they were all armed with eight 6-in guns and two 3-in high-angle anti-aircraft guns. Four of the 6-in guns were fitted forward of the bridge and four were aft on 'A' deck.

Rawalpindi was assigned to the Northern Patrol and *Rajputana* to the South Atlantic. *Ranchi* joined the East Indies fleet, and *Ranpura* spent the first few months of the war in the Mediterranean before being deployed to the South Atlantic. The heroic and tragic story of the *Rawalpindi* is well known, but what is perhaps not so well known is that ironically she took the place of the AMC HMS *Jervis Bay* on that fateful patrol in November 1939. *Jervis Bay* had been sent to the Tyne for repairs to her windlass machinery, and so *Rawalpindi* sailed north to the icy waters between the Faroes and Iceland to enforce the blockade of Germany. It was in the afternoon of November 23 1939 that she sighted the German battlecruisers *Scharnhorst* and *Gneisenau*. The German vessels ordered her to heave-to, but Captain E.C. Kennedy RN (the father of Ludovic Kennedy) decided to fight them both.

The terrible unequal action lasted for 40 minutes before, at 4.15 pm in the rapidly fading light, *Rawalpindi* sank but not before she scored at least one hit on the German ships. 26 survivors were taken prisoner and 11 were rescued next day by *Chitral*, but 265 men were lost in this first surface action of the war and Captain Kennedy was one of them. As the Prime Minister Neville Chamberlain said, 'Those men must have known as soon as they sighted their enemy that there was no chance for them but they had no thought of surrender. They fought their guns until they could be fought no more, and many of them went to their deaths, thereby carrying on the great traditions of the Royal Navy'. Six months later, at the end of May 1940, *Rawalpindi*'s motor boats which had been left in London, helped the armada of little ships in the evacuation of Dunkirk.

Meanwhile *Ranpura* and *Rajputana* were based at Halifax, Nova Scotia and were engaged in convoy escorts. In November 1940 while both ships were escorting convoys across the Atlantic *Ranpura* handed over her convoy to HMS *Jervis Bay* and returned to Canada. Two days later the *Admiral Scheer* sank *Jervis Bay*, which fought gallantly allowing most of the convoy to escape. *Rajputana* was approaching the area with her convoy, and so they were turned back to Sydney on Cape Breton Island, Canada, until the situation was cleared up. However, in April 1941 *Rajputana* was ordered to Iceland to fuel and then to take up patrol duties in the Denmark Strait. On April 11 she reached the patrol area 150 miles south of Iceland, and two days later at 6.00 am a torpedo from *U-108* crashed into the engine room on the port side. Although she was disabled, *Rajputana* was far from being sunk. The submarine was sighted and the gunners opened fire, but at 7.30 am another torpedo hit her and she began to sink rapidly. At 8.40 am the order to abandon ship was given and she sank soon afterwards. 41 men were lost, although 283 were rescued by destroyers and landed at Reykjavik. The war was less than two years old, and both of the Harland and Wolff built ships had been lost to enemy action.

For three and a half years *Ranchi* had served with the East Indies fleet and had steamed some 300,000 miles when, in March 1943, she went in to Thorneycroft's yards at Southampton to be refitted as a troopship. Meanwhile, *Ranpura* was now part of the East Indies fleet, having arrived there in August 1942; but in October 1943 she too left for the UK, arriving in the Clyde shortly before Christmas. The Admiralty had decided to purchase her outright and convert her to a heavy repair ship. In the New Year of 1944 she moved to Portsmouth for a refit which was to last over two years. *Ranchi* commenced her service as a troopship in the Mediterranean. In the weeks following the Allied invasion of Italy, she followed the advance up the peninsula disembarking troops at Taranto and Naples. In November 1944 she had a lucky escape, when she was the flagship of an eastbound convoy north of Benghazi. The whole convoy came under attack from the air, and a 500 lb bomb hit *Ranchi*. Fortunately it was deflected from its target, the ship's bridge by a wire span on the forecastle, and passed without exploding through a troops' latrine into the sea.

After the war in Europe came to an end in May 1945, she moved to the eastern theatre of war. In August of that year she carried troops to Malaya as part of 'Operation Zipper'. It had been planned originally as an opposed landing on the west coast of Malaya around Port Dickson, but fortunately Japan surrendered before the invasion fleet arrived. In April 1946 *Ranpura* was commissioned at Portsmouth as a heavy repair ship. She sailed soon afterwards for Singapore where she was to join the British Pacific Fleet. She reached Malta on May 30, and it was decided to keep her there as part of the Mediterranean Fleet. Later that year she was sent to Corfu to stand by the damaged destroyers HMS *Saumarez* and HMS *Volage*, which had both hit mines off the Albanian coast.

In early 1947 she returned to home waters and was used for a time to augment apprentice training facilities at the shore facility, HMS *Caledonia* in Rosyth. In June that year *Ranchi* was finally released from government service, and she went to Harland and Wolff's yards at Belfast to be refitted. Nevertheless it was clear that she would no longer be one of the company's crack mail steamers and she was reconditioned to carry 950 passengers in one class tourist accommodation, most of whom would be people emigrating to Australia on government assisted passages. On her return voyages, however, she did carry tourist class passengers on the company's account. Like other P&O emigrant ships she retained her pre-war black hull but she never regained her after funnel. She made her first voyage in this new role on June 17 1948 and served the company for just over four years. In August 1950 she was chartered by the Netherlands government in order to evacuate Dutch nationals from Indonesia. Her last sailing was on October 6 1952, and on her return to London on New Years Day 1953 she was sold to the British Iron & Steel Corporation for demolition. In mid January she arrived at Newport, Monmouthshire where she was to be broken up. This left *Ranpura* as the sole survivor of the 'R' Class.

Between October and December 1956 *Ranpura* took part in 'Operation Musketeer' (the Suez operations). She moored just inside the breakwater at Port Said, astern of HMS *Forth*, for the brief Anglo-French occupation of the Canal Zone. On November 23 1958 she was put into reserve at Devonport, and in April 1961 she was sold to Italian shipbreakers for over £200,000. She arrived at La Spezia in May that year and so 36 years after they had all entered service the last of the 'R' Class departed from the scene.

It is only fitting that the final paragraph in the story of the 'four R's' should be devoted to the gallant *Rawalpindi.* On September 19 1969 the Hull trawler *Kingston Sapphire* was fishing north of the Faroes when her nets were caught fast on a large seabed obstacle. Her radar showed a large object rising 85 ft (27.72 m) from the seabed. When she returned to port her chart was handed to Kelvin Hughes radar experts, who confirmed that the trace had all the appearances of a twin screw vessel of *Rawalpindi*'s dimensions. The Decca fix given for the wreck of 63° 40'N, 11° 29'W, coincides almost exactly with the last position given by *Rawalpindi*, 19 minutes before the final exchanges were fired. Thus 30 years later her wreck had been located.

Technical data

Gross tonnage: 16,585 *(Ranpura)*, 16, 650 *(Ranchi)*, 16,618 *(Rawalpindi)*, 16,568 *(Rajputana)*
Net tonnage: 9,268, *(Ranpura)*, 9,316 *(Ranchi)*, 9,416 *(Rawalpindi)*, 9,414 *(Rajputana)*
Length overall: 569 ft 8 in (173.61 m) *(Ranpura, Ranchi, Rajputana)*, 570 ft (173.73 m) *(Rawalpindi)*
Breadth: 71 ft (21.64 m)
Depth: 38 ft (11.58 m)
Cargo capacity: 344, 160 cu ft *(Ranpura, Ranchi)*, 356,600 cu ft, *(Rawalpindi)*, 352,865 cu ft *(Rajputana)*
Boilers: Oil-fired, six double-ended marine multitubular boilers, 215 psi *(Ranpura, Ranchi)*; oil-fired, six cylindrical open-ended boilers, 215 psi *(Rawalpindi, Rajputana)*
Main engines: Twin screw, two sets quadruple-expansion reciprocating engines, 15,000 IHP, 17 knots; 1930, *Ranchi* fitted with Bauer-Wach exhaust turbines
Ships company: 357 *(Ranpura)*, 366 *(Ranchi)*, 372 *(Rawalpindi)*, 408 *(Rajputana)*
Passengers: First class 305, second class 282 *(Ranpura, Ranchi, Rajputana)*; First class 307, Second class 288 *(Rawalpindi)*

The Rawalpindi *on her trials in August 1925 — this view shows off the lines of the 'R' Class to their best advantage* (Harland & Wolff).

Above Rajputana *prior to the Second World War* (P&O).

Below Ranpura *in P&O service before World War Two* (P&O).

Left *The first class lounge on board* Ranpura, *it would serve as the ward-room during her service as an AMC* (P&O).

Below left *The first class dining saloon on* Ranpura. *This lovely room was to become the coppersmiths' shop later in her naval service* (P&O).

Top right *SS* Ranchi *prior to World War Two* (P&O).

Right *A rare view of the gallant* Rawalpindi *as an AMC* (P&O).

Above *HMS* Rajputana *undergoing her conversion from luxury liner to armed merchant cruiser at Esquimalt in Canada* (P&O).

Below *A view of* Rajputana's *main armament, the ancient 6-in guns on the after section of 'A' deck* (P&O).

Above *HMS* Ranpura *as an armed merchant cruiser in the North Atlantic 1941, still in her P&O livery* (F.T. Grover).

Below *HMS* Ranpura *after her conversion to a heavy repair ship* (Wright & Logan).

Above *HMS* Ranpura *at Grand Harbour, Malta in 1954. She was a familiar sight in the port during the 1950s* (Michael Cassar).

Below *SS* Ranchi *after rejoining the P&O fleet in 1948. The stump which used to be her dummy funnel can be clearly seen* (P&O).

HMS Ranpura, *the last of the 'R' Class in reserve at Devonport. Brunel's Saltash Bridge can be seen in the background* (Rolf Meinecke).

Viceroy of India 1929

The building of the 19,627 ton *Viceroy of India* in 1929 was a bold step for the P&O company, for she was a 'one off' vessel designed for the Bombay service and for cruising. She was the first European owned turbo-electric ship, and she was ordered in April 1927 from the Glasgow shipbuilders Alexander Stephen and Sons. Originally it had been intended to name her *Taj Mahal*, but this was changed to *Viceroy of India* prior to her launch.

Viceroy had accommodation for 415 first and 258 second class passengers, and she carried a crew of 417. She also had a cargo capacity of 217,749 cu ft (6,166 cu m). She was the first liner to have all single berth first class cabins which could be converted into two or three berth rooms by means of interconnecting doors, which made the allocation of the cabins remarkably flexible. The first class public rooms were sited amidships and on 'A' deck. The lounge furnishings and decorations were in an 18th century design, as was the music room. The main smoking room was a reproduction of an old baronial hall complete with a huge fireplace, crest, suit of armour and a small museum of medallions and effects of Bonnie Prince Charlie. The first class dining room reproduced an 18th century French style and was panelled in English walnut. There was also an indoor Pompeiian style swimming bath. All the decoration and furnishings were designed by Lord Inchcape's daughter Miss Elsie Mackay. It was the last of the company's ships she was responsible for, because on March 13 1928 she accompanied Captain W.R. Hinchcliffe, an experienced Imperial Airways pilot, from Cranwell airfield in his Stinson-Detroiter monoplane, in an attempt to break the transatlantic flight record. They were last seen 170 miles off the Irish coast heading west into heavy snowstorms, and it is believed they were forced down into the Atlantic and drowned.

One of *Viceroy*'s most interesting features was her main propulsion machinery. When during the preliminary discussions on the vessel's design the question of machinery came up, turbo-electric had been suggested and Mr R.T. Clarke, P&O's Superintendent Engineer, had looked thoroughly at the possibility and had advised the company to adopt it. So the liner was driven by twin electric motors of 17,500 SHP, the power being supplied by two turbo alternators. Steam was provided by six oil-fired Yarrow water tube boilers at 350 psi and superheated to 740° F. When cruising at lower powers one alternator could supply current to both electric motors enabling two boilers to be shut down, thus obtaining the maximum fuel economy. All the electric machinery was built by the British Thomson Houston Company of Rugby.

The launching ceremony took place on Saturday September 15 1928, and her sponsor was Lady Irwin, the wife of the Viceroy of India. Among those present was Lord Inchcape, his daughter Lady Janet Bailey, and Mr F.J. Stephen. Her preliminary trials took place in the Firth of Forth between February 18 and March 6 1929 and were completely successful. However, in the severe weather which prevailed at the time, a Lloyds surveyor was killed when a pin broke from a shackle. *Viceroy* was handed over to P&O on the following day and made her maiden voyage from London on March 29 1929 bound for Bombay via Marseilles, Malta and Suez. She arrived in Bombay on April 26 and during her eight-day stay in the port an incident of enormous significance took place, which, although it had no immediate effect, was to profoundly alter the role of the ocean liner in the years to come. It was the first non-stop flight from London to Karachi by two RAF officers in a Fairey monoplane.

Viceroy returned to Tilbury on May 24 1929 and spent the summer months cruising from the UK, one of the cruises being to the Norwegian fjords which was to become something of an annual event. Her next voyage to India was on August 30 that year, and it was not long before she broke the London-Bombay speed record with a time of 16 days, one hour and 42 minutes.

On September 5 1935, the Cunard White Star liner *Doric*, with over 700 passengers on board, collided in thick fog with a French coaster *Formigny* off the Portuguese coast. *Doric's* forecastle was badly holed and she put out an SOS. Fortunately *Viceroy* was only 40 miles away, returning home from a cruise, and she raced to the rescue arriving at the scene at 5.30 am that day, shortly before the *Orion*. *Viceroy* took on 241 passengers from the *Doric*, the remainder being rescued by the *Orion*. Both ships then landed their unexpected guests at Tilbury two days later. On April 11 1937 *Viceroy* herself was in trouble when she was northbound in the Suez Canal and high winds forced her aground. She was stuck fast all day, not being refloated until 11.00 pm that night after part of her cargo had been discharged into lighters. Later when divers inspected her hull it was found that her rudder was damaged, but she was able to proceed to Tilbury where repairs were carried out.

The next two years passed without incident, and on Saturday February 11 1939, while she was on a three-week cruise to South America, she made the first P&O call at Tristan Da Cunha. The island headman was

Viceroy of India *on one of her cruises to the Norwegian Fjords* (P&O).

received on board and to the crew's surprise he arrived wearing a blue uniform with P&O buttons. A number of gifts were left, including a sewing machine, a record player and a chest of tea. *Viceroy* made several more round voyages to Bombay before starting her cruising season from Southampton in the summer. She made an Atlantic Isles cruise in July, followed by a three-week cruise to the northern capitals, sailing on August 4. It was to be her last cruise, and indeed her last peacetime voyage, for when she arrived back in Southampton on August 25 P&O announced that, 'owing to the political situation' her next 13-day cruise to Lisbon and the Atlantic Isles, was cancelled. In fact *Viceroy* was to take over the voyage to India and Shanghai which should have been made by the ill-fated *Rawalpindi*. She sailed via Suez returning by the same route, and on reaching UK waters called at Avonmouth and Plymouth, arriving in Southampton on December 26 1939.

She made three more passenger sailings to the Far East, the last one being from Liverpool on July 22 1940 and going via Cape Town and Mombasa. While she was on this voyage on the weekend of August 11 she went to the assistance of the Shaw Savill liner *Ceramic* and the cargo vessel *Testbank* which had been in collision off Cape Town. Neither vessel was seriously damaged, but *Ceramic*'s passengers were transferred to *Viceroy* as a precautionary measure and landed at Cape Town. She returned to Liverpool on November 12 1940, and six days later on the Clyde she was partially fitted out as a troopship. She made one trip in this role to Port Said, sailing round the Cape and returning on February 19 1941 to Liverpool, where she spent the next month being fitted out completely as a troopship. Her next sailing was to Bombay on March 23 calling at Freetown and Cape Town. She made two more trooping voyages to Suez between January and September 1942, and in April she was in Liverpool for repairs to a turbo-alternator.

On October 26 1942 she left the Clyde as part of an 'Operation Torch' convoy. She arrived safely in Algiers on November 7 and disembarked her troops and stores. She left the port at 6.00 pm on November 10, bound for the UK with 432 crew and 22 passengers. Just over ten hours later at 4.28 am on November 11 she was in a position 31 miles north of Oran (36° 26'N, 00° 25'W), when she encountered the German submarine *U-407* on the surface charging her batteries. The U-boat fired a torpedo which hit *Viceroy* in the engine room on the port side, killing two engineer officers and two Indian firemen. She was obviously sinking and her crew abandoned ship, being picked up by HMS *Boadicea*. At 8.07 am that morning *Viceroy of India* sank by the stern. Her crew were eventually repatriated from Gibraltar by the *Llangibby Castle*. It was a very sad end to P&O's most outstanding ship built between the wars.

Technical data
Gross tonnage: 19,648
Net tonnage: 10,087
Length overall: 612 ft (186.54 m)
Breadth: 76 ft 2 in (23.22 m)
Depth: 41 ft 6 in (12.65 m)
Cargo capacity: 217,749 cu ft (6,166 cu m)
Boilers: Oil-fired, six Yarrow watertube boilers, superheated steam at 350 psi, 740°F
Main engines: Twin screw, two synchronous three-phase, 3,150 volt air cooled electric motors. Power supplied by two 9,000 kW turbo-alternators. 17,500 SHP, 19 knots
Ship's company: 417
Passengers: First class 415, Second class 258

Left *The first class smoking room was a replica of an old baronial hall complete with a huge fireplace, crest, suit of armour and a small museum of medallions and effects of Bonnie Prince Charlie* (P&O).

Right *The first class dining saloon reproduced an 18th century French style and was panelled in English walnut* (P&O).

Above Viceroy*'s second class music room* (P&O).

Below *A sad sight,* Viceroy of India *sinking by the stern after being torpedoed by the German submarine* U 407. *It was an unlucky encounter, the U-boat was on the surface charging her batteries* (P&O).

Strathnaver and *Strathaird* 1931 and 1932

Without doubt the first two 'white sisters' *Strathnaver* and *Strathaird* set the style and standards for all the future P&O mail steamers for three decades. At 22,500 gross tons they were the largest ships to be built for the company at that time. The order for the two liners went to the Barrow in Furness shipbuilders Vickers Armstrong Ltd, although Lord Inchcape in his speech at *Strathaird*'s launch joked that the contract had been arranged in a Monte Carlo casino in December 1929, by himself and Sir Basil Zaharoff, who had been authorised to negotiate on behalf of Vickers. With their white hulls and buff funnels they were readily distinguishable from any other P&O vessels, although this was not an entirely new idea, having been used as early as 1894 on the *Caledonia*. Nevertheless it was the first time it had been chosen for the company's express mail steamers. Another new idea was the system of nomenclature, and this break with tradition drew a certain amount of criticism initially. *Strathaird* was derived from the title of Sir William Mackinnon, the founder of the BI line, and was taken from a headland on the Isle of Skye. *Strathnaver*'s name came from the first title of Lord Inchcape, and was taken from a valley to the north of Loch Naver in Sutherland.

The two ships had accommodation for 500 first class and approximately 670 tourist class passengers. Originally the tourist section of the ship had been planned as third class, but this was altered in order to meet the needs of regular travellers for moderate fares combined with a reasonable degree of comfort. The first saloon passengers were accommodated forward on 'A', 'B', 'C', 'D' and 'E' decks. The lounge, smoke room, reading & writing room, corridor lounge, verandah cafe and children's playroom were all on 'B' deck. Both dining saloons were on 'F' deck, separated by the galleys and pantries. The tourist class two and four berth cabins were on 'G' and 'H' decks, with smoking room and promenade on 'E' deck, the lounge and children's nursery on 'E' deck, and a verandah cafe and swimming pool on 'D' deck. A large deckhouse at the aft end of 'D' deck was arranged as a general and isolation hospital. Once again P&O had decided to install turbo-electric propulsion machinery, and the twin screws were driven by two synchronous three phase electric motors, the power being supplied by two 750 kW turbo alternators. The steam generating installation consisted of four oil fired Yarrow water tube boilers, which supplied steam at 425 psi, superheated to 725°F. The machinery developed 28,000 SHP and gave the ships a speed of 22 knots. Although they had three funnels, the first and third were dummies and were fitted to cater for public prejudice against 'less powerful' single funnel ships.

Strathnaver was launched on Thursday February 5 1931 by Lady Janet Bailey, the second daughter of Lord Inchcape. Fitting out was well under way when *Strathaird* took to the water on Saturday July 18 1931. It had been intended that Lady Inchcape should perform the naming ceremony, but owing to her poor health she asked her eldest daughter Lady Margaret Shaw to take her place, which she did. Just over a month later on August 26 *Strathnaver* steamed down the Walney Channel for the Clyde to undergo her trials, and having successfully completed them she arrived in Tilbury on September 4, the company having taken her over from the builders two days previously. She sailed on her maiden voyage to Brisbane on October 1, sailing via

Marseilles, Suez, Bombay and Colombo. She was four weeks into her second voyage to Australia on February 12 1932, when *Strathaird* left Tilbury on her maiden voyage, which was also to Brisbane.

On May 23 1932 the Earl of Inchcape died on board his yacht *Rover* at Monaco, and he was succeeded as Chairman of the P&O company by his son-in-law Mr Alexander Shaw, who was an ardent campaigner for the cause of British shipping. Earlier that month he had entertained the Lord Mayor of London to a dinner on board *Strathnaver* and he made a speech appealing to Britons to travel in British ships. On September 11 1937 *Strathnaver* was delayed on her first Australian voyage after her UK cruising season, when she collided with the quay at Tilbury. In March 1938 one of *Strathaird*'s passengers who had embarked at Bombay, died in Fremantle from smallpox and all her first class passengers were quarantined. She arrived at Sydney in early April and although no new cases were reported, a planned cruise to Fiji was cancelled.

On July 7 1939 *Strathnaver* left London for Brisbane, and ten days later *Strathaird* left Fremantle for London, arriving alongside Tilbury Landing Stage at 8.00 am on August 18 1939. Her next voyage was to have been on September 6, but this was cancelled. Meanwhile *Strathnaver* arrived in Brisbane on August 22, and sailed on to Rabaul in New Britain where she arrived four days later. She was on the return voyage to Sydney when war was declared and she had to continue her journey darkened and at increased speed. On arrival at Circular Quay the crew painted the white hull and buff funnels a uniform grey; from the depths of number six hold packing cases emerged, the contents of which, two ancient guns, one 6-inch and one 3-inch, were mounted on pre-positioned placings on the poop. She finally arrived home in Liverpool in mid-October 1939. Both ships were partially refitted as troop transports and in January 1940 *Strathnaver* sailed from Sydney with troops for the Middle East, joining up with a troop convoy from New Zealand which included *Strathaird*. In May that year *Strathaird*, which was homeward bound, embarked all the British women and children from Aden (which would be within bombing range of Eritrea if Italy came into the war) and went back to Bombay where they were disembarked. She then returned to Southampton via Mombasa, Durban, Cape Town and Las Palmas, arriving in early June. From there she went to Liverpool to be completely fitted out as a troopship, and was in the middle of this refit when she was called away and ordered to Brest. When she arrived there, only days before the fall of France, she embarked 6,000 troops and hundreds of civilians, including 200 children. She also took on the gold from British banks in Paris. All of her passengers were landed safely in Plymouth on June 18.

During 1941 and 1942 both ships made trooping voyages to South Africa, the Middle East and India. In March 1941 *Strathaird* was involved in a collision with the *Stirling Castle*, and her voyage from the Clyde to Suez had to be abandoned. In early 1942 she brought the first US infantry division across the Atlantic to Northern Ireland, and in November that year both ships took part in the landings in North Africa. *Strathnaver*'s voyage out from the UK was largely uneventful until the US merchant ship *Thomas G. Stone* was hit by a torpedo, which damaged her propeller. She fell out of the convoy and the other ships came under surveillance from enemy aircraft but there were no other attacks that day. *Strathnaver* arrived at Algiers on November 11 and was ordered alongside a berth. While she was approaching, an enemy air attack developed and a heavy bomb fell close to her port quarter. Later that day there were more heavy air attacks and more near misses for *Strathnaver*.

At 8.00 pm the same day she sailed for Bougie, and arrived at 6.45 am on November 12. As she approached the harbour she ran into heavy torpedo and minelaying attacks by enemy aircraft. The electricity supply to the winches was cut off to minimise the fire risk, but even though the ship was under heavy attack the Lascar seamen carried on hoisting the three-ton derricks by hand. All that day, until 10.00 pm when she cleared the harbour, *Strathnaver* was under heavy air attack. Captain E.M. Coates her commander, in his official report, praised his crew and particularly the Lascars. The only damage sustained by *Strathnaver* was while going alongside at Algiers, when a frame buckled and a port strained in the firemen's fo'c'sle. During the action she expended 3,204 rounds of Oerlikon, 216 rounds of Bofors, and 750 rounds of .303 ammunition. Fortunately there were no casualties on board. In May and June of 1943 *Strathnaver* took part in exercises in the Red Sea for the Italian landings, and later followed the Allied forces up Italy as they advanced. In 1944 both ships continued their trooping duties to South Africa, the Middle East and India. After the war in Europe had ended, *Strathaird* was employed repatriating New Zealand forces from Italy back to their homeland.

Strathaird was the first of the two sisters to be handed back to P&O in September 1946 and she returned to the builder's yard at Barrow to be reconditioned. *Strathnaver* was to stay in government service for another two years. On October 10 1946 she rammed and sank a small cargo ship *Fluor* at Southampton. She completed her last trooping voyage on October 3 1948 and went to Harland & Wolff's yards at Belfast where she too was to be re-converted for the P&O passenger service. During their refits the only alteration to the two ships was the removal of the dummy funnels, which modernised their appearance and provided the passengers with more open space on 'A' deck.

Strathaird resumed the service to Australia on January 22 1948, and on her return voyage from Sydney on March 10 she carried with her as passengers the Australian test cricket team, under their captain, Don Bradman, *Strathnaver* made her first post-war voyage from Tilbury on January 5 1950, after ten years in government service. 12 days later *Strathaird* was involved in a rescue off the Cocos Islands in the Indian Ocean. 18 of the islanders had put off in two boats to intercept *Strathaird* to obtain fresh food, but the heavy weather had overturned one boat and the second was in difficulties. Fortunately *Strathaird* arrived on the scene and rescued the men, who were later disembarked in Perth.

On June 15 1953 *Strathnaver* took part in the Coronation Fleet Review at Spithead, having been chartered by the government to take official guests round the fleet. Ten days later it was announced that with the arrival of the *Arcadia* and *Iberia* into service in 1954, *Strathnaver* and *Strathaird* would be converted to carry 1,200 tourist class passengers. This also coincided with the withdrawal and breaking up of the 1923 sisters *Mooltan* and *Maloja*. However, before the conversion was completed *Strathnaver* was delayed in Australia for over a week in December 1953 with engine trouble. In the spring of 1954 the two 'white sisters' made their first sailings as one class vessels, and to accommodate the larger number of passengers 174 upper pullman berths had been fitted in former first class cabins.

In February 1958 *Strathaird* made an unexpected call at Djakarta, during a voyage home from Australia, to evacuate Dutch nationals. The passengers were moved

Strathaird *in the early years of her career with three funnels, the first and third being dummies* (Vickers Shipbuilding).

Strathnaver *on her trials in August 1931* (Vickers Shipbuilding).

into the forward accommodation so that the refugees could be accommodated aft. She disembarked them at Rotterdam, on March 13 and arrived at Tilbury the next day. In June 1959 she rescued the crew of an aircraft which had crashed off Singapore and three months later she was delayed in Australia with engine trouble.

In early 1961 the two ships were 30 years old and it was clear that their careers were drawing to a close. *Strathaird* was the first to go. On March 24 1961 it was announced that on her arrival in London on June 18 that year she was to be withdrawn from service. She was sold to the Shun Fung Ironworks in Hong Kong and left Tilbury on June 24 1961 in ballast, arriving in the colony on July 24. She was handed over to the shipbreakers three days later, having been sold for £382,500. There was a condition of sale that demolition had to begin two months after delivery and to be completed a year later. In November 1961 it was announced that the steel from *Strathaird* was being melted down and re-rolled into reinforcing bars to be used in the construction of the new skyscraper blocks being built in the colony. Ironically, even the new buildings at Kai-Tak airport used much of the liner's steel in their construction.

A month later on December 11 1961, P&O announced that *Strathnaver* was to be withdrawn on the completion of her current voyage from London to Australia begun four days earlier. Her withdrawal had been planned for later in 1962, but owing to the Australian government's decision not to take up large numbers of berths provisionally reserved for British emigrants during the first five months of 1962, the date was brought forward. She arrived alongside the Tilbury Landing Stage at 6.30 am on February 23, 1962 and once disembarkation was completed she was moved to

33 berth in Tilbury docks. She left London for her delivery voyage a week later at 5.00 pm on March 1, like her sister going to the Shun Fung Ironworks in Hong Kong for £325,500. She arrived in the colony on March 31 1962; two days later she was handed over to the shipbreakers and made her final short voyage to the Ngautaukok breakers yards near the airport.

Technical data
Gross tonnage: 22,547 *(Strathnaver)*, 22,544 *(Strathaird)*
Net tonnage: 13,620 *(Strathnaver)*, 13,485 *(Strathaird)*
Length overall: 638 ft 7 in (194.64 m)
Breadth: 80 ft (24.38 m)
Depth: 46 ft 6 in (14.17 m)
Cargo capacity: 441,000 cu ft
Boilers: Oil-fired, four Yarrow water tube boilers, superheated steam at 425 psi, 725°F
Main engines: Twin screw, two synchronous three-phase, 3,000 volt air cooled electric motors. Power supplied by two 750 kW turbo-alternators. 28,000 SHP, 21 knots
Ship's company: 500
Passengers: First class 498, Second class 670 *(Strathnaver)*; First class 500, Second class 688 *(Strathaird)*; 1954, both ships 1,252 one class tourist, plus 82 children in cots.
War service
Troops carried: 129,000 *(Strathnaver)*, 128,961 *(Strathaird)*
Miles steamed: 352,000 *(Strathnaver)*, 387,745 *(Strathaird)*

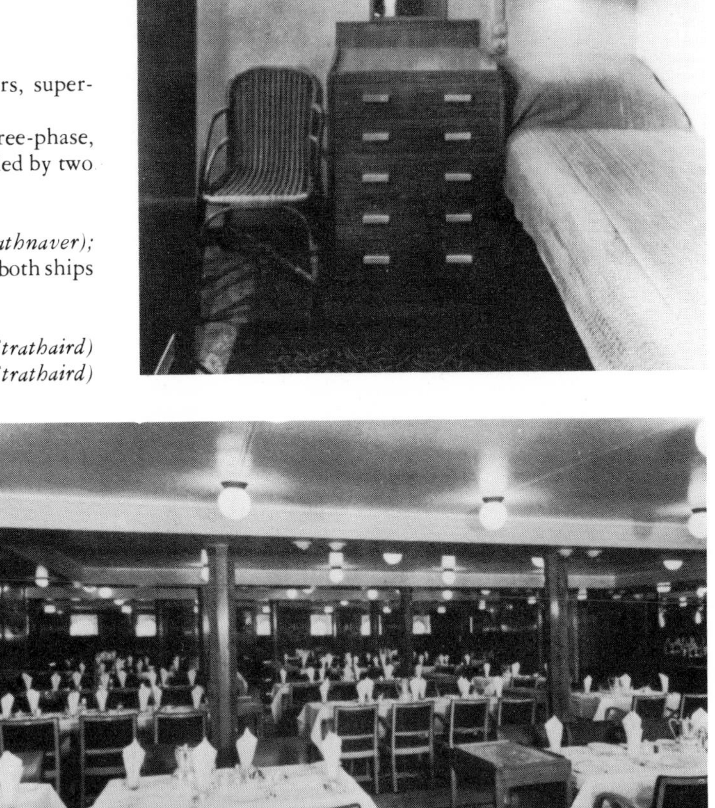

Above right *A tourist two berth cabin,* Strathnaver (author's collection).

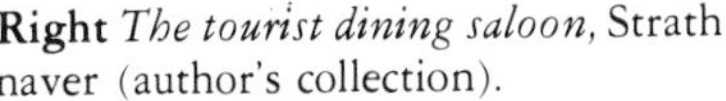

Right *The tourist dining saloon,* Strathnaver (author's collection).

Left *The tourist nursery,* Strathnaver (author's collection).

Below Strathnaver *as a troop transport at Grand Harbour, Malta, in May 1948 only five months before she started her conversion back to passenger liner* (Michael Cassar).

Right Strathnaver *at Sydney after her post-war refit* (P&O).

Below right Strathaird *arrives in Hong Kong in July 1961. Soon her steel was being melted down and re-rolled into reinforcing bars to be used for the construction of the new skyscraper blocks being built in the colony* (P&O).

STRATHNAVER

Corfu and *Carthage* 1931

By 1930, with the outdated 'K' Class as the mainstay of the P&O route to China and Japan, the time had come to build a new tonnage, and the order for two 14,000 ton ships went to Alexander Stephen & Sons of Glasgow. Although they would be slightly smaller, the design of the new vessels was to be very similar to the earlier 'C' Class of 1925, the one major difference being the main propulsion machinery. At last P&O had broken away from the reciprocating engines and had the new vessels fitted with geared turbines. This gave them a speed of 18 knots, sufficient power to beat any competitor and to maintain the mail service without undue difficulty. Originally it had been intended to name the two ships *Cheefoo* and *Canton*, but this plan was altered while they were on the stocks and they were renamed *Corfu* and *Carthage* respectively. Both retained the black livery and two funnels as seen in earlier P&O liners.

The first of the two sisters to be launched was *Corfu*. She took to the water on Wednesday May 20 1931, her sponsor being 15-year-old Miss Patricia Mackay, the eldest daughter of Viscount Glenapp, and Lord Inchcape's granddaughter. Her father represented the company at the ceremony, and in a speech on behalf of the builders, Mr Frederick J. Stephen referred to the launching of the German battleship *Deutschland* by President Hindenburg, and he joked about how much better Miss Mackay had carried out her launching ceremony. *Carthage* was launched three months later on Tuesday August 18 1931 and once again the naming ceremony was performed by one of Lord Inchcape's granddaughters, Miss Jean Shaw, the daughter of the P&O Deputy Chairman Mr Alexander Shaw, who was present on behalf of the owners. The depression of the times was reflected in the fact that once *Carthage* was completed, the yards of Alexander Stephen & Sons at Linthouse would be empty.

By September 25 1931 work on *Corfu* was finished and she was ready to undergo her trials, which were carried out over two days and attended by Lord Inchcape in his yacht *Rover*. She then left for London and sailed on her maiden voyage to Yokohama on October 16 that year. A few weeks later on November 24 *Carthage* started her trials on the Clyde. Four days later she left for London docking there on December 1. Lord Inchcape, who had travelled down from the Clyde, expressed himself well satisfied with the two new ships. A week later *Carthage* left on her maiden voyage commanded by Captain Hugh M. Jack. The day before she called at her first port, Marseilles, she passed *Corfu* homeward bound. The route to the Far East took *Carthage* via Suez, Aden, Colombo, Penang, Singapore, Hong Kong, Shanghai, Kobe and Yokohama.

She arrived in Shanghai on Sunday February 14 1932, a few weeks after Japanese troops had started military operations to capture the city. There was a lot of fighting in the city, and shells landed close to the Ningpo Wharf where *Carthage* was berthed, giving those on board a tense few hours. One shell landed close to the ship killing two ratings from HMS *Suffolk* and injuring Chinese civilians. *Carthage*'s surgeon gave assistance during the time she was in port and it was lucky that the ship herself escaped damage. It seems that the Chinese army had mistaken her for a Japanese troop transport bringing reinforcements to the city. By the time that *Carthage* returned to the city on March 8 on her homeward voyage, the fighting had stopped, so there were no problems and she arrived home on April 15 1932. Her second voyage a week later was to Brisbane, and *Corfu* followed her on this route on May 20; after this one trip to Australia both ships resumed the service to the Far East. In February 1935 while entering Keppel Harbour in Singapore, *Carthage* collided with and sank a lighter and four years later in February 1939 she struck the pier at Yokohama, but in both cases she suffered only minor damage.

Carthage left London for Yokohama on June 30 1939, and *Corfu* left Japan on July 25 that year. As with the other twin screw liners of a similar size in the P&O fleet, it was intended to convert the two sisters to armed merchant cruisers in time of war. The fleet they would serve with would largely depend on their position when war was declared. *Corfu* left Suez for her northbound transit of the canal on August 27 1939 and was detained without explanation at Port Said for a time. War was actually declared while she was in the Mediterranean, and she received the news on calling at Marseilles. *Carthage* was in Hong Kong at the time and she was ordered to Colombo where all passengers and cargo were discharged and she then went on to Calcutta where she was taken over by the Royal Navy for conversion. *Corfu* completed her voyage and then went to Belfast where the conversion was carried out by Harland and Wolff. She was commissioned on November 25 1939, and sailed the following day to join the Northern Patrol. *Carthage* commissioned on December 20, and after a shakedown cruise in the Bay of Bengal she joined the East Indies fleet.

Unlike the AMCs of the 1914-18 war there was to be no dual role of warship and cargo vessel. The new AMCs had to be completely altered. They were ballasted to compensate for lack of cargo, and their holds were filled with buoyancy tanks; whole sets of cabins were torn out to make room for armouries and mess rooms. The public rooms in *Corfu* and *Carthage* took on strange new roles; the first class smokeroom became the officers' ante room. Both ships lost their rear dummy funnels which altered their profile and they were armed with eight 6-in guns and two 3-in anti-aircraft guns, although this armament was improved upon as the months went by. At the end of her service as an AMC *Corfu* had nine 6-in, four 4-in guns and two seaplanes.

In June 1940 *Corfu* was transferred to Freetown and a few weeks later she was involved in a collision which kept her out of action for over a year. She left Freetown at 8.50 am on July 9 1940 as part of the escort for a slow convoy to Greenock, and at 3.02 am the next day the aircraft carrier *Hermes* collided with her tearing a 30 ft hole in her starboard bow plating. The two ships were locked together and at 3.30 am the majority of *Corfu*'s crew were evacuated to the flight deck of HMS *Hermes*. It was nearly two hours later at 5.20 am that she drew clear of *Hermes*, and with the cruiser *Dorsetshire* in company she set course to Freetown at slow astern. At 6.00 pm the same day *Dorsetshire* attempted to take her in tow, but after 30 minutes her bollard was carried away, and *Corfu* had to continue at slow astern until the next morning when tugs arrived. She finally arrived back in Freetown at 11.15 am on July 13, and as she had lost her anchors she was beached in the harbour.

It was clear that it was going to take at least three months for temporary repairs to be effected and so it was decided to re-draft a great proportion of her crew. Almost immediately the Army authorities at Lagos requested that they be allocated *Corfu*'s 6-in guns to assist with the defences there and at Takoradi. In the event only two were given on loan for three months, because to have removed any more would have upset the ship's trim. In January 1941 *Corfu* sailed for Calcutta where she remained until August for permanent repairs to be carried out. In September 1941, with her trials completed, she joined the East Indies fleet and remained on this station for the next year.

Meanwhile *Carthage* had been employed in the Indian Ocean, mainly on convoy escort duties. In June 1940 she made a visit to Diego Suarez to show the flag and to boost the morale of the French authorities there. On November 3 1941 *Carthage* was part of a force of vessels attempting to intercept a convoy of Vichy French ships south-west of Madagascar *en-route* to Europe. The cruiser *Devonshire* confronted the French sloop *D'Iberville*. However, the Captain of the French warship backed down and set course back to Diego Suarez while the French merchant vessels did what they could to immobilize themselves. *Carthage* sent a boarding party to the SS *Cap Padaran* but then had to tow her into Port Elizabeth, a distance of 362 miles. *Carthage*'s Engineer, the late W.J. Fiddes RNR, was awarded the MBE for his part in repairing the *Cap Padaran*'s sabotaged engines. In April 1942 *Carthage* went to Southampton for a refit, during which she suffered a serious fire in number four hold. However, by July 1942 the work was completed, and in August she left the UK once again for the Indian Ocean as escort for convoy WS 22. On November 24 that year, together with the cruiser HMS *Birmingham*, she searched an area in the Indian Ocean (7° 36'N, 61° 8'E) for survivors from the BI ship *Tilawa* which had been torpedoed the day before. But after a long search she was only able to find four Indian seamen on a raft.

In September 1943 it was decided to convert *Carthage* to a troop transport, and she sailed for the Clyde via Suez on her last convoy escort. On October 11 she berthed in Kings Dock, Swansea, where she was emptied of stores. The white ensign was lowered for the last time on October 29, and two weeks later she sailed in convoy for Norfolk, Virginia, where her conversion was to be carried out. In September 1942 *Corfu* left the East Indies for the UK, and then Freetown to join the escort force. In January 1944 she too was converted to a troopship and her naval commission ended in Halifax, Nova Scotia, on February 17 that year. The P&O crew had joined the ship the day before, and at the end of the month she went into the dockyard at Mobile, Alabama, for her refit.

On completion of their conversions both vessels served mainly in the eastern theatre for the remainder of the war, *Carthage* being based at Calcutta. When Japan surrendered on August 14 1945, *Corfu* sailed two weeks later in a large convoy with troops to re-occupy Singapore. Although they were delayed for some time while minesweepers cleared the shipping lanes on the Malacca Straits, they entered Singapore on September 5. A few days later she left for Southampton with 1,134 ex-prisoners of the Japanese, and they arrived on the afternoon of October 7 to a great reception. However, on April 9 1946 she had some far less appreciative passengers on board. She was about to sail for India with 1,205 troops aboard who had been home on leave, when about 450 men walked off her and refused to sail. They complained of conditions on board. About 100 of them went back on board after being seen by the district commander and *Corfu* sailed at 3.00 pm. Eventually all but 34 of the remainder sailed on the *Durban Castle* three days later, but the 34 were charged with 'deserting from the troopship *Corfu* with intent to avoid sailing overseas', and were court martialled at Aldershot.

Later in 1947 *Carthage* returned to her builders yard

Carthage *in her pre-war livery with two funnels* (P&O).

Corfu *as an armed merchant cruiser during the Second World War* (Imperial War Museum).

on the Clyde to be reconditioned for her Far East passenger/cargo service again, and she was followed in 1948 by *Corfu*. Both ships were left with only their forward funnel which was lengthened and changed to the company's new buff colour, while the hulls were painted white. In the words of an ex-P&O Commodore, the new look gave them 'a certain yacht-like grace'. *Carthage* made her first peacetime sailing to the Far East in July 1948, and *Corfu* in February 1949, three and a half years after the end of the war. But their voyages east were very different from the route they had plied in the 1930s. Shanghai was a closed port and Japan was a conquered enemy, so the turn round port was now Hong Kong.

For the next 12 years the two sisters maintained the Far East service, interrupted only by the Suez Crisis in November 1956. *Carthage* was homeward bound when the crisis broke and she was re-routed via the Cape; *Corfu* was outward bound and she too was similarly re-routed. But by April 1957 the Canal had been reopened and things settled down to normal again. By late 1960 both ships were nearly 30 years old. They were now outdated, and it would have cost far too much to install air conditioning and carry out other modernisation work. Then in early 1961 P&O had the opportunity to purchase the two Belgian 13,000 ton Belgian liners *Jadotville* and *Baudouinville* to replace the two sisters.

Carthage arrived in King George V Dock for the last time on February 13 1961. She had been sold to the Japanese shipbreakers Mitsui Bussan Kaisha of Osaka for one cargo voyage, then demolition. She was renamed *Carthage Maru* and left London for the last time on February 28. Her bell was presented to the Tunisian Ambassador to London and it remains in the Embassy to this day. *Corfu* arrived in London on April 13 and after discharging her stores, she too was handed over to Mitsui Bussan Kaisha. She was renamed *Corfu Maru*, and like *Carthage* she made her delivery voyage under the Japanese flag. The two ships had provided a good reliable service, and they had served their country and company well for 30 years.

Technical data

Gross tonnage: 14,251 *(Corfu)*, 14,304 *(Carthage)*
Net tonnage: 7,665 *(Corfu)*, 7,810 *(Carthage)*
Length overall: 522 ft 6 in (159.26 m)
Breadth: 71 ft (21.64 m)
Depth: 46 ft (14.02 m)
Cargo capacity: 361,889 cu ft in six holds
Boilers: Oil-fired, four Yarrow water tube boilers, 425 psi
Main engines: Twin screw, two sets Parsons single reduction geared turbines, 15,500 IHP, 18 knots
Ship's company: 279
Passengers: First class 177, Second class 214

Above Corfu *in her role as a troop-ship in Grand Harbour, Malta* (P&O).

Left *The tourist class dining saloon,* Carthage (author's collection).

Above right Carthage *at Southampton in the late 1950s* (Keith Byass).

Right Carthage Maru *leaves the Thames for the last time on February 28 1961, bound for the breakers yards in Osaka* (A. Duncan).

Strathmore 1935

In 1934 P&O placed the order with Vickers Armstrong at Barrow in Furness for the third of the *Straths*. She was the 23,580 gross ton *Strathmore*, and having had plenty of opportunity to assess the performance of the first two 'white sisters' they were able to make a number of distinct improvements to the new ship. The most obvious modification to the design of *Strathmore* was her single funnel, instead of the three in the earlier ships. The major difference was the main propulsion machinery. The company had decided to revert to the geared turbines, instead of turbo-electric machinery because of the lower capital cost and the fact that the machinery could be built in Vickers' own yards at Barrow.

Strathmore was launched on Thursday April 4 1935 by the Duchess of York, who is now Her Majesty the Queen Mother. The Duke and Duchess visited Barrow for the day, and the launching of *Strathmore* was the first engagement of a very busy schedule. The ceremony took place at 10.53 am, when the Duchess pulled the lever which released the launching triggers, saying, 'I name this ship *Strathmore*. May God bless all those who sail in her.' The ship glided steadily down the slipway, and was taken over by tugs which brought her safely alongside the *Orion*, launched four months previously. *Strathmore* was a very appropriate name for the new ship as it was the title of her sponsor's father, the Earl of Strathmore.

Strathmore's accommodation was very similar to the earlier sisters, having berths for 445 first and 665 tourist class passengers. The layout of her public rooms was very similar to the other two *Straths* with the first class section amidships on 'B' and 'C' decks. Over the fireplace in the first class library and writing room was a portrait of HRH the Duchess of York by Mr Simon Elwes, while in the first class dining saloon on 'F' deck was a large needlework tapestry panel depicting Glamis Castle situated in the wooded plain of Strathmore, with the hazy outline of the Grampian Mountains in the background. An additional refinement in this room was an air conditioning plant which enabled an equable temperature to be maintained in any climate.

Strathmore sailed north to the Clyde on September 13 1935 from Liverpool where she had been drydocked and, despite heavy squalls of wind and rain, she ran a successful series of trials off Arran, and two days later the P&O house flag was hoisted at the masthead. Her maiden voyage was a two-week cruise to the Atlantic Isles, Dakar, Cadiz and Lisbon, sailing from Tilbury on September 27 1935. Although she was designed for the Australian route, her first few voyages east were to Bombay. Despite the fact that her maiden sailing east was delayed by tidal conditions on the afternoon of October 26, she made good progress and arrived in Bombay at noon on November 10 1935. She made the run between Marseilles and Bombay in exactly ten days, beating the previous best run of 11 days made by the Italian liner *Victoria*.

She left London on her third round voyage to Bombay on February 15 1936 but five days later she limped into Gibraltar with engine trouble. After a three-day delay she sailed once more, arriving in Bombay on March 8 and leaving for London again the following day. Her next voyage to Bombay was on March 28 when she carried the new Viceroy of India,

Lord Linlithgow and brought back the outgoing Viceroy, Lord Willingdon and his wife, thus breaking a long tradition that the old and new Viceroys did not meet on Indian soil. On April 22 1937 when entering Bombay she collided with Ballard Pier and damaged her bow, but after urgent repairs in drydock she was able to sail two days later for London, carrying a large number of distinguished guests for the coronation of King George VI. She arrived in Tilbury on Sunday May 9, three days before the ceremony.

For the next two years *Strathmore* sailed between London, Bombay and Sydney, and on April 14 1939 she left Tilbury for Australia on her last pre-war round voyage. She arrived back in London on July 21 and a fortnight later she left on a two week cruise to the northern capitals, returning to Southampton on August 18. The next day she left on a three week cruise to the Mediterranean, but four days later it was announced that she had been ordered to alter her itinerary and was to proceed to Casablanca and Bermuda returning by way of the Azores. She arrived back in Southampton on September 10, seven days after the outbreak of war. Five days later she sailed for Australia, making the cancelled voyage of *Mooltan*. It was not long, however, before she was taken up by the Ministry of War Transport as a troopship, and during the next eight years she served in most theatres of war, coming through safely. One of her memorable voyages was from Bombay to Southampton, when she brought 3,000 men of the 2nd Division home from India. In March 1946 she made a trooping voyage to Kure in Japan, and in May 1948 she completed her last voyage on government service and then went up to Vickers Armstrong's yard on the Tyne to be reconditioned.

She made her first post-war voyage to Australia on October 27 1949, and nine months later she made P&O's first call at Marseilles since the end of the war. Although these calls were customary before the war on both outward and homeward voyages, only homeward bound ships were to make them in the early 1950s. At 9.30 am on Wednesday January 14 1953, *Strathmore* left Tilbury Landing Stage with 973 passengers bound for India and Australia but less than an hour later she developed engine trouble and had to be towed back to Gravesend. It was clear that she would have to go into drydock, and the next day fleets of coaches took 700 of

The launching of Strathmore. *Her sponsor was the Duchess of York* (P&O).

the passengers to London hotels, the remainder making their own arrangements. A week later after repairs were completed and her passengers had embarked once again, she was due to sail at 2.30 pm on January 21. Then one of London's thick fogs dropped over the Thames and she was delayed for a further 24 hours.

Three years later in October 1956 when *Strathmore* was inward bound and moving to anchor off Gravesend, she was in collision with a small Norwegian cargo ship the *Baalbek*. Fortunately there were no injuries and only slight damage was done to a rail on 'E' deck. In 1961, with the withdrawal of *Strathaird, Strathmore* was converted to a one class ship with berths for 1,200 tourist class passengers. But her new role did not last long, for on November 20 1962 it was announced that the three remaining pre-war P&O Orient liners, *Strathmore, Stratheden* and *Orion* were to be withdrawn from service during the next 18 months, although it had not been decided how they would be disposed of. Then 11 months later, on October 22 1963 came the announcement that both *Strathmore* and*Stratheden* had been sold to the Greek shipowner Mr John S. Latsis of Athens. Their new owner proposed to use the ships for most of the year as hotel ships and in other periods as pilgrim ships.

Her Majesty the Queen Mother had always taken a special interest in the ship which she had launched and P&O presented her with several items of personal interest. These included the tapestry of Glamis Castle, the portrait of her as Duchess of York and one of her as Queen Mother, which were all taken from the ship when she docked in Southampton for the last time on October 27 1963. Four days later she left for Piraeus where she was handed over to her new owner a week later. *Strathmore* was renamed *Marianna Latsi*, and three years later this was changed again to *Henrietta Latsi*. Her career lasted another three years, and in June 1969 she was sold to Italian shipbreakers for breaking up at La Spezia. She always had a special place in the minds of P&O sea staff, and she was considered by far the best of the five *Straths*.

Technical data

Gross tonnage: 23,580
Net tonnage: 13,993
Length overall: 665 ft (202.69 m)
Breadth: 82 ft 2 in (25.04 m)
Depth: 47 ft 6 in (14.48 m)
Cargo capacity: No figures available
Boilers: Oil-fired, six Babcock & Wilcox watertube boilers, superheated steam at 440 psi, 725°F
Main engines: Twin screw, two sets Parsons single reduction geared turbines 24,000 SHP, 20 knots
Ship's company: 515
Passengers: First class 445, Second class 665; 1961, 1,200 tourist class

Below left Strathmore *at Sydney* (Vickers Shipbuilding).

Right *The first class writing room; the portrait of the Duchess of York is on the left above the fireplace* (author's collection).

Right *A first class deluxe cabin,* Strathmore (author's collection).

Right *The second class lounge,* Strathmore (author's collection).

Stratheden and *Strathallan* 1937 and 1938

To complete the building programme which was started in 1930 with *Strathnaver*, P&O ordered two more liners, again based on the very successful design worked out between the P&O and Vickers Armstrong naval architects. As before the orders went to Vickers Armstrong, and the two ships were built at their Barrow yards. They were to become the *Stratheden* and *Strathallan* and, like the *Maloja* of 1911, the latter's career was all too brief as she became a victim of the Second World War. The two new vessels, at 23,722 gross tons, were slightly larger than *Strathmore*, and there were some improvements in the design.

One of the most obvious differences was the increased funnel height, and on board, the first class swimming pool was moved one deck higher to the promenade deck, which gave more deck space for passengers of both classes, and allowed six more bathroom cabins to be added to the first class. The tourist dance space was considerably improved as the area formerly taken by the swimming pool tank was now available. Another improvement was the siting of most of the tourist class cabins on 'H' deck rather than 'G' deck, although the number of passengers carried was slightly reduced, the two new ships having accommodation for 530 first class and 450 tourist class. Like *Strathmore* the new vessels were powered by single reduction geared turbines, capable of 20 knots.

The first of the new sisters to be launched was *Stratheden*, a name derived from the valley of the river Eden in Fifeshire. An unexpected difficulty arose in the months before the launch took place, when it was found that an Aberdeen trawler already bore this name. A representative of P&O called on Messrs Johnstone, the trawler's owners, to enquire whether an arrangement could be made to change the trawler's name. An agreement was worked out and the trawler was renamed *Earnmore*. Her owner was invited to the *Stratheden*'s launch, which took place on Thursday June 10 1937, in brilliant sunshine. The ceremony was performed by the Duchess of Buccleuch & Queensbury, Mr Alexander Shaw, the Chairman of P&O, appealed in his speech for friendship between Britain and Germany, for the clouds of war were already building up over Europe. *Strathallan*, whose name was taken from a valley in central Scotland near Gleneagles, was launched three months later on Thursday September 23. She was christened by the Countess of Cromer, whose husband was a member of the P&O board of directors. Once again the P&O Chairman Mr Alexander Shaw, now Lord Craigmyle, was present.

On December 5 1937 *Stratheden* left Barrow for Birkenhead where she was drydocked, and a week later she arrived off Greenock to begin her trials. The weather was bad with heavy snow squalls, but even so she achieved a speed of 21.8 knots. She was handed over to P&O on December 16, and sailed on her maiden voyage to Brisbane eight days later on December 24 1937. She did not arrive back in London until April 1 1938. Meanwhile *Strathallan* left Tilbury for her maiden voyage to Brisbane on March 18 1938, and the two sisters met for the first time a week later in Marseilles. *Stratheden*'s second voyage was to Bombay via Tangier, Gibraltar and Suez, and on her return to the UK in May 1938 she spent the summer months carrying out a full cruising programme, not sailing for Australia again until September that year. *Strathallan* arrived back at Tilbury from her maiden voyage on June 24 1938, and like *Stratheden* she then spent the summer months cruising from the UK. She made only three more round-trips to Australia before the war, leaving Tilbury on her final peacetime round voyage on June 9 1939. On her arrival in Brisbane she then spent four weeks cruising from that port, before leaving for London. She left Bombay on August 26 1939, and eight days later war was declared. On her return to the UK she was immediately requisitioned as a troopship. *Stratheden* meanwhile, had spent the summer months of 1939 cruising from Southampton. In June she visited the fjords, and in July she sailed on a two week cruise to Madeira, Dakar and Casablanca. She left Southampton on August 12 1939 for the last cruise of the season, sailing to the Mediterranean with Athens and Malta among her ports of call. She arrived back at Tilbury at 3.00 am on Monday August 28 1939 and four days later she left for Australia.

It was March 1940 before *Stratheden* was requisitioned by the Ministry of War Transport as a troopship. She then carried Australian troops to the Middle East and in 1942 she carried Canadian troops from Halifax, Nova Scotia, to the Clyde. In early 1942 both sisters made trooping voyages to the Middle East and India. In the autumn of 1942 *Stratheden* went to Liverpool where additional anti-aircraft guns were fitted, and in early October she sailed to Loch Na Keal in the west coast of the Isle of Mull, where she took part in troop landing exercises in the run up to 'Operation Torch'. Later that month both *Stratheden* and *Strathallan* embarked troops at Greenock for the landings in Algiers. Both ships sailed from the Clyde on October 26 1942 in the second convoy, which consisted of 39 fast troop transports and their accompanying escorts. The voyage was uneventful apart from the torpedoing of the US transport *Thomas G. Stone* near Gibraltar. Just after sunset on November 7 the convoy, which had been sailing east in the Mediterranean, turned due south for Algiers. The assault on the beaches took place at 1.00 am the following day, and once the troops and stores had been disembarked both ships returned to Glasgow. They sailed once again for Algiers and although the weather was bad *Stratheden*'s trip was without incident and she returned home for Christmas. But for *Strathallan* it was to be her final voyage.

On her second voyage *Strathallan* was carrying on board 4,408 troops, which included a proportion of the headquarters staff of the US First Army, and 296 British and American nurses. She was the commodore ship of the convoy and was commanded by Captain John Henry Biggs, a most excellent Captain and well loved man. The Algiers and Oran sections of the convoy had just separated and *Strathallan* was steering an easterly course in the Mediterranean, zigzagging in bright moonlight and smooth seas when, at 2.25 am on December 21 1942, a torpedo fired by the German submarine *U-562* struck the ship in the engine room on the port side, making a large hole and damaging the bulkhead between the engine and boiler rooms. Two engineer officers and two engine room crew were killed in the explosion, but fortunately no other lives were lost. All the lights in the ship failed and she listed 15° to port. The explosion had been very violent, sending a huge column of water over the ship and blowing number eight boat over the head of the davit where it became jammed.

The emergency generator was quickly started and lighting was restored; the troops and crew were mustered and orders were given to lower the boats. By now the list had been corrected to about half of what it had been, and the Chief Engineer reported that the bulkheads were holding. Emergency bilge pumps were started and at 6.30 am water levels in the boiler room were reported to be decreasing. The situation was looking slightly more hopeful. There were still about 3,000 troops on board and they were ordered to the starboard side to ease the list.The destroyer HMS *Laforey* came alongside to assist, and Cadet J.F. Wacher (later Commodore J.F. Wacher CBE RD) recalls hearing a voice calling over a loudhailer in the darkness, '*Strathallan* are you all right?' Eventually *Laforey* took the crippled vessel in tow at five knots towards Oran and at 11.15 am HMS *Verity* signalled that she had picked up the nurses and troops from the lifeboats. At 12.30 pm that day a destroyer came alongside and disembarkation of the remaining troops began.

At 1.00 pm it appeared that *Strathallan* might reach Oran, the only setback being that the emergency bilge pump was failing and could not cope with the leak. The tug *Restive* came alongside to assist but at 1.15 pm flames shot out of the funnel and continued to burn fiercely. It appeared that oil carried on the rising flood water in the boiler room had been ignited by the residual heat from the boiler brickwork. Captain Biggs went below and found that all the bulkheads amidships were red hot, with the paint and woodwork smouldering. As he returned to the bridge through dense smoke, flames shot up through the 'B' deck lounge to the officers' quarters.

Although attempts were made to fight the fire and ammunition was thrown overboard, the fire proved too fierce. Soon Captain Biggs and Cadet McKibben, the last two men remaining aboard, were forced to abandon ship. They both had to drop over the fore side of the bridge and run through dense smoke to the starboard side of 'C' deck amidships where they boarded the *Restive*. *Laforey* had ceased towing at 2.00 pm, but this was taken up again by the *Restive*. Towing continued until 4.00 am on December 22. Twenty minutes later in a position 36° OI'N, 00° 33'W, only 12 miles from Oran, *Strathallan* rolled over onto her port side and sank. The 'Torch' landings had been a success, but the P&O company had suffered heavily, losing five liners in the space of six weeks. Commodore Wacher recalls the kindness of the US troops ashore towards the survivors. The crew were repatriated in the troopship *Duchess of York*, and on their return they were ordered not to tell anyone that *Strathallan* had been sunk, although as Commodore Wacher has recalled, his rail ticket from Liverpool to London had 'survivor of the *Strathallan*' stamped on it. One of the quirks of war.

During 1943 and 1944 *Stratheden* made trooping voyages to the Middle East and India. When the war in Europe ended in 1945 she repatriated British troops, including the 'Men of Arnhem' — men who had survived the battle and had been held as POWs. In October that year she carried 2,000 Australian and New Zealand troops and airmen home, and returned on December 4 with over 3,000 service men and women from the Far East. On July 27 1946 her days as a troopship were over, and she left Tilbury for Barrow-in-Furness where her builders were to recondition her for ordinary passenger service. In her six years on government service she had steamed 468,000 miles, and carried 149,697 personnel. It was thought that she would be ready to resume the service to Australia in early 1947, but with the immediate post-war shortages it was June that year before she made her first sailing to Sydney. The first class fares ranged from £110 to £185 (£94 to £130 in 1939) and the tourist class fares from £64 to £100 (£43 to £71 in 1939).

In 1950 *Stratheden* was chartered by Cunard to make four round voyages between Southampton and New York to supplement their summer service across the Atlantic. She returned to Tilbury from Australia on May 20 1950, and then sailed down to Southampton to prepare for her first voyage to the USA via Le Havre, due to start on June 7. Her other three sailings from Southampton were on June 30, July 24 and August 15, leaving New York for the last time on August 26 to return to Tilbury in readiness for her next voyage to Sydney. Five years later on March 11 1955, *Stratheden* left Port Said on the final leg of a voyage from Brisbane. Two days later at 11.20 am an SOS was received from a Greek trawler, the *Iason*, which was sinking off southern Italy. *Stratheden* reached her position at 4.12 pm that day and, despite the fact that there was a gale blowing and a considerable sea, a lifeboat was away from *Stratheden* three minutes after her arrival. Then the tragedy which unfolded was witnessed by many passengers and crew aboard *Stratheden*. The lifeboat covered the half mile to the stricken ship and the *Iason*'s crew jumped into the water, to be picked up by the boat which, as it returned to *Stratheden*, seemed to swerve a little off course and was suddenly overwhelmed by a huge wave which threw the occupants into the water. Although another rescue boat was got away, there was a delay when the engine would not start. Eight of the *Stratheden*'s crew lost their lives, including the Third Officer and Quartermaster. Only four of the Greek ship's crew of 17 were rescued. *Stratheden* remained in the area until 9.00 am the following day but there were no other survivors, and with all hope of further rescue gone she resumed her voyage. It had been a gallant rescue attempt which almost succeeded, and there were many tributes including one from the Greek government.

In December 1956 *Stratheden* was due to return from Australia with 450 passengers but in Melbourne she developed engine trouble and although she was able to steam back to London under her own power, all the passengers had to be left behind. It would have been difficult to supply them with fresh water on what turned out to be a 46-day voyage.

On a happier note, in April 1961 she visited the Cape

Verde Islands and to commemorate the event the use of a special franking stamp was authorised, made up of an illustration of the ship and the caption 'Tourist Voyage — Cape Verde — SS *Stratheden*'. Over 5,500 letters and postcards were franked with it. Later that year, and just before the withdrawal of *Strathnaver*, *Stratheden* was converted to a 'one class tourist' configuration with berths for 1,200 passengers. On November 7 1962 she made her first sailing after the conversion, from London to Sydney. However, this service did not last long, for a year later came the announcement that she was to be withdrawn within 18 months. She left Sydney for the last time bound for Tilbury on September 15 1963 on her 55th roundtrip between Britain and Australia.

It had already been announced that she was to be chartered to the Travel Savings Association during December 1963 and January 1964 and after a brief lay up at Portland she made her £2 a day cruises for the association, two nine-day cruises to the Atlantic Isles and a 33-day cruise to the West Indies. P&O provided the crew and 'one class tourist' services, while booking, berthing and itineraries were arranged by the charterers. It was while she was on one of these cruises on December 23 1963, that she was involved in her last drama at sea, when she went to the aid of the Greek liner *Lakonia*, on fire 180 miles north of Madeira. She was not the first rescue ship on the scene but her medical services, which included a fully equipped hospital, were invaluable and some of the worst injured survivors were transferred to her from the *Montcalm* in order that they could receive expert medical attention.

At the end of 1963 *Stratheden* had been sold to Mr John S. Latsis of Athens and she was handed over to the Latsis company in Piraeus on February 18 1964, being renamed *Henrietta Latsi*. Her employment with the new company was very similar to that of *Marianna Latsi* (ex-*Strathmore*), and in 1966 the two ships exchanged names. They were both sold to shipbreakers at La Spezia in Italy in June 1969 for more than £1 million. There is no doubt that the five *Straths* were a major success in the story of the Australian mail service, and a credit to both Vickers Armstrong and P&O.

Technical data

Gross tonnage: 23,722
Net tonnage: 14,134
Length overall: 664 ft 6 in (202.54 m)
Breadth: 82 ft 2 in (25.04 m)
Depth: 47 ft 6 in (14.48 m)
Cargo capacity: 374,000 cu ft
Boilers: Oil-fired, six Babcock & Wilcox watertube boilers, superheated steam 450 psi
Main engines: Twin screw, two sets Parsons single reduction geared turbines. 24,000 SHP, 20 knots
Ship's company: 563
Passengers: First class 530, Second class 450; 1961, *Stratheden* 1,200 one class tourist

The first of the new sisters was Stratheden, *a name derived from the valley of the River Eden in Fifeshire* (Vickers Shipbuilding).

Above left *The ill fated* Strathallan (Vickers Shipbuilding).

Left Strathallan *burning off Oran, the tug* Restive *is alongside her* (P&O).

Above *The tourist class lounge in* Stratheden *during the early 1950s* (P&O).

Right *A tourist class cabin,* Stratheden (P&O).

Canton 1938

The arrival of the *Canton* in 1938 marked the end of an era for the P&O company. She was the last liner to enter service before the outbreak of the Second World War, the last in the traditional black livery, and she was also the last liner to be built for the company by Alexander Stephen & Sons of Linthouse, Glasgow. She was a handsome vessel, and her single funnel gave her a profile very similar to that of *Strathmore*. Like *Corfu* and *Carthage* she was designed for the Far East route to China and Japan.

Canton was launched on Thursday April 14 1938, the naming ceremony being performed by Miss Thalia Shaw, the daughter of Lord Craigmyle, who, although he had recently retired as Chairman of the company because of ill health, represented P&O at the launch. She was the largest ship to take to the water in the Clyde since the *Queen Mary* in 1934. *Canton* was a twin screw vessel with a service speed of 18 knots. She had accommodation for 298 first and 244 tourist class passengers and ample cargo space. As she prepared for her maiden voyage, the political situation in Europe was deteriorating rapidly, but in September 1938 the Munich agreement was signed, and for a time things looked more hopeful.

On the evening of October 7, *Canton* left London on her maiden voyage to Yokohama. She was fully booked for the voyage, and shortly after leaving she grounded on a mudbank at Blackshelf off Grays. Fortunately she was refloated within ten minutes and most of the passengers were unaware of the occurrence. She had less than a year of service ahead of her before the Second World War broke out, but it was to be an eventful ten months and she was in the news twice. The first incident took place in March 1939, while *Canton* was homeward bound from Japan and about to enter Hong Kong when, in dense fog, the French liner *Marechal Joffres* collided with her. There were no casualties, although *Canton* was holed in the starboard side near the engine room. She spent the next three weeks in drydock in Hong Kong undergoing repairs, and finally left the colony on March 31 for Shanghai. The next incident occurred on May 10 1939 as she was homeward bound on the same voyage and *en route* to Colombo, when she went to the aid of the little Danish liner *Alsia* which had caught fire nine miles off Galle in Ceylon. *Canton* was able to rescue 35 passengers and some of her crew and landed them safely in Colombo.

She made only one more round voyage being requisitioned by the Admiralty, leaving Penang for London on August 26 1939. She was in the Indian Ocean when war was declared but she completed her voyage and was then sent up the yards of her builders on the Clyde for conversion to an armed merchant cruiser. Armed with eight 6-in and two 3-in high-angle guns, she was commissioned in November 1939 and started her war service on the Northern Patrol. In early January 1940 she was on patrol between the Faeroes and Iceland, when it was decided in the Admiralty to transfer her to the east coast of South America. Consequently she left the patrol line on January 9 for Greenock. The weather was bad, and the sea rough when, at 11.18 pm the following day, breakers were sighted from the bridge. Two minutes later she ran aground on the rocks of Barra Head, on Lewis in the Outer Hebrides. She was badly damaged forward and two holds were flooded. Bulkheads were shored up and the crew went to abandon ship stations 20 minutes later when attempts to go astern at full power failed. It was 3.30 am on January 11 before she finally got clear of the rocks under her own power. Then with the destroyer *Impulsive* and the AMC *California* standing by she set course for the Clyde, where she arrived at 12.30 pm two days later. Being down by the head and with the pumps unable to control the leaks, she was beached in Holy Loch. A week later, after temporary repairs, she went into Princes Dock, Glasgow, where Barclay Curle & Co made her seaworthy once more.

The refit was completed on April 15 1940 and she came under the orders of the Commander-in-Chief Western Atlantic, carrying out patrol and escort duties. Two months later on June 17 1940, while escorting a convoy from Freetown to the UK, she was involved in a running battle with a U-boat pack off the west coast of Ireland, and she was narrowly missed by a torpedo. In January 1941 she was refitted at Greenock, and was back in service the following month. Shortly after this, on the morning of February 24 1941, she was involved in an incident with the submarine HMS *Thunderbolt* (formerly the ill-fated *Thetis*). Two signals were received at the Admiralty as follows:- '08.30, 24/2/41 from *Thunderbolt*, Sighted merchant ship speed 15 knots, challenged but vessel opened fire with several guns, accurate fire. Forced to dive. Am endeavouring to shadow. Position 54° 19'N, 26° 43'W.' Five minutes later the following was received from *Canton*, '08.35, 24/2/41, Opened fire on enemy submarine, believed hit, vessel submerged. Position 54° 19'N, 26° 43'W.' Fortunately *Thunderbolt* had not been hit and the Admiralty was able to signal both vessels with their identities. On April 18 1941 *Canton* went to New York for a refit which was completed two months later on June 9.

A few weeks later, shortly after sunset on July 10 1941, while *Canton* was on patrol duty in the Atlantic Ocean, she sighted the German cargo vessel *Karnak* 300 miles north of St Pauls Rocks. She was flying the Dutch flag and the name *Hermes* had been painted on her bows. As *Canton* went to investigate, the German vessel altered course and increased speed. After a two hour chase *Canton* overhauled the vessel and signalled her to stop. When there was no response *Canton* opened fire with her 6-in and Lewis guns on the *Karnak*'s boats. Almost immediately a number of scuttling charges were heard to go off and her superstructure burst into flames. *Canton*'s boarding party were unable to get near the ship because of the ferocity of the fire and the danger of further explosions. Three boatloads of survivors were picked up by *Canton* and she stood by until the enemy vessel sank.

Although she had been unable to prevent the scuttling, *Canton* had helped to scotch a blockade breaking plan which had been organised by the German Transport Ministry and thus prevented a valuable cargo of rubber reaching Germany. Four months later at the end of November 1941 *Canton* searched for survivors from the German raider *Atlantis* which had been sunk in the Atlantic by HMS *Devonshire*. The next six months were spent patrolling from Freetown and Simonstown, and in July 1942 she arrived in the Clyde for a long refit.

By January 1943 *Canton* was at sea again destined for the East Indies station as escort for convoy WS26. She remained east of Suez for the remainder of her naval service. By now she was quite a formidable AMC, being armed with nine 6-in guns, two twin 4-in guns, two two-pounder pom-poms and 16 Oerlikons. In early March 1944 it was decided to convert *Canton* into a troopship, and on the 21st of that month she sailed for Port Suez which she reached ten days later. She remained there for two weeks under a 'care and maintenance' party, and on April 15 1944 a P&O crew arrived to take over. Shortly afterwards she sailed for Cape Town where her conversion was to take place. By the time the war ended in August 1945 she had steamed 278,797 miles on government service, 257,967 of these as an AMC.

In August 1946 she was released by the government and she then returned to her builders on the Clyde for an overhaul and to be refitted as a passenger liner. Originally it had been intended that she resume her P&O service in May 1947, but with the delays in delivery of essential materials and the shortage of skilled labour, it was September 28 that year when she completed her trials. Structurally there was very little alteration, but the biggest change to her external appearance was her new livery. Like *Corfu* and *Carthage* the black hull and funnel had given place to a white hull and superstructure, surmounted by a buff funnel. There is no doubt that this new livery was a great improvement. Almost three weeks later on

October 17 *Canton* sailed from Tilbury bound for Hong Kong, thus marking the first P&O passenger sailing to the Far East since the end of the Second World War. At last, nine years after first entering service, she was able to settle down to her intended role. *Canton* soon became a firm favourite with travellers to the east, especially Colonial and Foreign Office personnel either outward bound or returning to the UK on leave.

At the time of the Suez crisis in early November 1956, *Canton* was already in the Far East having completed her outward voyage. The return trip was made via Cape Town and, like all the other company vessels, she continued to use that route until well into 1957. On October 15 that year she was in King George V Dock, London, about to sail for Hong Kong when, shortly after midnight, clouds of smoke were seen billowing from one of her holds. It turned out that a cargo of toilet tissue had caught fire; the East Ham fire brigade soon extinguished the blaze and there was little damage, but her sailing was delayed.

By early 1962 it was becoming obvious that her days were numbered. *Corfu* and *Carthage* had been replaced by the ex-Belgian vessels *Cathay* and *Chitral*. Both of these ships and *Chusan* were air conditioned and *Canton* was not. She had been built for a different era, and now passengers travelling east by sea demanded more modern facilities. Not least of all, the general decline in liner voyages had begun. So on April 5 1962, P&O announced that *Canton* was to be withdrawn from service on her arrival in the UK on August 26 that year. At that stage it was undecided what her future would be, but she was 24 years old and it was soon known that she would be sold to shipbreakers. She was given a fond farewell at each port along her homeward route. In Singapore a pipe band turned out to play her off, and on Sunday August 26 she arrived in King

Canton *undergoes her trials on the Clyde in 1938* (P&O).

George V Dock for the last time. Two days earlier P&O had announced that she had been sold to the Leung Yau Shipbreaking Company of Hong Kong.

At 3.15 pm on the last day of August 1962 *Canton* left London for her final delivery voyage. A moving account of her departure was given by Mr A.B. Weeks, her ex-Third Radio Officer, who was amongst a small group of people who had turned out to bid her farewell. 'As she moved down the docks towards the lock guided by a pair of fussy tugs, *Canton* passed the company's cargo vessel *Somali*. The latter cheered her white sister and bade her farewell on the whistle, a signal *Bon Voyage* fluttering from the signal halyards and ensign dipped in salute. *Canton* gracefully acknowledged the signals and bowed out of the lock stern first.'

She arrived in Hong Kong on Wednesday October 2 1962 and was handed over to the breakers the following day. Captain W. Eade, her commander, presented the ship's bell to the Ying-Wa college in the colony. So passed from the scene another pre-war P&O express mail liner.

Technical data
Gross tonnage: 15,784
Net tonnage: 9,255
Length overall: 568 ft 5 in (173.2 m)
Breadth: 73 ft 5 in (22.38 m)
Depth: 41ft 9 in (12.73 m)
Cargo capacity: 385,000 cu ft
Boilers: Oil-fired, four watertube boilers with forced draught and superheaters, 435 psi
Main engines: Twin screw, two sets Parsons single reduction geared turbines, 18,500 SHP, 18 knots
Ship's company: 350
Passengers: First class 302, Second class 244

An impressive aerial view of Canton *off the Isle of Wight* (Skyfotos Ltd).

Above *The first class verandah café,* Canton (P&O).

Below *A first class deluxe cabin,* Canton (P&O).

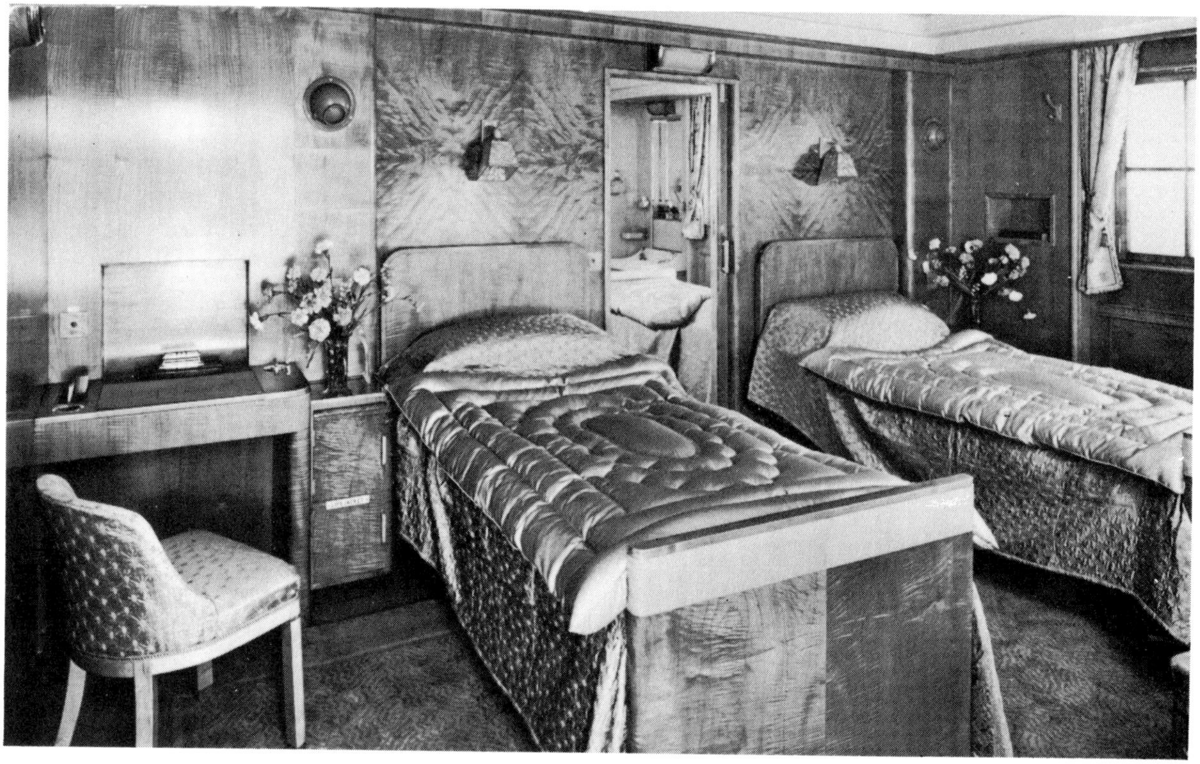

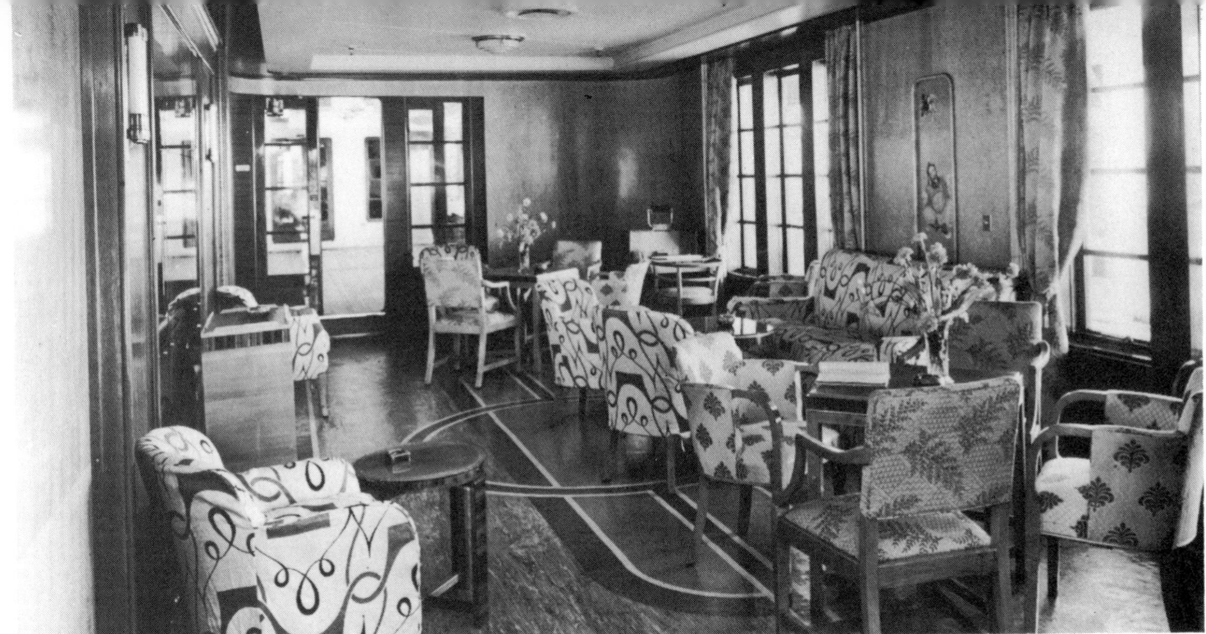

Above *the first class corridor lounge,* Canton (P&O).

Below Canton *during her later years at Southampton in 1958* (Keith Byass).

Above *A stern view of* Canton (Keith Byass).

Below Canton *looking every inch a warship during her war service as an AMC* (Imperial War Musuem).

Passage Bookings: · Bangkok—Wednesdays 0915

Telephone 5021 (15 lines)

P. & O. and B. I.

MAIL LINE

Canton	for London ..	sails	28 Jan.
Carthage	" " ..	"	24 Feb.
Corfu	" " ..	"	21 Mar.
Canton	" " ..	"	22 Apr.
Carthage	" " ..	"	19 May
Corfu	" " ..	"	15 June
Canton	" " ..	"	15 July

CARGO SERVICE

Surat from P. Swettenham	due	30 Jan.
Somali from U.K./P. S'ham	"	8 Feb.
Trevince "	"	11 Feb.
Trevelyan "	"	14 Feb.

For Genoa/Marseilles/Havre/London/
Antwerp/Rotterdam/Hamburg.

Trevanion .... In Port.

APCAR LINE

Sirdhana due from Japan/
Shanghai/H'Kong .... 1 Feb.
Sails for Penang/Rangoon/
Calcutta .... 3 Feb.

MADRAS LINE

Rajula from Madras/N'Patam/
Penang .... 3 Feb.
Sails for P. S'ham/Penang/
N'Patam/Madras .... 6 Feb.

BOMBAY LINE

Padana loads for Bombay,
Karachi .... sails 1 Feb.

BANGKOK LINE

Kistna .... In Port .... ETD 1 Feb.

AUSTRALIAN LINE

Chanda loads for Cairns/
Brisbane/Sydney .... 8 Mar.
Dongola due from Australian
Ports .... February.
Sails for Madras/Calcutta ....

PENANG
TEL 1086

ISLAY KERR & CO., LTD.

SINGAPORE
TEL. 5457.

ANGLO-CHINESE SHIPPING CO., LTD.

Agents: MOLLERS' (MALAYA) LTD.

Frequent Service between Singapo re Sarawak & North Borneo Ports.

Extract from the Singapore Straits Times *January 27 1949, showing the sailings list of P&O* (B. Meston).

Himalaya 1949

By the time the Second World War ended in August 1945, the P&O company had suffered terrible losses, the shipping group itself having lost 182 vessels totalling nearly 1,250,000 tons. The rebuilding of the passenger fleet started in January 1946, when P&O ordered their 28,047 gross ton liner *Himalaya* from Vickers Armstrong at Barrow-in-Furness. She was their yard number 951, and her keel was laid on April 29 1946, seven months after the Orient liner *Orcades* had been laid down. P&O and its Orient subsidiary had been persuaded that it would be advantageous to have the two ships from the same 'mould', although each company used their own individual style for their respective ships.

It had been intended that *Himalaya* should be completed and enter service between London and Sydney in early 1948, but with all the post-war austerity and shortages in Britain, it soon became clear that there was little hope of this being achieved. It was Tuesday October 5 1948 before *Himalaya* was launched, and at 12.43 pm that day Lady Currie, the wife of the P&O group Chairman*, sent the great ship down into the waters of the Walney Channel. In late August 1949 *Himalaya* sailed north to the Clyde to begin her acceptance trials, and these were completed during a three-day voyage to Southampton. For the run down the Irish Sea and English Channel she had on board hundreds of special guests, as well as representatives of the press and travel agencies. At dawn on Tuesday August 30 she slid smoothly out into the Atlantic and began the passage to Wolf Rock off Lands End, reaching the English Channel soon after midday. Speed had to be reduced shortly after this when thick fog was encountered off Start Point in Devon. However, trials were eventually resumed and successfully completed, and she arrived at an anchorage in Cowes Roads on the evening of August 31. The following day she was handed over to P&O at a small ceremony in Southampton Docks which was attended by Sir William Currie.

Himalaya was the largest ship to be completed anywhere in the world during 1949, and it was refreshing to see luxury returning to the country after ten years of austerity. She had accommodation for 758 first and 401 tourist class passengers, and carried a crew of 572. Most of the first class public rooms were situated amidships on the promenade deck. One of these, a corridor lounge on the port side called the Australia Room, included wall panelling made from Australian scenes by Mr John S. Loxton of Melbourne. It was the first time that the company had identified a particular room so closely with the Commonwealth, and it would be very appropriate in the case of *Himalaya*, particularly in her later years. There were also two reminders of other company vessels of the same name. The ship's bell from the first *Himalaya* of 1854 was donated by Sir George Hammick of Axminster, who had bought it at a sale of surplus equipment at Devonport dockyard in 1931. It was fitted in the first class foyer, at the entrance to the lounge on the promenade deck. The second *Himalaya* of 1892 was remembered in an oil painting which was hung in the same foyer.

*Sir William Crawford Currie GBE, succeeded Lord Craigmyle in March 1938.

The tourist class public rooms were situated aft on 'B', 'C' and 'D' decks and they were tastefully decorated and furnished. The most important feature which contributed to passenger comfort was to be found down below in the machinery spaces; this was a Weir evaporating plant for distilling water which could convert sea water to fresh at the rate of 350 tons per day. 30-35 tons were double distilled for boiler feed water, the rest was for domestic use and was made palatable by a special aeration system. It was estimated that this saved 1,700 tons in weight, and £1,500 on a ten-week round voyage. She was the first liner to be fitted with an evaporating plant, and this was certainly a distinct advantage over earlier ships. So it was a very proud ship and crew which docked in Tilbury on the afternoon of Sunday September 11 1949 to prepare for her maiden voyage to Australia.

Himalaya left for Bombay and the Australian ports just over three weeks later on October 6, commanded by Captain D.M. Stuart, DSC, Commodore of the P&O fleet. He had a distinguished career with the company, and had commanded the *Cathay* when she was sunk by bombs in 1942 during the North African landings. *Himalaya* immediately reduced the passage time to Bombay from its pre-war 20 days to 15, and cut the passage to Melbourne to 28 days. She was an instant success with travellers, and it was obvious even at this early stage that she was going to be very popular. She returned to Tilbury three days before Christmas that year, and Captain Stuart retired from the sea, being succeeded by the Staff Captain H.C.C. Forsyth. In the summer of 1950 *Himalaya* was released from the Australian route for a short cruising season based in the UK. These were the first such cruises undertaken by P&O since the summer of 1939, and *Himalaya* made two 14-day trips into the Mediterranean. First class fares ranged from £65 to £85, and those for tourist passengers were from £36 to £48. There were over 12,000 applicants for places in that summer cruising programme and only 5,000 berths, which left a lot of disappointed people.

By March 1951 P&O were able to announce that *Himalaya*'s distillation plant was an unqualified success, and that it was producing over 40,000 tons of fresh water a year, at a cost of nine pence per ton. Three months later *Himalaya* opened the UK cruising season with a 20-day cruise to the Mediterranean, and once again she was fully booked. Later that year she was in drydock at Southampton for repairs to her main engines, but after the work was finished high winds on the south coast unfortunately delayed her departure for Sydney. In 1953 *Himalaya* was fitted with a 'Thorny-croft funnel top', in an attempt to overcome the age-old problem of soot falling on passengers decks. This added 12 ft to the height of the funnel, and the fins gave the ship a very distinct appearance which was instantly recognisable the world over.

On August 27 1956 *Himalaya* left London for Australia, and three days later, when she was at the entrance to the Mediterranean, there was an explosion in a domestic refrigeration plant. The ship's first refrigeration engineer, a cook and a steward were killed instantly, and 13 crew members were injured, some seriously. The ship made an unscheduled stop off the breakwater at Valletta in Malta to land the injured; unfortunately a fourth man died shortly before the landing, and another died four days later in the naval hospital. It seemed the explosion had been caused by a gas leak which had occurred near a working alleyway adjoining the Goanoese stewards' accommodation. It was a tragic accident in an otherwise trouble-free career, and by the end of November 1957 *Himalaya* had completed 30 voyages to Australia, which included three via Cape Town during the Suez affair. She had also made 14 cruises from the UK and seven in the Pacific, and she had steamed 866,000 miles.

In June 1959 she went into drydock at Tilbury, where stabilisers were fitted. She sailed again for Sydney in early July that year, and on the 13th of that month she was delayed for 24 hours at Port Suez, after damaging a propeller as she left the canal. The remainder of the voyage was completed with the damaged screw out of action, and on arrival at Sydney she went into the Australian navy's Captain Cook drydock where repairs were effected. The Australian defence ministry sent P&O a bill for the emergency docking, amounting to £18,311. When she arrived back in London again, it had been decided that she would be fitted with air conditioning, the contract for which had been awarded to the Rotterdam Dry Dock Company, who had submitted the lowest tender; this created a minor stir in the press. It was a sign of the times that *Himalaya* was spending more and more of each year cruising, and in order to fit in with this new image the dining rooms were designated as restaurants, the change being made in November 1960 while the liner was in Tilbury dock for her annual overhaul. The first class saloon became the 'Drake Restaurant' and the tourist saloon the 'Tasman Restaurant'. *Himalaya* spent the Christmas and New year following these changes on a cruise from Sydney, which took her to New Zealand and on to Fiji and Hawaii.

In the autumn of 1963 she was converted by R & H Green & Silley Weir at Tilbury for one class tourist operation with accommodation for 1,416 passengers, and she made her first voyage from Tilbury in this new role on November 21 1963. Ten months later in September 1964 she was at Tilbury when fire broke out in her funnel uptakes. Although it burned for two hours and the local fire brigades attended, there was very little damage caused, and it was described by a fire chief as 'only a large chimney fire'. By the late 1960s she was primarily employed on cruising duties, and in June 1968 she left Tilbury for a world voyage which took her 66,884 miles, calling at 51 ports and carrying in all a total of 14,734 passengers. It was to be her longest voyage, and she returned to London in December that year. The following year the P&O company's long passenger association with Tilbury came to an end, and from October 1969 their passenger vessels began using Southampton as their terminal port. The event did not go unheralded, and a special luncheon was held aboard *Himalaya* on October 9. The following day the last link with Tilbury was broken as *Himalaya* left the port's Passenger Landing Stage. She and the other ships of the P&O — Orient Lines would soon become a familiar sight alongside the long stretch of Southampton's Western Docks. On April 9 1970, while on a Pacific cruise, *Himalaya* steamed into Kobe, Japan and thus became the first ship to use the port's new passenger terminal. Her master, Captain J.W. Terry, and some of the passengers were invited to the opening which took the form of a Shinto religious ceremony.

Himalaya made her last cruises from Southampton in the spring of 1974 to the Mediterranean, with a short three-night voyage to Amsterdam, arriving back in Southampton on May 15. It had been announced earlier that month that she was to be withdrawn at the end of the year, and so when she left for Sydney to spend her last few months cruising from that port, many turned

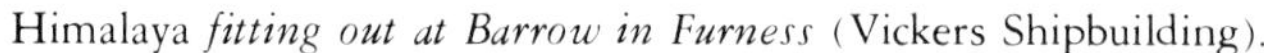
Himalaya *fitting out at Barrow in Furness* (Vickers Shipbuilding).

out to wish her farewell. Five months later it was the turn of Sydney to say goodbye when, on Friday October 19 1974, she sailed on her final passenger voyage to Hong Kong. It was a farewell to a very popular ship which will long be remembered. Hundreds of ex-*Himalaya* passengers turned out to pack Circular Quay, as the grand old lady of the P&O fleet pulled away from the Overseas Passenger Terminal. The liner was dressed in bunting and her paying off pennant fluttered in the breeze. As the last of *Himalaya*'s mooring ropes was let go, a Scottish pipe band played *Auld Lang Syne*, as only a pipe band can. All the small craft in the harbour rallied with whistles and hooters as *Himalaya* slowly turned under Sydney Harbour bridge, and the great liner replied as she let her siren blast. As she moved forward down the harbour she was followed by scores of small craft, including ferries and hydrofoils, and a special Department of Trade ferry, chartered for the occasion at the request of hundreds of members of the public. A few days later she was given a similar send off from Brisbane, as crowds of people lined Hamilton Wharf to watch the tugs assisting her into the Brisbane River, ending her 25-year link with Australia. Her final voyage would end in the breakers yards at Taiwan. She had become a victim of increased oil prices, and was the fifth of the group's liners to go within four years, but P&O still remained the world's largest passenger ship operator.

Technical data

Gross tonnage: 28,047
Net tonnage: 15,443
Length overall: 709 ft (216.1 m)
Breadth: 90 ft 6 in (27.58 m)
Depth: 50 ft (15.24 m)
Cargo capacity: 435,000 cu ft
Boilers: Oil-fired, two large and two small Foster Wheeler watertube, controlled superheat boilers, 525 psi, 600°F-800°F
Main engines: Twin screw, two sets Parsons double-reduction geared turbines, 34,000 SHP, 22 knots
Ship's company: 572
Passengers: First class 758, Tourist class 401, 1963, 1,416 one class tourist

August 1949, Himalaya *on her trials in the Clyde* (P&O).

HIMALAYA
LONDON

Left *A stern view of* Himalaya *in drydock at Southampton* (British Transport Docks Board, Southampton).
Above Himalaya *leaving Keppel Harbour, Singapore in 1956* (P. Crunch).
Below *Aerial view of* Himalaya (Skyfotos Ltd).

Chusan 1950

In May 1946 P&O ordered a new vessel for the Far East service as part of their post-war revival programme. As with the *Himalaya*, there were delays in her building due to the shortages at the time; it was planned to have the new ship completed by May 1948, but it was two years after this before she was delivered. The new liner, at 24,215 gross tons, was to be the largest ship to be built by the company for the Far East service and was to be called *Chusan*, a name derived from the Chou-Shan archipelago off Shanghai. But, sadly, she was also to be the last. Once again the contract for the construction of the new vessel went to Vickers Armstrong at Barrow, and the keel was laid in February 1947. By the end of 1948 building was well under way, although visitors to the yard in November that year would have been surprised to find an arc cut out of the liner's stem. In fact this had been done to facilitate the use of a light railway and allow its engines to pass underneath. Vickers had started a substantial modernisation programme and eventually the railway track was moved, so that the missing portion of stem could be welded back into place.

Chusan was launched on Tuesday June 28 1949, with the naming ceremony being performed by the Viscountess Bruce, whose husband was a former Prime Minister of Australia and a director of the P&O line. The ceremony was a great occasion at Barrow, and at 1.00 pm that day, just before the ship was launched, thousands of people gathered to witness the event. The launch itself was not without its drama. As the *Chusan* went down the slipway, she rolled precariously to starboard just as she entered the water. One of the launching cradles on the starboard bow had broken as she ran down to the water, but fortunately, it did nothing worse than make her roll as she became water-borne and there was quite a sense of relief as the huge hull righted itself. It was to be still another year before she was completed.

Three years and four months after the keel was laid *Chusan* was finally completed. Originally it had been estimated that she would cost £2,244,000, but with all the delays the amount had risen to £3,250,000. So the total cost to P&O for the *Himalaya* and *Chusan* was nearly £7 million, and allowing for depreciation and interest charges, the two ships would each need to earn £700,000 a year for 20 years to be economical. It can be seen that with such huge building costs, the post-war building programme would have to be more limited than that of the 1920s, although with the changing world circumstances in the 1950s, the role of the ocean liner would be much reduced anyway. *Chusan* left Barrow in early June 1950 for Liverpool where she was drydocked, then a few days later on June 9 she sailed for the Clyde to begin her trials. A week later she was in Southampton, and on her arrival there was a small formal ceremony when the ship was handed over to P&O. A form of transfer was signed on behalf of P&O by Mr A.O. Lang, the Deputy Chairman, and the company houseflag replaced that of Vickers Armstrong. The following day she sailed to Rotterdam with British officials who were attending a freight conference at The Hague, together with some members of P&O staff and their families, returning to Southampton three days later on June 18.

There is no doubt that *Chusan* was the most sophisticated ship built for the Far East route, and the most luxurious. She could accommodate 474 first and 514 tourist class passengers, and she had a crew of 572. The first class passengers were carried amidships and they had six decks, from the boat deck to 'D' deck. The boat deck was devoted to leisure and recreation and it included a 'sun trap' abaft the bridge. The public rooms were situated directly beneath on the promenade deck, and overlooking the forepeak was the children's nursery. Then working aft came the library and writing room, the main lounge, the ballroom, a verandah cafe and the swimming pool. Perhaps the most striking feature of these rooms was in the library, and this was a fine mural painting of an Italian style arcaded colonnade. 'A' deck, which was the next one down, was given over mainly to cabins, but there was also a shop and hairdressing salons. Tourist class passengers were accommodated aft on 'A' to 'E' decks, but they also had a games and sunbathing area at the after end of the promenade deck. On 'A' deck was a verandah cafe and swimming pool, and below this on 'B' deck was the main lounge and ballroom. The children's nursery was on 'C' deck and ran the whole width of the ship.

The dining saloons for both classes were on 'D' deck, and were separated by the galley and kitchens. Like *Himalaya*, one of *Chusan*'s main features which made a large contribution to passenger comfort was down below in the machinery spaces. She was the first liner to be fitted with Denny-Brown stabilisers, which had already been successfully adopted for cross-channel ships and some small warships. The decision to fit them in *Chusan* had been taken only two months before she was launched and from trials conducted on the Clyde and in the English Channel when the rolling had been induced, they had proved an unqualified success.

Chusan's maiden voyage was a nine-day cruise from Southampton to Madeira and Lisbon, sailing on July 1 1950. She was fully booked with 988 passengers who had paid fares ranging from £25 to £60, with supplements for extra facilities. This trip was followed by three further cruises, the first to Madeira, Casablanca and Lisbon and the other two into the Mediterranean. The cruise programme was completed at the end of August, and *Chusan* then went up to London to load cargo and embark passengers for Bombay, sailing on September 15. Additional sailings of passenger liners to Bombay in the early autumn were customary before 1939, and they were usually taken by *Viceroy of India*, so it was something of a nostalgic trip. It was November 7 1950 before *Chusan* made her first trip to Hong Kong, returning to London in January 1951. On her second voyage east there was an outbreak of influenza on board, and she was delayed in Bombay until quarantine arrangements could be made for the passengers disembarking there.

In May 1952 *Chusan* returned to the UK and was due to start a series of cruises in the middle of June. Before this, however, she was fitted with a 'Thorneycroft funnel top'. It had been designed in Southampton, but the prefabrication of the material, and the fitting were undertaken by R & H Green & Silley Weir at Tilbury. On June 16 she left for her first cruise after this modification, and the effects of the new funnel top were studied at regular periods. It was found that smoke did not touch any part of the ships's superstructure and there were no fumes on the after decks as smoke did not tend to curl downwards behind the funnel. Later that year it was announced that *Chusan* would call at Japanese ports, so after 13 years the Far East route was back to what it had been before the war. Three months later in January 1953 her first commander, Captain R.E.T. Tunbridge, retired, his place being taken by Captain E.R. Bodley.

On Friday June 12 1953 *Chusan* sailed from Tilbury for a three-week Mediterranean cruise but only a few hours after sailing she was in collision with the 6,000 ton cargo ship *Prospector* off the Goodwins. She was forced to return to Tilbury with a 25 ft gash in her bows and spent the next two days alongside while repairs were carried out. The passengers on board continued to enjoy all the usual facilities and entertainment and eventually they sailed again after a 55 hour delay. Although only one port of call had been cancelled, P&O made a 10 per cent refund of the fare to all the passengers. In September 1954 *Chusan*'s annual overhaul was carried out at Rotterdam because of a dock strike in London, and in March 1955, on a voyage from Kobe to London, a passenger with smallpox was landed at Port Said. But the most dramatic incident involving *Chusan* in the 1950s happened on September 2 1955 when she was in Naples.

An anonymous message was received at Scotland Yard that a bomb had been placed on board; messages were flashed to the Captain and an exhaustive search was made, but nothing was found. Special restrictions were made on visitors to the ship and the cruise passed off without incident. This was obviously an early example of the 'bomb hoax' which is all too common today. Two years later in July 1957 *Chusan* paid a visit to the tiny island of Porto Santo to disembark two stowaways from Madeira. The two youths had been discovered in a waste bin two hours after the ship left Funchal homeward bound for Southampton.

In April 1959 *Chusan* left London for a 92-day voyage around the world, during which she steamed some 32,000 miles and called at 24 ports. A problem cropped up during the trip when it was proposed that she make a two-week cruise from San Francisco, making a three-day visit to Honolulu before going on to Vancouver. After a complaint by Senator Warren Magnuson of Washington, it was found that that the visit would breach the US customs law which forbids the carriage of people between US ports by non-US ships. However, by cutting down the length of the stay in Honolulu the cruise was able to go ahead. Later that year she went to Harland and Wolff's yard at Belfast where she was given a thorough refit. Her accommodation was improved by the addition of more private facilities in cabins, and by fitting air conditioning throughout the ship. In October 1960 her dining saloons were re-designated as restaurants, and in June 1963 she was transferred from the Far East to the Australian route. Like other P&O ships, cruising was beginning to play a greater role throughout the year.

Once she started sailing to Australia she spent a great deal of time cruising in the Pacific, but she was still seen occasionally in home waters. On February 8 1970 she made P&O's last scheduled passenger call at Bombay, and to mark the occasion she was played out of harbour by the Indian Navy band. In the following month she made a call at Colombo when homeward bound, thus ending the P&O passenger service to that port which had lasted over a century. Later in the year she initiated P&O's first cruising programme from Cape Town for South Africans, and amongst her passengers was the famous heart transplant surgeon Dr Christian Barnard. 1971 was her penultimate full year of service, and she was in the news twice. In March she was some 500 miles out of Sydney when a 69-year-old passenger needed an urgent operation on his leg. After radioing for assistance, an RAAF Hercules dropped urgently needed drugs and equipment and the liner's surgeons were able to operate. The second incident was in July 1971, shortly after the ship docked at Southampton. Soot had caught fire in the funnel uptakes, and firemen had to be treated for heat exhaustion as they fought the blaze in temperatures of 200° F before bringing it under control in just over an hour.

In December 1972 it was announced that *Chusan* was to be withdrawn, and she made a final series of cruises from Cape Town in the early months of 1973, before sailing for Southampton in March that year. Loyal devotees of the liner were able to make a last voyage on

her by flying out to Tenerife and joining her for the last leg to Southampton on March 19. When she arrived back in the UK a week later on March 26 she was put up for sale. It was inevitable that she should be sold to the shipbreakers of Taiwan, and she left Southampton Water for her final voyage east on May 12 1973. This time there were no streamers or happy cruise passengers, just a sad empty ship which had fallen victim to the jet age. An obituary appeared in the personal column of *The Times* of May 8 1973, which read, '*Chusan* — a grand old lady sadly mourned by all who sailed in her'.

Technical data
Gross tonnage: 24,215
Net tonnage: 13,445
Length overall: 672 ft 6 in (204.98 m)
Breadth: 85 ft 2 in (25.96 m)
Depth: 36 ft 2 in (11.02 m)
Cargo capacity: 481,000 cu ft
Boilers: Oil-fired, four Foster Wheeler controlled superheat boilers, 525 psi, 600°F-850°F
Main engines: Twin screw, two sets Parsons double-reduction geared turbines, 42,500 SHP, 23 knots
Ship's company: 572
Passengers: First class 474, Tourist class 514

Below left Chusan *before her Thorneycroft funnel top was fitted* (author's collection).

Right *The first class lounge,* Chusan (author's collection).

Right *The first class children's nursery,* Chusan (author's collection).

CHUSAN

Above *Aerial view of* Chusan (Skyfotos Ltd).

Left Chusan *in drydock* (British Transport Docks Board, Southampton).

Below Chusan *at Hong Kong* (P&O).

Arcadia 1954

Of the four liners which were constructed in the post-war rebuilding programme, the *Arcadia* made the transition from ocean liner to cruise ship and managed to survive in this competitive world until February 1979, a career of 25 years. Her story begins in early 1952 when she was ordered from John Brown & Co Ltd, and her keel was laid in the Clydebank yard. The hull was constructed in the same berth as the Cunard liner *Queen Elizabeth*, and she was the largest P&O passenger ship to be built on the Clyde. She was named after the mythological district of the Peloponnese, the region of rural happiness in southern Greece. On April 16 1953 the Queen and Duke of Edinburgh visited John Browns yard to launch the royal yacht *Britannia*, and while they were there they visited the *Arcadia* whose hull was being painted, although on board the cabins on 'E' and 'F' deck were virtually complete.

Arcadia was designed for the P&O mail service between London and Sydney, and she was launched on Thursday May 14 1953, her sponsor being Mrs D.F. Anderson, wife of the P&O Deputy Chairman. It was something of a unique day in British shipbuilding, for on the same day at Barrow the Orient Line launched the *Orsova*. In one day the two closely related companies had put into the water 58,000 tons of shipping which had cost some £12 million. By January 20 1954 the *Arcadia* was completed and she left John Brown's yard for the Mersey where she was drydocked for the painting of the underwater hull, returning in the following week to the Clyde for her trials. These were completed on January 30 when she was handed over to P&O after which she sailed for Tilbury with Sir William Currie and over 300 guests on board, including Mr A.T. Lennox-Boyd, Minister of Transport. On the voyage along the south coast she put into Torbay on the evening of Sunday January 31 and two days later she arrived back in Tilbury where fitting out for her maiden voyage continued.

Arcadia's accommodation catered for 670 first class passengers in one, two and three-berth cabins, including eight two-berth de-luxe cabins. In the tourist class she carried 735 passengers in two, four and six-berth cabins. She had 16 public rooms, nine of which were in the first class section. One of the most popular of these was the 'Lookout Bar' situated on the boat deck, immediately below the bridge. This room was fitted with long windows on three sides which gave the passengers a panoramic view of the sea around them with decoration maritime in character. The floor covering featured two map panels showing the eastern and western hemispheres and figureheads stood on either side of the bar, copied from those of old wooden sailing ships. The centre piece was in the form of a chart table fitted with a compass and chronometer, and flanked by terrestrial and celestial globes.

The majority of the first class public rooms were on the promenade deck amidships and included the children's nursery, the library and writing room, the first class lounge and ballroom, the verandah cafe and the swimming pool itself. The lounge was a large, high room with windows on either side; the central section of the ceiling was circular in shape with a panelled perimeter arranged to carry concealed lighting. At the after end, between the glazed doors leading to the ballroom, was a wide, deep mural painted on a concave panel. It was based on an Arcadian scene and designed in rhythmic sequence in low colour tones. The tourist class rooms were on 'A', 'B' and 'C' decks, with the swimming pool at the after end of the promenade deck. Dining saloons for both classes were on 'D' deck separated by the galleys, and both were air-conditioned. All the furnishings and decoration were designed by A. McInnes Gardner & Partners, and many renowned artists provided murals to tone in with the colour schemes. Externally *Arcadia* was a handsome vessel with two masts and a large funnel topped with what has become known as a 'Clydebank' funnel. A great deal of research was carried out by John Brown & Co and Thermotank Ltd to perfect this design and the desired effect was achieved with the soot and smuts being carried well aft of the long sports deck.

Arcadia sailed on her maiden voyage from Tilbury to Sydney on February 22 1954. She was commanded by Captain Geoffrey C. Forrest, who had joined P&O just before the First World War, and who had served on the *Kalyan, Borda, Rajputana, Strathnaver, Canton* and *Stratheden.* He was to command the ship for her first two years of service, before retiring in October 1956. At Port Said the Governor of the Canal Zone, Mr Mohamed Riad, was entertained on board by Sir William and Lady Currie; and when the ship reached Australia she was given an enthusiastic reception. She returned to London in early May and took *Himalaya*'s place in the summer cruising programme, the latter ship remaining on the mail run. It was during this series of cruises that *Arcadia* made her first visit to Southampton on June 4 1954.

Arcadia's first three years of service were not spectacular, but she gained a reputation for quiet efficiency and comfort. However, on December 30 1957 she was in the news when, on the final leg of a voyage from Australia, she encountered severe gales in the Bay of Biscay, and several passengers and crew members were injured when the liner was caught in winds of up to 70 mph. Dinner was being served when there was some violent rolling and the ship heeled over about 40°; passengers were thrown from their chairs and hundreds of pieces of crockery were smashed. Two passengers suffered broken bones and some stewards were scalded by boiling water in the galleys. At about 10.00 pm all the passengers were ordered to their cabins for safety, and *Arcadia* hove to during the night to give them a chance to sleep. The storm abated after 24 hours, and in the event she was only four hours late arriving at Tilbury. Captain E.R. Bodley, who was completing his first voyage in command, said that it was the worst storm he had encountered in 36 years. In December 1958 it was announced that *Arcadia* was to make her first Pacific cruise in November the following year, but first she was to go to Belfast to be modernised.

She arrived at Harland & Wolff's yard at Queen's Island on Wednesday April 1 1959, and was berthed at Thompson Wharf. The contract, which was worth £500,000, was for the whole ship to be air-conditioned throughout. Six days after she arrived in Belfast, at 11.45 pm on April 7, a fire was discovered in one of the after holds and within minutes the stern of the ship was enveloped in pungent smoke from burning plastic. The Belfast fire brigade was called and they were able to confine the blaze to its seat of origin and bring it under control within an hour. It seems that workmen had been working in the hold earlier that day and the cause was accidental. Despite this setback, Harland & Wolff completed the refit by June 11 that year, well ahead of schedule. To celebrate the occasion Sir William Currie entertained 400 officials and foremen from Harland & Wolff to dinner on board.

Arcadia sailed for Tilbury the following day and called at Liverpool on the way to pick up 400 guests for the voyage south. Later that year she started her Pacific cruise programme and in November 1959 she became the first cruise liner to sail up the Queen Charlotte Sound and land passengers at Picton on the South Island of New Zealand. Just over a year later in January 1961 *Arcadia* ran aground on a coral reef just outside Honolulu while entering harbour. She had stuck bow first 300 yards off Okahu Island and she took a list of three to four degrees. Two hours later she was freed by a fleet of tugs and was taken to her berth in the harbour; after a survey it was found that she had suffered only a small dent in the keel plate and was able to sail on schedule for Sydney via Suva and Auckland. Three months later, after an inquiry into the incident had been held, the pilot who had been on board at the time was suspended for two months. In early February 1963 she was on her way home from Australia with 1,040 passengers on board when, just outside Bombay, she developed engine trouble. However, after a two-day delay in the port she was able to resume the voyage, cutting her call at Aden to make up lost time.

By 1968 *Arcadia* was spending more of her time in the Pacific, and in December that year she received clearance from the US authorities to make scheduled cruises from the USA to the Caribbean. In April 1970 *Arcadia*'s mainmast was removed and the foremast was shortened by 18 ft at Thorneycroft's in Southampton, which enabled her to clear low power cables in Alaskan harbours.

In April 1972, after a voyage to Sydney via Panama and the west coast of the USA, she returned to Southampton by the same route and made two cruises from the port. She then sailed once more for Sydney, this time via Cape Town and Durban, returning once again after Pacific cruises via the USA and Panama, arriving in Southampton on December 3 that year. One unusual call was a four-hour stay in Cherbourg while homeward bound. The first few months of 1973 were spent on a world cruise, which took her to Lisbon, Bermuda, Port Everglades, Bahamas, Acapulco, the west coast of the USA and Canada, Honolulu, Suva, Auckland, Sydney, Singapore, Hong Kong and Japan, returning via Panama and arriving back in Southampton on April 10. She was then converted to an open class vessel with berths for 1,350 passengers, and she made her first cruise as a one class ship in June 1973 on the west coast of North America. She continued to be based there, cruising to Alaska, Mexico and across the Pacific until early 1975. On March 21 that year she returned to Southampton after an absence of nearly two years, and following a refit by Vosper Thorneycroft she made three cruises from that port. The first two were to the Atlantic Isles and were of a two-week duration, and the last one was a four-night voyage to Amsterdam and back. After completing this cruise she was stored and prepared for a positioning voyage to Sydney, sailing on May 17 via South Africa. She was to take *Himalaya*'s place on the Australian station.

In the spring of 1976 she made a few spring cruises from Southampton, but thereafter she was based permanently in Australia. Her exclusion from the 1977 UK cruise brochure led to rumours that P&O were about to sell her, but this was strongly denied by the company. In actual fact the rumours were groundless and she had another two years of her career left.

By the middle of 1978 *Arcadia*'s suitability for her role of cruise liner was in question; the Australian cruise market was a highly competitive business and it was inevitable that as she was 24 years old some thought would be given to replacing her. Then on September 1 1978 P&O announced that the recently purchased *Sea Princess* would take over from *Arcadia* in February 1979. On January 29 1979 *Arcadia* returned to Sydney from her last full Pacific cruise. She disembarked her 1,250 passengers and prepared to embark 650 more who were to go on a unique adventure cruise, during which they would 'ring out the old and ring in the new'. On the voyage they called at Rabul, Hong Kong and Singapore, where the passengers transferred to *Sea Princess* for her first cruise. As *Arcadia* left Sydney on the evening of January 29, thousands of people turned out to wave goodbye. It was a public holiday as the country celebrated 'Australia Day', and as *Arcadia* sailed down the harbour scores of small craft escorted her to Sydney Heads, while on shore a band played *Scotland the Brave*, recalling *Arcadia*'s Clydeside origins. She was commanded by Captain Anthony Dallas, and her Chief Radio Officer Mr Kenneth Gibson had sailed on her maiden voyage as a junior radio officer. It was a nostalgic goodbye from a city which had grown to love the ship, and the evening air resounded to a cacophony of whistles and car horns as *Arcadia* left for the last time.

She disembarked her passengers in Singapore on February 17 and ten days later she was sold to the Nisshoi-Iwai Co of Tokyo to be broken up in Taiwan. *Arcadia* arrived in Kaohsiung on February 28 and was berthed alongside a Greek tanker the *Andros Apollan*. She was visited on March 6 that year by the American author and shipping enthusiast Mr James L. Shaw, and at that time stripping operations were in progress. Furniture and bedding were being lowered over the side, and lifeboats were being used as tankers to take off her excess fuel. On board, wooden decks were being taken up and the carpeting in most public rooms had been cut and rolled up. Most nautical items were stripped by employees of Rainbow Enterprises Ltd, and would be exported all over the world. A few months later Mr Roger Chapman, one of her ex-radio officers, visited her at Kaohsiung and found only the foremast and about 200 ft of hull left. She must have disappeared altogether soon afterwards and Mr Chapman must have been the last of her ex-crew members to set eyes on her. During her 25-year career she had steamed, 2,650,000 miles and carried 430,000 passengers.

Technical data

Gross tonnage: 29,871
Net tonnage: 16,077
Length overall: 721 ft 4 in (219.86 m)
Breadth: 90 ft 8 in (27.63 m)
Depth: 40 ft (12.19 m)
Cargo capacity: 320,792 cu ft
Boilers: Oil-fired, three Foster Wheeler controlled superheat boilers, 620 psi
Main engines: Twin screw, two sets of Parsons double-reduction geared turbines, 42,500 SHP, 22 knots
Ship's company: 716
Passengers: First class 679, Tourist class 735; 1973, 1,350 open class passengers

Above left
Arcadia *takes to the water on May 14 1953, the largest P&O passenger ship to be built on the Clyde* (Scottish Record Office).

Right Arcadia *in the Indian Ocean, outward bound to Australia in November 1960* (author's collection).

Above Arcadia's *first class dining saloon* (P&O).

Below *The first class lounge,* Arcadia (P&O).

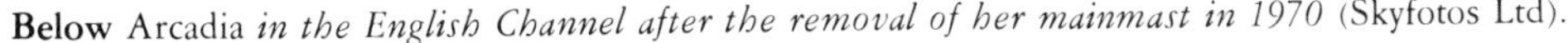

Above Arcadia's *first class observation lounge showing the wooden figureheads on either side of the bar* (P&O).

Below Arcadia *in the English Channel after the removal of her mainmast in 1970* (Skyfotos Ltd).

Arcadia *in drydock at Southampton* (P&O).

Iberia 1954

On February 8 1952 the keel was laid for the last liner to be built in P&O's post-war reconstruction programme. The new ship was to be a sister to the *Arcadia*, and she was built by Harland & Wolff at Queen's Island, Belfast. She was to be named *Iberia*, which revived the origins of the line when, in 1836, the first *Iberia* provided the Peninsular Steam Navigation Company's service to Vigo, Oporto, Lisbon, Cadiz and Gibraltar. The new *Iberia* was a splendid ship of 29,614 gross tons, and she was launched at noon on Thursday January 21 1954 by Lady McGrigor, the wife of the First Sea Lord Sir Roderick McGrigor, who was also present. The ceremony went without a hitch, and to loud cheers from the workforce and guests *Iberia* took to the water for the first time. A few hours after the launch the old *Mooltan* steamed by Belfast Lough on her way to the breaker's yard; she had been built at Harland & Wolff's yard 30 years earlier. Sadly *Iberia* would serve only 18 years with the company before competition from air travel and mechanical trouble brought about an early end to her career.

By September 7 1954 work on *Iberia* was completed, and that evening she left Belfast for the Clyde to undergo her trials. Three days later she made her runs over the measured mile off the Isle of Arran and achieved a speed of 24.9 knots, which was nearly three knots faster than her intended service speed. Later that day in a short ceremony on the first class promenade deck Sir William Currie accepted her on behalf of the P&O company. She then sailed for Tilbury, arriving three days later on the morning of September 13 to prepare for her maiden voyage to Australia on September 28.

Iberia's profile was very similar to *Arcadia*'s, with a curved, rounded stem, a cruiser stern, and two masts. She had a single elliptical-shaped funnel designed to throw fumes and soot clear of the vessel's upperworks which gave *Iberia* such a different appearance from her sister. The company had been testing various types of funnel from the 'Thorneycroft' top to the French 'Valensi' design (as fitted seven years later to the *France*). Serious thought was given to fitting this type in *Iberia*, but the appearance of an aircraft wing when viewed from forward and aft made them continue the search for a more suitable funnel top. With the result of wind tunnel tests established, the 'Clydebank' top was fitted to *Arcadia*, but further experiments in the national Physical Laboratory resulted in *Iberia*'s funnel shape, in which the dome was replaced by a coaming to disguise an otherwise odd appearance.

Iberia had accommodation for 674 first and 733 tourist class passengers, which in common with *Arcadia* was P&O's highest tourist/first class ratio. The layout of the accommodation was the same as that in *Arcadia*, with the first class observation lounge on the boat deck overlooking the forecastle, and the remainder of the first class public rooms on the promenade deck. The tourist class public rooms were on 'A', 'B' and 'C' decks, and included a lounge, smoke room, ballroom and verandah cafe. Dining saloons for both classes were on 'D' deck, the first class seating 366 and the tourist class 376 passengers, and both saloons were air-conditioned.

Iberia left Tilbury as scheduled on Tuesday September 28 1954, commanded by Captain C.E. Pollitt, arriving in Bombay on October 14 and Sydney on

November 1. She sailed back to London in time for Christmas, and left in late December 1954 for her second voyage to Australia. When she reached Port Said on the afternoon of December 31 she found that the canal was blocked. The 10,000 ton Liberian tanker *World Peace*, which was second in line in a northbound convoy, had collided with one of the piers of the El Ferdan swing bridge and had then run aground on the west bank of the canal. Although nobody had been injured, the collision had caused the metal structure of one of the wings of the bridge to collapse across the tanker's deck, and both lay athwart the canal. Owing to the danger of explosion and fire the crew were evacuated, and the seven ships which had been following were moved to a safe distance. Altogether 200 ships were held up, *Iberia* being the largest. Fortunately by the evening of January 2 1955 the obstruction was cleared and two days later *Iberia* was able to continue her voyage. The delay to the ship cost the company £14,000.

Just over a year later *Iberia* herself was involved in a collision. On Thursday March 29 1956 she was off Colombo while outward bound for Australia when the 10,000 ton Liberian tanker *Stanvac Pretoria* collided with her on the port side amidships, causing damage to the promenade and boat decks. That same day she went into Colombo where over the next four days temporary repairs were carried out. She sailed again on Monday April 2 1956 with her 1,300 passengers on board bound at reduced speed for Fremantle. Once there she was met by senior dockyard officials, and plans were drawn up to replace the damaged decks. When she arrived in Melbourne, dockyard workmen marked out and labelled all the steel decking and fittings which needed replacing. As soon as she arrived in Sydney work began on cutting away the damaged decks, and continued day and night for 18 days. On May 2 she was ready for sea once again, and Sir William Currie sent a telegram of appreciation to the Chairman of Cockatoo Dockyard for the speedy accomplishment of the repair work. She sailed soon afterwards for London, where the first of her summer cruises due to begin on June 2 had to be cancelled.

In August 1958 *Iberia* made her first visit to Spain, where her Captain was presented with a vase commemorating the occasion. Unfortunately the Mediterranean cruise she was on ended a week later in Southampton on September 7 when ambulances took a dozen of her passengers to hospital with gastro-enteritis; altogether about 50 passengers had been taken ill during the cruise. Also that year *Iberia* made her first cruise to New York, and two years later she took her share of the transpacific cruise duties. Then on January 15 1961 she went into the yards of John I. Thorneycroft & Co of Southampton for a major overhaul and modernisation for cruising. This involved air-conditioning the whole ship, and providing all first class cabins not already having them with self contained shower, hand basin and toilet facilities. The first and tourist class dining saloons were designated as restaurants and all the passenger and crew accommodation was repainted. She was docked for 70 days in all, and the whole refit cost P&O £500,000. On March 27 that year, with the work completed, she left Southampton for Tilbury to prepare for a voyage to Australia, New Zealand and Japan. Ten days later she left London for the voyage and then returned to the UK afterwards for a summer cruising season.

During the 1960s *Iberia* was a familiar sight on the west coast of the USA and she became a popular cruise-ship with American passengers. In 1967 she again became a familiar sight at Cape Town and Durban as the Suez Canal was closed for the second time in ten years. *Iberia* would never sail via Suez again, the canal not being re-opened until three years after she had gone to the breakers. Unfortunately by 1968 she was beginning to prove mechanically unreliable, and on October 2 that year she was delayed in Madeira after a breakdown in the power system. She was on a cruise from Southampton to the Atlantic Isles, and all her 900 passengers had to spend two nights in hotels ashore. During 1969 her mainmast was removed, and on December 10 1969 she limped into Southampton at reduced speed a day behind schedule. She had completed a troublesome seven-week Pacific voyage from Australia, during which mechanical trouble had plagued her all the way. While she was in Pago-Pago the funnel was on fire for 15 minutes and rained red-hot soot down onto the passenger decks. She arrived 24 hours late in Honolulu after an electrical failure in the engine room, and at Acapulco the starboard engine failed which slowed her down for the rest of the voyage. But her troubles were not over yet and on November 27 1969 at Curacao, one of the first class baggage rooms was flooded with fuel oil while the ship was bunkering.

She went straight into drydock and sailed again on December 23 1969 for Australia via Cape Town and Durban. However, this trip did not start well. On Boxing Day in the Atlantic, with a gale blowing from the starboard quarter, the stabilisers were put out of action by an electrical power failure and later, for a time, there was a full electric power failure. After this was put right she was able to reach Las Palmas the next day. On leaving Durban on January 9 1970, *Iberia* took the Great Circle Track to Fremantle, arriving in Sydney later that month. By June 18 she was back in Southampton for the summer cruising season, and few observers realised that she had less than two years left in service. She was the newest of the post-war replacements, but the first to be withdrawn.

On her return from the Pacific in August 1971 she made her final cruises from Southampton, the first being for two weeks in the Mediterranean. The second of the series lasted a week, calling at Bergen and Copenhagen; the last was an eight day cruise to Madeira, Lisbon and Vigo, arriving back in Southampton on the morning of September 19 1971. *Iberia* made her final departure for Sydney on November 5 1971, sailing via Cherbourg, Panama, the USA and Canada, arriving in Australia on December 21. She spent the next three months cruising in the Pacific, and on February 4 1972, over a month before she left for home again, P&O announced that she was to be sold on her return to Southampton. The introduction of the wide-bodied Boeing 747 aircraft had taken away passengers from the route to Australia, and the liners were sailing only 60 to 70 per cent full. So with the passenger lists getting shorter all the time, it was decided that ships would have to be withdrawn, and because *Iberia*'s mechanical performance had not been up to scratch, she was the first choice. She left Sydney on March 16 1972 and returned to Southampton via Durban and Cape Town, arriving in the port a month later on April 19. She spent the next two months laid up in Southampton's Western Docks, while many wondered what her fate would be.

It soon became clear what was to happen to her when it was announced that she had been sold to Mitsui & Co of Japan for demolition in Taiwan. It was a sad day when she left 107 berth in Southampton Docks on June 28 1972, for her delivery voyage. She slipped quietly from the Solent for her final voyage, carrying only one lifeboat on either side of her hull, the rest having been removed. Steaming round the Cape she bunkered at Durban and arrived at Kaohsiung on September 8 1972. She was handed over to the Nan Feng Steel Enterprise Co and became the first of a long line of

A great liner takes shape, Iberia *on the stocks at Belfast* (Harland & Wolff).

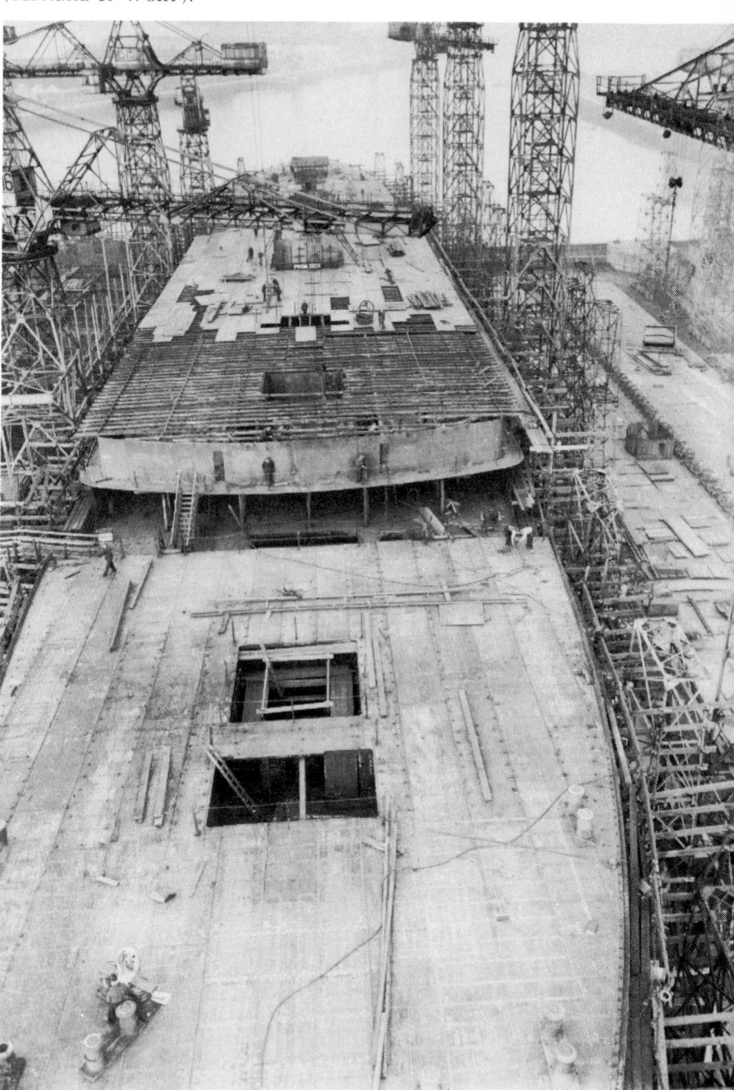

post-war P&O Orient Line ships to depart from the scene in the early 1970s.

Technical data
Gross tonnage: 29,614
Net tonnage: 15,885
Length overall: 718 ft 8 in (219.05 m)
Breadth: 90 ft 8 in (27.63 m)
Depth: 49 ft 9 in (15.16 m)
Cargo capacity: 304,930 cu ft
Boilers: Oil-fired, three Foster Wheeler controlled superheat boilers, 530 psi, 600°F-800°F
Main engines: Twin screw, two sets Parsons double-reduction geared turbines, 42,500 SHP, 22 knots
Ship's company: 709
Passengers: First class 674, Second class 733

Below Iberia *was launched at noon on Thursday January 21 1954 by Lady McGrigor, the wife of the First Sea Lord Sir Rhoderick McGrigor* (Harland & Wolff).

Right *Work on* Iberia *nears completion. Also at her fitting out berth is Shaw Savill's* Southern Cross (Harland & Wolff).

Above Iberia *off the Needles, outward bound from Southampton* (Harland & Wolff).

Below Iberia *in the English Channel soon after her mainmast was removed in 1969* (Skyfotos Ltd).

Cathay and *Chitral* 1961

Although these two ships became well known under the P&O flag in the 1960s, their origins went back to 1954 and the Antwerp headquarters of the Compagnie Maritime Belge (CMB). This Belgian shipping company was formed in 1895 and ran a passenger/cargo service to the Belgian Congo. In 1954 plans were laid to build two new passenger/cargo liners for the route. They were to be larger and faster than any ship seen before on the Congo run, and would eventually replace two of CMB's ageing 7,000 tonners built in 1938, the *Copacabana* and the *Mar Del Plata*, which were to be withdrawn from service in 1958. The order for the first of the two sisters went to a French company, SA des Chantiers et Ateliers of St Nazaire, and she was launched on November 30 1955 as *Jadotville*, being named after a town in the Congo. She completed her trials and entered service with the CMB in July 1956, on the Antwerp — Matadi route. Meanwhile, the order for the second ship had gone to SA Cockerill — Ougree of Hoboken, Antwerp. She was launched in January 1957, and named *Baudouinville* after the King of the Belgians. She entered service with the CMB in November of that year on the same route as her sister.

Both *Jadotville* and *Baudouinville* were single screw ships of over 13,000 gross tons, with a service speed of 17 knots. They had the unmistakable air of the continental passenger liner; their tall superstructure amidships was dominated by a 'lascroux' designed funnel, a type which had proved successful in a number of European vessels, notably the *Provence* and *Cristoforo Colombo*. The Belgian sisters wore the light grey livery of the CMB, with white upperworks and yellow funnel. The two ships had one class accommodation for 300 passengers, including 26 children, and a crew of 137. They had seven passenger decks, from the boat deck down to 'E' deck. The public rooms were on 'A' deck; overlooking the forecastle was the 'grand salon', aft of this the smoking room, and further aft a verandah cafe. On the boat deck was the swimming pool, and down on 'D' deck the dining saloon.

By January 1958, both ships were established on the Antwerp — Lobito and Matadi service. They cut the passage time on this route to 14 days, and there is no doubt that had not political events intervened, their careers with CMB would have been longer. Many of their passengers were Belgian government officials taking up their posts in the Congo, but in early 1960 the airlines were making inroads into the route and taking passengers from the CMB. It was not the airliners, however, that finally ended CMB's passenger service to the west coast of Africa. In June 1960 the Belgian Congo became independent, and the political catastrophe which followed saw the repatriation of the Belgian officials. The decline was irreversible and it was necessary for the CMB to act quickly, so in December that year the board made the brave decision to sell their largest liners, *Jadotville, Baudouinville* and *Thysville*.

It was an ideal opportunity for the P&O company when the two sisters were put up for sale, for with the *Corfu* and *Carthage* coming to the end of their careers, the Belgian ships would make excellent replacements. But they had to make a quick decision because both Greek and Italian interests wished to buy the ships and on January 11 1961 a deal was successfully negotiated with P&O purchasing the two sisters for £3 million.

The first of the two to be handed over was *Jadotville*, and when she arrived in Antwerp on Saturday Janaury 28 1961, key P&O officers joined the ship. Three weeks later on February 17 she left for London, where she arrived the following day. Two days later her main crew joined and she went alongside *Carthage* in King George V Dock for the transfer of stores. On February 23 she went back alongside the dock, and in a short ceremony she was renamed *Chitral*. In his speech Sir Donald Anderson, the chairman of P&O congratulated the CMB on the design of the two ships, and on their maintenance, which he described as exceptional. He finished his speech with these words, 'We can assure them (the CMB) that we shall give these ships a good home, treat them with respect, and try to look after them no less well than they have been looked after already, and if the owners have to haul down the Belgian flag and the CMB house flag, I hope they may feel that the Red Ensign and the P&O house flag are the next best thing'.

On the last day of February 1961 *Chitral* left London for Southampton and then for the Far East, arriving in Yokohama on June 23 1961. Although P&O officials had inspected *Baudouinville* on January 4 1961, she did not complete her last voyage for CMB until February 11 that year, and after key P&O personnel had joined the ship she sailed for London at 5.00 pm on March 30. Ten days later she left for Southampton and after transferring stores and the bulk of her crew from *Corfu*, she sailed on April 14 1961 for her maiden voyage east as the *Cathay*.

The two ships now wore P&O's white livery with buff funnel, and the accommodation was altered to cater for 235 passengers in one class. In addition to the Far East service both ships operated cruising voyages in European waters, another role for which they were well suited with the fall in passenger traffic on all liner routes. In December 1961 *Chitral* was in the news when she collided with a junk in thick fog two miles outside Hong Kong as she was leaving the port for Japan.

Fortunately, the crew of the junk were unharmed and two of them were picked up by *Chitral*, the remainder by a fishing boat. A Far East round voyage for *Cathay* and *Chitral* took just under three months, most of the catering stores being taken on before leaving London. The chef's order sheet would include ten tons of meat, five tons of fish, four tons of bacon, 18,000 eggs and 1,000 gallons of milk. It was quite a shopping list and a well known hotelier who travelled in *Cathay* in October 1965 was full of praise for her high standards, and called her a fine example of a 'floating hotel'. In March 1966 *Cathay* was at Yokohama in Japan, and she took part in the port's celebrations to welcome *Canberra* on her first visit. It must have been quite a sight to see both ships dressed overall and tied up at Yokohama's South Pier.

Although the passenger trade was falling off, once again it was politics and war which drastically changed the careers of *Cathay* and *Chitral* and brought about another change of companies. In the summer of 1967 the Middle East war closed the Suez Canal once more. It soon became obvious that it would be closed for a long time, and P&O had to reorganise its passenger/cargo routes. Between March and September 1970 it was decided to experiment with *Chitral* to test the Continental cruise market. The P&O company had wanted to establish itself in the very important European holiday market for a long time, and so *Chitral* was scheduled to undertake a programme of 12 cruises from Genoa. It was planned that her passengers would be mainly from Germany, Holland, Italy and Belgium, with only a few from the UK. However, although she completed the programme, it was not a total success for the company. Both *Cathay* and *Chitral* had to utilise the large cargo capacity as well as the passenger space in order to be completely viable. There was some thought of increasing the number of passengers they could carry, but it was decided that the cost of doing so and maintaining acceptable standards would prove insuperable barriers. It was fortunate for both ships that it was decided to transfer them permanently to eastern waters, and to the Eastern & Australian Steamship Company Ltd, a P&O subsidiary.

The origins of the E&A went back to 1873, with a service from Brisbane to Singapore, which was soon expanded to cover a passenger/cargo service from Australia to most of the Far East. In 1946 75 per cent of the shares of E&A were acquired by P&O and this famous and respected company became a member of the P&O group. The *Cathay* was to replace the E&A's *Aramac*; she was Cunard's *Parthia* until 1962, and in November 1969 went to the breakers at Kaohsiung. On November 14 1969 *Cathay* arrived in Hong Kong at the end of her final voyage for P&O. Her crew were flown home and the crew from *Aramac* transferred to their new ship as she commenced her career with the E&A. In January 1970 *Chitral* brought to an end P&O's UK — Far East passenger service which had been operating for 134 years, and on September 7 1970 completed her final Mediterranean cruise programme.

She sailed that evening for Hong Kong, calling at Dakar, Durban and Singapore, arriving at 8.00 am on October 12. Both ships were to operate the E&A service between Australia, the Far East and Japan, and soon became a familiar sight in those waters, retaining the white livery and buff funnel of the P&O company. In common with E&A tradition, the ships' officers were Australian and their crews Chinese. New ports were added to E&A's itinerary in the east, and both ships soon became very popular with Australian passengers. In 1972 Guam was added to the list as a port of call on the southbound voyage back to Australia. During the early 1970s the two ships successfully carried the E&A's cargoes to the Far East and Japan, but by 1975 it had become clear that containerisation was reducing the amount of traffic and the E&A was forced to close the service in the latter half of that year. *Chitral* was the first to go, and on December 3 1975 she was sold to Choy's Iron & Steel Company for demolition in Taiwan.

But *Cathay*'s story was not yet over. When she made her final sailing from Sydney in December 1975 this marked the end of regular shipping services maintained by the E&A between Australia and the Far East. She had been sold to the Nan Yang Shipping Company of Macao for use as an officers' training ship and was handed over to her new owners on January 28 1976, in Hong Kong. It soon became clear that in fact she was to serve under the flag of the Peoples Republic of China, having been renamed *Kenghsin*, and precise details of the next five years of her career are difficult to obtain.

She was resold to the China Ocean Shipping Company of Peking, and by early 1979 she had been renamed *Shanghai*. For the past few years she has been engaged on a regular passenger and cargo service between Shanghai and Hong Kong, carrying 451 passengers in three classes. She caters mainly for

The CMB's Jadotville, *the first of the two sisters* (CMB).

Chinese, that country's cuisine being all that is available, although Europeans are able to travel in her, particularly now that China is encouraging tourism from the west. *Shanghai* wears a pale green hull livery, with a dark green boot-topping and white upperworks. Her funnel is yellow with a red band bearing a yellow star and waves. She provides a weekly service and in Shanghai uses the old passenger ship terminal just below the Bund and Soochow Creek. In Hong Kong she anchors in the western part of the harbour, between Kowloon and Stonecutters Island. Passengers are disembarked by tender and landed at Tai Kok Tsui Ferry Pier in Kowloon.

One European who travelled aboard her during 1983, recalls that the cabins and public rooms seemed little changed from her E&A days and they were kept quite clean although they were a little worn and threadbare. Externally around the decks, he felt that little effort was made to maintain 'passenger ship' standards, and he thought it was doubtful whether the decks had seen a holystone since the Chinese had taken her over. The decks, he remembers, were in poor condition with the planking dirty, split and otherwise damaged. Many of the dowels were missing leaving the rusting bolts beneath exposed, in addition to which runner wires were just coiled on decks and not cleared away or tied up. So as she enters her 28th year the career of the little Belgian ship continues on the other side of the world from where she first set sail.

Technical data
Gross tonnage: 13,921 *(Cathay)*, 13,789 *(Chitral)*
Net tonnage: 7,572 *(Cathay)*, 7,451 *(Chitral)*
Length overall: 557 ft 9 in (170 m)
Breadth: 79 ft 10 in (24.33 m)
Depth: 40 ft 7 in (12.37 m)
Cargo capacity: 404,244 cu ft *(Cathay)*, 430,778 cu ft *(Chitral)*
Boilers: Both ships oil-fired, three watertube boilers, 670 psi
Main engines: Single screw, Parsons double-reduction geared turbines, 9,500 SHP, 17 knots
Ship's company: 138
Passengers: 235 on one class

Cathay *at sea* (Ray Catterall).

Above Cathay *whilst in service with the E&A* (Keith Byass).

Below *The* Shanghai, *looking in need of a coat of paint* (CMB).

Above left *The lounge on board* Shanghai, *little changed since her P&O days* (China Merchants Steam Navigation Co).
Below left *The restaurant on the* Shanghai (China Merchants Steam Navigation Co).
Above *The reading room,* Shanghai (China Merchants Steam Navigation Co).

Canberra 1961

On January 23 1957 P&O surprised the shipping world when they announced that they had ordered a 45,000 gross ton passenger liner from Harland & Wolff of Belfast. It was not so much her size that caused the surprise, but the unusual nature of her design. This hinged on the fact that her machinery was to be placed aft, and her lifeboats would not be carried at the traditional height of the boat deck, but were to be stowed three decks down, lying in flush with the ship's side. The fullest advantage was to be taken of this layout with the whole midships section of the ship being given over to passenger accommodation. Having just started to extend their routes into the Pacific, P&O wished to shorten the sailing times by means of greater speeds. It was doubtful if ships the size of *Arcadia* or *Iberia* could achieve the speeds required and, with increased building costs, it would have been impossible to make them pay. So the requirement was for a larger and faster ship, but at the same time a ship which could negotiate the Suez Canal and could be handled at the major ports *en-route*. So the scene was set for the building of the 45,000 tonner, known as yard number 1621.

The keel of the new ship was laid on slipway 14 of the Musgrave Yard on September 23 1957, and in March the following year it was announced that the new ship would be named *Canberra*. It was chosen because it symbolised the part played by P&O in Australian trade and commerce. It is generally accepted that the name comes from the Aboriginal and means 'meeting place by the water'. *Canberra* was launched on Wednesday March 16 1960, which in fact was two weeks later than had originally been planned, the delay having been caused by disputes at the yard. Her sponsor was Dame Pattie Menzies GBE, wife of the Prime Minister of Australia, and she performed the ceremony gracefully with a bottle of Australian wine. Just before the ceremony she added a personal gesture to the proceedings by attaching a sprig of white heather to the launching ribbon. Congratulatory telegrams poured in to Harland & Wolff's yard, including one from the Queen and another from Sir Robert Menzies. It was a successful day and a remarkable ship had taken to her natural element. The event was overshadowed only by the fact that Harland & Wolff had lost a great deal of money in the building of *Canberra*. Indeed, by the time she was completed the builders had lost nearly £2 million. However, when she left Belfast on April 29 1961 for drydocking at Southampton, the public knew nothing of this. While in drydock she was visited by Prince Philip, and after the underwater hull had been repainted she sailed for the Clyde and her trials. After logging a speed of 29.27 knots on her full power trials, she was handed over to Sir Donald Anderson on May 19. At 8.45 pm the following day, with several hundred special guests on board, she sailed on a two day trip to Southampton to prepare for her maiden voyage.

Canberra was indeed a remarkable ship, with her wide open sun decks, the terraced superstructure surmounted by one swept back mast, and aft the slender twin funnel uptakes, totally different from anything seen before. She is powered by turbo-electric machinery capable of developing 85,000 SHP; two 1,500 kW turbo alternators provide the power for two synchronous electric propulsion motors. In the boiler room *Canberra* has three main Foster Wheeler external superheat boilers, providing steam at 750 psi and 960°F, and one auxiliary boiler. At the time of her completion she had accommodation for 548 first and 1,690 tourist class passengers, which was a significant increase in tourist class berths to cater mainly for the emigrants to Australia from the United Kingdom. She has ten passenger decks ranging from the sun deck to 'G' deck. The first class public rooms were amidships on the games and promenade decks, and the tourist class public rooms were aft on the games, 'B' and promenade decks. The most spectacular room was the first class observation lounge at the forward end of the games deck, the 'Crows Nest Lounge'. The forward bulkhead had 41 full height windows with a magnificent view over the sea, while the after bulkhead looked out onto an enclosed games area. Two large screens which concealed the bar, and pantry areas contained illuminated relief maps of Sydney Harbour and Southampton Water, her two main ports of call.

Aft of the main foyer was the 'Bonito Club', a ballroom which opened out aft onto the first class swimming pool. Forward on the promenade deck was the first class lounge, the 'Meridian Room', with its spiral staircase which went up three decks to the 'Crows Nest'. Aft of this was the bureau area, the focal point being the brightly lit floor to ceiling showcases of the shop and hairdressing salons. In the tourist class the main lounge, the 'William Fawcett Room', was on the promenade deck; also on this deck were the 'Peacock Room' which provided a quiet atmosphere for reading, the 'Pop Inn', a teenagers, rumpus room equipped with drink dispensers and juke box, and the 'Cricketers Tavern'. This was the main tourist class bar, and on the walls hung life size portraits of famous cricketers and a montage of bats, wickets, caps and other cricketing ephemera.

Aft on 'B' deck was the 'Alice Springs Bar' which opened out onto one of the two tourist class swimming pools. On the games deck aft of the children's playrooms was the tourist class ballroom, or 'Island Room'. Right aft on this deck was the lido area, which was the second tourist swimming pool. The task of furnishing and decorating the public rooms was carried out by a number of designers, notably Sir Hugh Casson, Mr John Wright and Miss Barbara Oakley, who were headed by Mr John West, the assistant manager of P&O Orient Lines.

Canberra sailed on her maiden voyage on June 2 1961, sailing via Suez to Sydney. There was a slight problem in Aden with leaky condenser tubes, but this was soon rectified and resulted in only minor delays. She received a terrific welcome in Australia, and after leaving Sydney she sailed on to Auckland, Honolulu, Vancouver, San Francisco and Los Angeles and at each port the welcome was rapturous. She returned home once again via Suez and arrived at Southampton on September 1 1961. During 1962 *Canberra* had trouble with her distilling plant which necessitated an early end to a Pacific cruising programme, but she suffered a real setback in the early part of 1963. She had left Southampton in late December 1962 for a voyage to Australia when, at 4 am on January 4 1963, there was an explosion in the main switchboard. The resulting fire destroyed the whole of the starboard side of the main switchboard, and *Canberra* lay crippled 150 miles west of Malta.

It was several hours before makeshift leads could be rigged up. Later, one main engine was started and she was able to reach Malta the next day. Most of the passengers were airlifted to their destination, and on January 16 *Canberra* was able to sail for Harland & Wolff's yards at Belfast. She was out of service until the end of May that year, and in a statement about the explosion P&O said that a member of the engine room staff had thrown a circuit breaker switch totally contrary to warning notices. The result was a short circuit arc of great severity and a fire which had been fed electrically by other generators. Fortunately the rest of the year passed without further incidents.

In May 1966 *Canberra*, along with many more British ships, was caught up in the seamen's strike which lasted for six weeks. She and *Arcadia* were tied up alongside each other at Southampton's 106 berth, and it resulted in the cancellation of her UK cruise programme. By 1972 it was clear that the days of the liner voyage were over, and some thought would have to be given to a full time cruising role for *Canberra*. In January 1973 she was sent over to New York for a series of cruises to the Caribbean, but despite the dropping of class divisions the cruises were not a success. For most of the following month she was laid up at the mouth of the Cape Fear River, near Wilmington, North Carolina. Although she was back in service by March, just over two months later it was announced that she was to be withdrawn from service and put up for sale. It was a surprise decision, which had been taken because it was thought she was unsuitable for cruising on account of her excessive draught.

Then a few weeks later on August 14, in a sudden reversal of thinking, it was decided that *Canberra* would stay with P&O and take up a cruising role. However, the doubts about her draught proved to be well founded when she ran aground twice. The first incident was in July off Grenada, and the second happened on the day her reprieve was announced, this time off St Thomas harbour in the US Virgin Islands. Fortunately she was refloated without difficulty and she returned to Southampton in September 1973 as planned.

In early 1974 *Canberra* was converted permanently to a 'one class' ship, her design lending itself to a conversion of this nature. The 'Stadium' on the games deck became an enclosed theatre and the 'Pop Inn' was turned into the photographer's shop, while the first class children's playroom became the card room. Her passenger capacity in this new role was cut to 1,737, mainly by converting fourth-berth cabins in what used to be tourist class, into two bedded cabins. During the summer season *Canberra* was based at Southampton, sailing on mainly two or three week cruises. Each autumn she spent a short period in drydock before setting out on a Christmas and New Year cruise, returning early in January. She then set sail on a three-month world voyage, which as the years went by became almost a ritual.

Canberra's cruising routine went largely unaltered for seven years, and as she sailed on her world cruise on January 6 1982 nothing at all seemed any different. Yet before the cruise ended *Canberra* would be on the front page of every newspaper the world over. On Friday April 2 1982 the Argentinian army invaded the British Crown Colony of the Falkland Islands, and the Prime Minister, Mrs Margaret Thatcher, told the nation that a 'task force' was to sail for the South Atlantic to free the islands. At the time of the invasion *Canberra* was in Naples, the last port of call on her long voyage, and two days later as she was off Gibraltar, *Canberra* was requisitioned by the government for service as a troop transport.

As soon as she berthed alongside 106 berth in Southampton Docks at 7.30 am on April 7 work began on her conversion. Guardrails and windshields on the sun deck were removed and a helicopter landing pad was built over the Bonito swimming pool. Similarly a flight deck was constructed on the observation deck forward of the bridge, and the 'Stadium' was converted into a hospital unit. All day on Wednesday April 7 men of the 3rd Battalion, Parachute Regiment, and 40 Commando, Royal Marines embarked for their journey south. After some delay *Canberra* finally sailed for the South Atlantic at 8.13 pm on April 9 to a resounding farewell from the people of Southampton. Eight days later she called into Freetown for fuel, and on April 20 she arrived off Ascension Island, which was to be the staging post for the British forces. There followed a 16-day wait around the island while the diplomats attempted to solve the deadlock, but by early May it was clear that only force would remove the invaders and on May 6 *Canberra* weighed anchor and set course for the Falkland Islands. By May 20 she and the other 18 ships of the convoy were only 110 miles north-east of Port Stanley. At 6.05 am the next day she anchored in San Carlos Water to disembark her troops. At 8.50 am that day she was attacked for the first time, when a Pucara counter insurgency aircraft fired rockets at her. From then until 4.00 pm that day the ships in San Carlos water were subjected to continuous air attacks at half hourly intervals, but *Canberra* survived and at 11.15 pm she left the North Falkland Sound for the safety of waters north-east of Port Stanley.

On May 25 she sailed for South Georgia, and two days later she rendezvoused with *QE2* at Grytviken, where troops of 5 Brigade were embarked. Then as *QE2* left for home *Canberra* sailed once more for San Carlos. This time when she anchored, on June 2, there was a welcome thick fog hanging over the sound, and she was able to disembark the troops safely before proceeding once again to sea. At 11.59 pm on June 14 the Argentine forces in the Falkland Islands surrendered to Major General J.J. Moore, and the problem arose of what to do with thousands of Argentinian prisoners. Once again the answer lay in *Canberra*'s huge bulk, and on June 15 she embarked 1,121 POWs in San Carlos Water, followed by a further 4,000 in Port Stanley over the next few days. After she had been guaranteed safe conduct *Canberra* sailed for Puerto Madryn in Argentina, where she arrived on Saturday June 19. She was escorted to a berth on a long jetty, where her passengers were disembarked to a rather cool reception in their home country. Two days later she was back in Port Stanley, and this time she embarked Royal Marines from 40, 42 and 45 Commando before sailing for Southampton and the end of a great enterprise.

Canberra's voyage home was far more relaxed than it had been on the way south and just over two weeks after she left the Falkland Islands she arrived off the Lizard. At 5.00 pm that day, July 10, the group Chairman, the Earl of Inchcape flew on board and as *Canberra* closed the shore those on board got some idea of the welcome in store. All the headlands were crowded with people and all varieties of small boats came out to greet her, their occupants cheering and waving. The climax came the next day when she arrived in Southampton Water. At 9.00 am the Prince of Wales went on board, and as she made her way up towards her berth she was surrounded by an enormous procession of boats, yachts, ferries and every kind of small vessel which can be imagined.

A tide of emotion followed the 'Great White Whale' as she returned to her home port. As she drew level with the Eastern Docks she came to a stop, almost as if she was unable to move for the masses of small boats gathered around her. She had, in fact, slowed down to allow the Prince of Wales' helicopter to get away before she berthed. As *Canberra* was edged into her berth, the

Canberra *is launched from slipway 14 of Harland & Wolff's Musgrave Yard on Wednesday March 16 1960* (Harland & Wolff).

whole emotional welcome reached its peak. The Royal Marine band struck up *Land of Hope and Glory* to the accompaniment of the 2,500 marines on board and the huge crowd ashore. There is no doubt the nation had taken *Canberra* to its heart. She had been away for 94 days, and had steamed a total of 27,187 miles.

On August 1 she went into drydock where she was refitted once again as a passenger liner. As well as the necessary work which was done at government expense, P&O themselves made a few changes such as the installation of a new bar in the 'Island Room'. On September 11 1982 she left Southampton for the first of three cruises from the port, before undertaking a positioning voyage to Sydney. For the next few years she was to spend the summer season in the UK and the winter cruising from Sydney, the world cruise having been taken over by *Sea Princess*. At the time of writing *Canberra* still cruises successfully, 12 years after she had been written off as 'not suitable for cruising'.

Technical data
Gross tonnage: 44,807
Net tonnage: 24,021
Length overall: 818 ft 6 in (249.48 m)
Breadth: 102 ft (31.09 m)
Depth: 32 ft 10 in (10 m)
Cargo capacity: 150,000 cu ft
Boilers: Oil-fired, three Foster Wheeler external-superheated 'D' type boilers (ESD), 750 psi, 960° F
Main engines: Twin screws, two synchronous three-phase, 6,000 volt air cooled electric motors. Power supplied by two 1,500 kW turbo-alternators. 85,000 SHP, 22 knots
Ship's company: 803
Passengers: First class 548, Second class 1,690; 1974, 1,737 one class; 1985, 1,750

Canberra *on her first visit to Southampton April 30 1961* (Skyfotos Ltd).

Above *Southampton Water in 1966* (Skyfotos Ltd).

Below *A verandah cabin on board* Canberra (Keith McCart).

Above *The 'Pacific Restaurant'* Canberra (Keith McCart).

Below *The games deck starboard side* (author's collection).

Above *The 'Cricketers' Tavern'* (author's collection).

Below *The 'Meridian Room'* (author's collection).

Canberra *sails to war, her decks lined with troops, April 9 1982* (P&O).

Spirit of London 1972

In February 1971 the P&O company announced that they had purchased a partially-built liner from the Italian shipbuilders Cantieri Navali Del Tirreno E Riuniti SPA of Genoa. There is no doubt that it was a terrific boost to the passenger division. It was thought the new ship would be launched in June 1972, just over 12 years after *Canberra* had been launched. This new vessel would set the standards for the future, being the company's first 'custom built' cruise liner, and designed to cater for the luxury cruise market.

The story goes back to the late 1960s, when the P&O company reviewed the whole concept of the passenger liner's role. The Batelle Institute of Geneva were commissioned to study the problem, and as a result it was decided that a 'two tier passenger fleet was needed. One part of the fleet would consist of the large traditional vessels already in service, all of which were over 20,000 gross tons and had been built for long voyages. They would continue to sail to the Far East, Australia and New Zealand, and would also operate cruise programmes in the off-peak season. The second tier of passenger liners were to be smaller ships of between 10,000 and 20,000 gross tons. They were to be purpose built for cruising, as this was a market which was growing at the rate of ten per cent a year. P&O were determined to increase their share of this international trade, particularly in the lucrative Caribbean cruise market. It was only fitting that the company which invented cruising back in 1844 should take the lead in this holiday business. In the late 1960s, the Norwegian shipping company Klosters Rederi A/S Oslo ordered two 17,000-ton cruise liners from Cantieri's of Genoa and work started on them in 1970 as yard numbers 288 and 290. However, financial difficulties soon caused the Italian company to break their contract with Klosters. Fortunately the Italian government came to the rescue with the necessary finance, but by this time Klosters had decided that they would only take the first of the ships they had originally ordered. She later became the *Southward*, and now cruises in the Caribbean for Norwegian Caribbean Lines. So the second ship was left partially completed on the stocks, and this turned out to be the opportunity P&O had been looking for, as they were able to step in and renegotiate the contract to purchase the vessel. There was some speculation about the price paid, but informed sources said it was £10 million, and this proved to be correct. P&O proposed to operate the new vessel in the Caribbean area, which is what Klosters had intended, so very few modifications to the original design were needed. In fact apart from the funnel uptakes, *Southward* and the new P&O vessel were to be almost identical.

In August 1971 P&O announced that the ship would be called *Spirit of London*, and that she would be based in San Francisco. P&O were laying the foundations to become one of the biggest cruise companies on the west coast of the USA, which without doubt was the largest potential cruising market in the world. The name had been chosen because with the ship operating from the USA, P&O wanted a name that would immediately link her with Britain. Secondly a theme was wanted which could be developed as the second tier of cruise liners was built up, although this plan was eventually dropped in the light of later events. P&O were determined to get things right for *Spirit of London* and in January 1972 they sent a purser to the Caribbean to sample various cruises and port arrangements. One of the vessels he visited was *Spirit of London*'s sister *Southward.* In April that year the *Spirit of London* was ready for launching, and the date was set for the 29th of that month. She was to be given a true Cockney send off, her sponsor being 69-year-old Mrs Beatrice Marriott, London's Pearl Queen. Unfortunately, she could only perform the naming ceremony that day as weather conditions prevented the launch. It must have seemed a strange ceremony for the Italian shipyard workers as Mrs Marriott named the ship, whilst a liveried 'Lloyds Waiter' and a London 'Bobby' looked on and a fanfare was played by four state trumpeters. Ten days later on May 11 *Spirit of London* finally took to the water. Four months later her fitting out was completed and she underwent her trials off La Spezia and the Italian Riviera, achieving a speed of 20.5 knots.

When she entered service *Spirit of London* wore the P&O livery of a white hull with one buff coloured funnel, which bore the P&O logo on both sides. She had the distinction of being the first diesel powered P&O passenger ship, being fitted with four medium-speed Fiat diesels geared to two shafts (two engines on each shaft), which developed 18,000 BHP, and gave her a normal service speed of 20 knots. She was also fitted with a bow thruster unit, which was driven by the main engines. As with all modern cruise-ships she was fully air-conditioned and to reduce pollution an incinerator was fitted, its exhaust fumes being fed through the funnel uptakes. The ship had a profile that was to become very familiar as more and more purpose built cruise-ships were built. She had a deep clipper bow, which was bulbous below the waterline, and a cruiser stern. There was a small radar pole above the bridge, and a single raked mast amidships above the observation desk. Her single conical funnel was right aft giving her a yacht-like appearance. She had a maximum passenger capacity of 874, but she normally carried 736. Her cabins were fitted out to a very high standard, each having its own toilet, bath or shower, and multi-channel radio. Her design emphasis was on high quality accommodation and entertainment facilities.

The interior design of her public rooms was by royal designer to industry Neville Ward, and with her name as his theme, he set out to create a variety of London's moods, from medieval times to the swinging seventies. The hub of the ship's social activities was the huge 'Churchill Room'. The 'Thames Restaurant', which seated 400 passengers, was decorated with a collage of London's landmarks. The 'Globe Theatre' situated on 'Chelsea' deck had seating for 200 passengers, and the shopping arcade was called 'Thames Street'.

On October 11 1972 *Spirit of London* was handed over to the P&O company and she sailed for Southampton, arriving there six days later. She was welcomed in the Solent by the Sea Cadet training brigantine *Royalist* under full sail, and a flotilla of fire boats. She was to stay in the UK for just over three weeks, for the finishing touches to be made to her public rooms and for storing. As soon as the work had been completed the liner became the venue for many important functions. The London Press Club's 400 members celebrated its 90th birthday on board, with all the guests staying overnight. The Southampton Master Mariners held their annual luncheon on board on November 8, and the following day there was a luncheon for Trieste Diesel Engines Ltd. There were also several open days for the public. She sailed on her maiden voyage from Southampton on November 11, with 400 American and 180 British passengers on board. Only a limited number of berths had been made available to the UK market, and these had been sold out within a week. She called at Madeira, Barbados, Grenada, Martinique, Antigua and San Juan in Puerto Rico. From there she made two Caribbean cruises before proceeding to San Francisco which was to be her home port, arriving there on January 17 1973. As she sailed into San Francisco Bay she passed *Arcadia* which was also based at the port at that time. Her welcome was marred slightly by the fact that P&O had called in Scotland Yard to investigate a series of petty thefts which had affected both passengers and crew all through the maiden voyage. One of these involved the opening of the captain's safe with a stolen key. However, once in port she began her first season of 15 cruises down to the Mexican coast. In the San Francisco press there was a two-week feature by a journalist who had taken a cruise with her. During the summer months she cruised north to Canada and Alaska, and she soon built up a regular cruising clientele. She played host to a variety of Hollywood stars, including Glen Ford and Elke Sommer, and the astronaut Colonel

Gordon Cooper. During an Alaskan cruise she was used for the filming of an episode of the detective series 'Colombo'. The film was seen by thousands of TV viewers in both the USA and the UK, but by that time she was no longer called *Spirit of London*.

During August 1974 P&O acquired the Los Angeles based Princess Cruises, and the cruise liner *Island Princess*. Following the purchase of this company P&O decided to operate both *Island Princess* and *Spirit of London* under the banner of Princess Cruises, and in September that year they announced that *Spirit of London* was to be renamed *Sun Princess*. That same month she went into the Burrard Yarrows shipyard in Victoria, British Colombia, for her annual refit and when she emerged on October 11 she was the *Sun Princess*. It was exactly two years since she had sailed from the builders' yard at Genoa to join the fleet. The most obvious difference was her change of livery. Her buff funnel was white with a black top, with the Princess Cruises motif, the head of a princess, featured on both sides. Her hull and upperworks were still white. More changes were made in the passenger accommodation. The 'Churchill Lounge' was renamed the 'International Lounge' and the 'Thames Restaurant' became the 'Continental Dining Room'. The 'Globe Theatre' became the 'Princess Theatre', although the 'Union Jack Bar' was retained. She kept to her original itinerary and continued to cruise to Mexico, Alaska and the Caribbean.

Soon after her change of identity *Sun Princess* was adopted by the Californian city of Brea, which is situated some 20 miles east of Los Angeles and at that time had a population of 23,000. In July 1975 the link between the ship and the city was cemented when 13 members of the crew were entertained by the mayor and local dignitaries. The following year marked the USA's 200 birthday, and *Sun Princess* celebrated the 4th of July bi-centennial in Glacier Bay National Park in Alaska. That evening she gave a huge firework display, for which special permission had been given by the park authorities. News of her part in the celebrations reached the White House and later that month her master, Captain J. Young, received an appreciative letter from President Gerald Ford.

Spirit of London *takes to the water ten days late, her bow thruster can be seen clearly* (P&O).

On March 30 1979 *Sun Princess* was at St Thomas, Virgin Islands, berthed aft of the Italian liner *Angelino Lauro* when the Italian ship caught fire and sank. Although she was in no immediate danger it was decided to move *Sun Princess* to a safer anchorage, but before doing so she took on 400 of the stricken liner's passengers. They were given refuge in the main lounge and provided with a buffet supper, then the entertainers organised an impromptu show. Fortunately most of them were found alternative accommodation ashore, but some stayed aboard *Sun Princess* and disembarked at San Juan. *Sun Princess* continued to break new ground in cruising itineraries. In December 1980 she called at the uninhabited Palm Island in the Grenadines, near Mustique, where her passengers were able to enjoy the sun soaked island, and a barbecue for all 700 of them. Then in the early hours of June 16 1983 she was involved in the dramatic rescue of the pilot of a Cessna aircraft, which had been forced to ditch in the sea 60 miles north of Ketchikan in Alaska. *Sun Princess* had received warning that the aircraft was in trouble, so when the pilot was forced down an hour later she was able to provide an illuminated ditching zone and to pick up the distressed airman quickly. As a result of this rescue a commendation was received from the US Coast Guard.

So *Sun Princess* continues to cruise successfully. She was the first of a new generation of P&O passenger ships, and there is no doubt that in 1972 she was a welcome addition to the P&O fleet, and a sure sign that the company was not going to abandon its passenger division.

Technical data

Gross tonnage: 17,370
Net tonnage: 8,885
Overall length: 536 ft 2 in (163.3 m)
Breadth: 75 ft 7 in (22.4 m)
Draught: 21 ft 4 in (6.5 m)
Main engines: Twin screw, four medium-speed geared Fiat diesels, 18,000 BHP, 19 knots
Ship's company: 319
Passengers: Maximum capacity 874, normally carried 736 in one class

Aerial view Spirit of London (Skyfotos Ltd).

Above *Aerial view* Spirit of London (Skyfotos Ltd).

Below Spirit of London *enters Southampton for her first and only visit to the port* (Keith Byass).

Left *The 'International Lounge'* Sun Princess (P&O).

Below left *The 'Continental Dining Room'* Sun Princess (P&O).

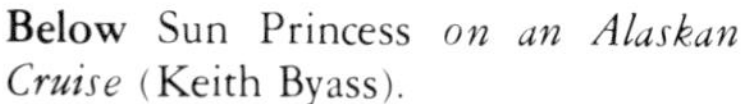

Below Sun Princess *on an Alaskan Cruise* (Keith Byass).

Island Princess and *Pacific Princess* 1974 and 1975

Just over a year after P&O made their first foothold on the west coast of the USA, they seized the opportunity to become one of the biggest cruise operators on the continent of America when, in the summer of that year, they acquired the Los Angeles-based Princess Cruises and the cruise ship *Island Princess*. She was a vessel of 19,907 gross tons, and had been built by the West German shipbuilders Rheinstahl Nordseewerke of Emden for Norwegian Cruiseships A/S of Oslo, a joint company formed by Oivind Lorentzen and Fearnley & Eger. She was launched on March 6 1971, and underwent her trials eight months later. On December 14 that year she was named *Island Venture* at Oslo, and she sailed for the United States in January 1972. Her first few months of service were spent cruising from New York to Bermuda and the West Indies. Later that year, in November 1972 she was chartered by Princess Cruises, a Los Angeles company headed by the industrialist Stanley B. McDonald. She was renamed *Island Princess* and left Fort Lauderdale for Los Angeles on November 28 1972. She was to cruise from the USA's west coast, but she remained under the Norwegian flag, with a Norwegian operating crew and an Italian hotel staff. Princess Cruises quickly built up an excellent reputation for comfort and high standards, and *Island Princess* became a very popular cruise-ship.

In September 1973 she was in the news when a well known US baseball player was convicted in Los Angeles of threatening to blow up the ship unless he was paid $250,000 by the company. He was later sentenced to nine months imprisonment. Then in May 1974 came the announcement that P&O were negotiating to buy Princess Cruises from Mr McDonald and the *Island Princess* from Fearnley & Eger. In August that year an agreement was reached with both parties so that Princess Cruises became the marketing name of P&O Inc and *Island Princess* their second purpose-built cruise-ship. In December 1972 she took on British registry and a British crew, but kept the name *Island Princess*.

Two months after they purchased Princess Cruises, P&O announced that they had also bought the sister ship to *Island Princess*, the 19,903 gross ton *Sea Venture*. She had been built in the same yards and for the same owners as *Island Venture*, and had been launched on May 9 1970. She made her maiden cruise from New York to Bermuda in June 1971, under charter to Flagship Cruises of New York with whom she was to remain until taken over by P&O. Although P&O's latest deal was concluded in late September 1974, *Sea Venture* was scheduled to complete her cruising programme for Flagship Cruises before being handed over on April 7 1975. Like her sister she was transferred to British registry and took on a British crew and her new name *Pacific Princess*. It was ten years since Princess Cruises had been incorporated, and now, with Mr Stanley McDonald as its president and as part of the P&O company, it was a major force on the west coast of the USA.

Both *Island* and *Pacific Princess* were purpose-built for cruising from the USA and they have accommodation for 650 passengers in luxury style. Both ships have just over 300 individually air-conditioned cabins, and seven passenger decks. These range from the uppermost 'Observation' deck down to 'Coral' deck where the 'Coral Dining Room' is situated. There is an impressive observation lounge at the forward end of the sun deck, and aft of this the lido swimming pool area, which can be covered by a glass dome during inclement weather. But most public rooms are situated four decks down on the 'Riviera' deck. From forward to aft they are, the 'Carousel Lounge' with its circular dance floor, the 'Princess Theatre' flanked by the 'International Lounge' and the 'Bridge Lounge', and the 'Pirates' Cove' which serves as the disco. Aft of this is the 'Carib Club' and the 'Carib Lounge' which looks out onto the 'Riviera' swimming pool. All of the de-luxe suites are on the 'Promenade' (or 'Boat' deck) directly above the public rooms, but most of the cabin accommodation is on the two decks below the 'Riviera' deck, the 'Aloha' deck and 'Fiesta' deck.

With three ships now based on the west coast of the USA, P&O was in a position to extend its operations. Initally the latest *Princesses* cruised to Mexico, the South Pacific and in the summer months to Canada and Alaska. Not surprisingly, the *Island Princess* cruises to Alaska from early July to September are very popular. Every eighth day she sails from Vancouver, up the Strait of Georgia and past Ripple Rock in the Seymour Narrows. Her first port of call is Ketchikan in south-east Alaska, followed by Juneau, the state capital, where she berths on the fourth day out from Vancouver. From there she sails up the Lynn Canal to Skagway, the most northerly port on the cruise, where passengers can sample some of the 1898 Gold Rush history. From Skagway she retraces her route south and spends the sixth day cruising in the spectacular Glacier Bay. After this the last port is Sitka, which was once the capital of Alaska and a Russian settlement. The last day is spent heading for Vancouver once again, where she arrives early the following morning to prepare for the next cruise at 9.00 pm that same day.

In December 1975 *Pacific Princess* arrived in Sydney at the end of a positioning voyage to undertake a

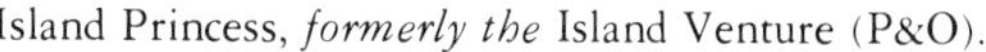

Island Princess, *formerly the* Island Venture (P&O).

programme of cruises from that port until May 1976. It was the first time she had visited the antipodes and she received a great welcome in both Auckland and Sydney. She was the first ship of the more luxurious class of cruise liner to operate from Sydney and all the cruises were sold out. In May 1976 she returned to the USA's west coast, her foray over the Pacific having been an unqualified success.

Most people in the UK have no opportunity to see the Princess ships, so perhaps it was a treat for ship lovers to see *Pacific Princess* playing the title role in the American TV soap opera series 'Love Boat'. Both ships have had their share of film and television stars travelling aboard on cruises, Charlton Heston and Michael Caine being just two. The crews of the two ships are popular ashore, particularly with the children of Mazataln Orphanage in Mexico, where they have done a great deal of voluntary work to improve life for the unfortunate youngsters.

Today Princess Cruises is definitely the most important growth area for P&O's cruise liners, and the two former Norwegian ships provide a wide variety of cruises around the Pacific and along the US west coast.

Technical data
Gross tonnage: 19,907 *(Island Princess),* 20,636 *(Pacific Princess)*
Net tonnage: 11,165 *(Island Princess),* 11,703 *Pacific Princess)*
Length overall: 554 ft 3 in (168.8 m) (includes bulbous bow)
Breadth: 80 ft 9 in (24.61 m)
Depth: 25 ft 3 in (7.7 m)
Main engines: Twin screw, four-geared Fiat diesels, each paired to each shaft by independent couplings, 18,000 BHP, 19 knots
Ship's company: 303
Passengers: Maximum 751, usually 644 in one class

Island Princess *cruising in the Caribbean* (P&O).

Above Pacific Princess in *drydock* (P&O).

Below *An impressive view of* Pacific Princess (P&O).

Sea Princess 1978

In June 1978 P&O announced that they had acquired the 27,670 gross ton liner *Kungsholm*, and that she was to replace *Arcadia* in the Australian cruise programme. Although certain areas of world shipping were under stress, the acquisition of *Kungsholm* demonstrated that there was a good potential in the specialised cruising trade and P&O intended to remain the market leaders.

The *Kungsholm* had been built on the Clyde in the shipyard of John Brown & Co for the Swedish-America Line. She had been designed for a dual role of sailing on the North Atlantic route during the summer months and cruising in the winter. Her keel was laid in 1964, and she was launched on Wednesday April 14 1965 by Mrs Dan-Axel Brostrom, the wife of the Chairman of the owning company. On November 19 1965, although she was far from completed, she began her trials on the Clyde early at the request of her owners and after they had been successfully completed she returned to John Brown's yard two days later. She was finally handed over to the Swedish America Line on March 17 1966 and sailed for her home port of Gothenburg, having cost £7 million to build.

Kungsholm was a lovely ship with truly aesthetic lines. She had a curved rounded stem and cruiser stern. Her balanced superstructure was surmounted by two funnels, the forward one being a dummy, and two masts. She was a twin screw vessel powered by two 12,600 BHP Gotaverken direct drive, slow-speed diesel engines, which gave her a service speed of 21 knots. It was intended that when cruising *Kungsholm* would sail as a one class ship carrying 450 passengers but when on the transatlantic crossing she would operate as a two class ship with berths for 750 passengers. She sailed on her maiden voyage to New York on April 22 1966, and when she arrived there ten days later she received a typical New York welcome, with foghorns and fireboats saluting her. However, it was significant for her future on the North Atlantic that she had only 304 passengers aboard. For the next nine years she was owned by Swedish America Line, but her transatlantic voyages were gradually reduced and she was used mainly for cruises.

In August 1975 she was sold to Flagship Cruises and for the next three years she cruised out of New York to the Caribbean. Then in June 1978 came P&O's announcement and *Kungsholm* was taken over by her new owners in September that year. P&O intended to operate her as a luxury ship of the same standard as the three *Princesses*, and in fact they had already announced that she was to be renamed *Sea Princess*. She was to undergo a refit which would include fitting 86 extra cabins, and a second swimming pool. Tenders were put out and at least a dozen British yards were interested. However, none of them could operate the complex work within the time limit, and so the order went to the Bremer Vulkan yard at Bremen, West Germany. So the *Kungsholm* sailed on her final voyage from New York to Bremen to undergo a three-month refit which was to transform her.

The most obvious changes to the ship's appearance were the removal of the forward funnel, the heightening of the remaining funnel, and the removal of the mainmast. Although P&O likened her new look to the other three *Princess* ships, it seemed to many people that they had made rather an 'ugly duckling' out of a once lovely ship, and there is no doubt that they destroyed her individuality. Fortunately, her interior passenger accommodation was improved. The 'Carousel Lounge' was built on the 'Promenade' deck, and aft of it the Carousel swimming pool. The additional cabins increased the passenger capacity to 840, and the ship retained a certain amount of her old Scandinavian atmosphere. By January 15 1979 the refit was completed and the official renaming ceremony took place that day when Mrs Jill Spanton, wife of the Chairman and Managing Director of P&O Cruises, unveiled a plaque commemorating the change from *Kungsholm* to *Sea Princess*. She now has nine passenger decks, from the 'Bridge' deck down to 'D' deck, which houses the indoor swimming pool, sauna and gymnasium. On the 'Bridge' deck, at the base of where the forward funnel had once been there is now a solarium. Below this is the 'Sun' deck, and beneath that the 'Promenade' deck. Working from forward to aft on this deck are the 'Lookout lounge', enclosed and open promenades, the children's nursery, and the 'Carousel Room' which serves as a lounge and a discotheque in the evenings. Beneath this is the verandah deck which accommodates the library, 'Princess Theatre', 'Tiffany's Bar', 'Verandah', 'Mayfair shop', the 'Pacific Lounge and Bar', casino and boutique. The upper and main decks are given over to cabin accommodation, and on 'A' deck there are more cabins and the 'Tasman Restaurant'.

Sea Princess was due to leave Bremen on January 16 1979, and P&O were to exhibit her at Southampton two days later. Unfortunately bad weather delayed her departure from Germany, and she only managed a very brief call at Southampton on January 21. A month later on February 17 she met *Arcadia* in Keppel Harbour, Singapore, and took on the former vessel's passengers to complete their cruise. Soon after her first arrival at Sydney she was visited by Sir Zelman Cowen, the Governor-General of Australia, who was given a tour of the ship and entertained to lunch. *Sea Princess* cruises from Australia took her round the ports of Australia, including Hobart in Tasmania, and to Singapore, Hong Kong, Manila, Jakarta, Bali, Rabaul and across to the Pacific islands. A two-week cruise costing anything between £500 and £1,000.

On May 1 1980 Mr Harry Spanton, the Managing Director of P&O Cruises, died. He had transformed the passenger division of P&O into the highly professional P&O Cruises of today, and he had expressed great confidence in *Sea Princess*. So it was a surprise when, in March 1981 P&O announced that it was transferring her to Southampton in the spring of 1982. It seemed that she had not been a total success in Australia, and the 22 year old *Oriana*, 'which offered the Australian market a wider variety of accommodation', was to be sent out to Sydney to replace her. During the 1981 season in Australia *Sea Princess* continued to make news, as in the summer of that year when she carried the 'slit drum of Vanuata' (formerly the New Hebrides) home after 85 years in Australia. The drum, which has enormous cultural significance in Vanuata, was returned to the republic by the Australian Museum to mark the first anniversary of independence. It was handed over to the President of the Republic by the Captain of *Sea Princess* and the dignitaries of the islands were entertained on board.

In early 1982 she left Sydney for her positioning voyage to Southampton, where she arrived on April 21 only 13 days after *Canberra* had sailed to war in the South Atlantic. She was due to make her first cruise on May 14, but suddenly everything was very uncertain as it seemed that *Sea Princess* might also be requisitioned as a troopship. During her stay in Southampton she was given a three-week refit by Vospers. Her four de-luxe suites were re-designed and all her public rooms were refurbished. Technical improvements included the fitting of bow thrusters to aid her manoeuvring in port. It was only 24 hours before she was due to sail that P&O finally heard that she was not to be taken over by the government, and she sailed on schedule for a 14-night cruise to the Mediterranean. She disembarked her passengers on May 28 and then spent the next nine days in the eastern Mediterranean, arriving back in Southampton on June 11. She made 14 more cruises that year, including three fly-cruises in the Mediterranean, three weeks to the West Indies, and on July 16 1982 she began a three week cruise which took her to Bermuda, Port Canaveral and to New York on July 28. It was her first return to the port since she left as the *Kungsholm* in September 1978, an absence of nearly four years. She completed the cruise programme on Monday January 3 1983, and three days later she sailed on a 90-day world cruise. Her route took her via Panama into the Pacific to Sydney, up to Malaysia and across the Indian Ocean to Durban and Cape Town, arriving back in Southampton on April 17 1983. She then went into drydock for her annual overhaul by Vospers before starting her next season of cruising in Europe. The rest of that month and all of May was spent in the Mediterranean, with the holidays marketed in the UK all fly-cruises. She was commanded for this season by Commodore John Wacher. It was his last year before retirement — he had spent a distinguished career with the company, starting 41 years previously on the ill-fated *Strathallan*.

During one cruise in August 1983 *Sea Princess* visited the Azores, and whilst she was off the islands she hit uncharted rocks damaging her starboard propeller. This was rectified at the end of the cruise when, with a day to spare before the next one started, she was drydocked and the ends of the blades were ground even. Her last cruise in the 1983 season was three weeks in the West Indies, after which she returned to Southampton to prepare once again for her world cruise. When she returned from this voyage in April 1984 there was an outcry when it was learned that her annual refit was to be undertaken at the Hapage Lloyd shipyard in Bremerhaven. But it turned out that the German shipyard had quoted a price 15 per cent lower than Vospers at Southampton, and as P&O were also faced with the threat of industrial action at the latter yard, they decided to accept the German tender.

When she emerged a month later in May *Sea Princess* had an entirely new sunbathing area on the 'Bridge' deck, and two new companionways had been built from the lido area to the 'Bridge' deck. The highlight of her 1984 cruise season was perhaps in September when she made a two-week 'food & wine' cruise in the Mediterranean. She had on board several experts in these subjects, including author and broadcaster Glynn Christian and Conal Gregory, one of only 115 Masters of Wine in the world. In 1985 she broke new ground when, on Saturday March 9, she visited Shanghai. It is over 44 years since P&O passenger liners were a regular sight in the port, and once again passengers will be able to stroll along the Bund and absorb the atmosphere of this great city and its past. They will witness the new China of today, and of course the Chinese too will see the new image of P&O in *Sea Princess*.

Technical data
Gross tonnage: 27,670
Net tonnage: 13,842
Length overall: 660 ft (201.17 m)
Breadth: 87 ft 1 in (26.54 m)
Draught: 28 ft 1 in (8.56 m)
Main engines: Twin screw, two Gotaverken direct drive, slow speed diesels, 25,200 BHP, 19.5 knots
Ship's company: 402
Passengers: 750 in one class

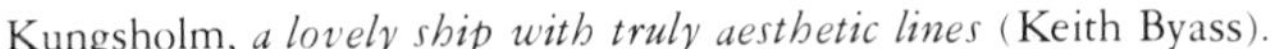

Kungsholm, *a lovely ship with truly aesthetic lines* (Keith Byass).

Above left Sea Princess, *the ugly duckling* (author's collection).

Left Sea Princess *leaving Southampton, August 7 1982* (author's collection).

Above Sea Princess *enters New York for the first time since she left as the* Kungsholm *in September 1978* (P&O).

Below *A choppy crossing of the Bay of Biscay* (Keith McCart).

The 'Carousel Room', Sea Princess (author's collection).

'Tiffany's', looking aft (author's collection).

Verandah, Sea Princess (author's collection).

Royal Princess 1984

On February 16 1982 Dr Rodney Leach, the Chairman of P&O Cruises, called a surprise press conference in London and stunned the shipping world with the announcement that P&O was going to place an order for an £80 million, 40,000 gross ton cruise liner with the Helsinki shipbuilders Wartsila, to be delivered in late 1984. It was to be the largest purpose-built cruise-ship ever constructed, and it was the most valuable single ship order ever placed with a Finnish shipyard. However, the headlines the next day ranged from 'P&O Order For £80m Liner Goes To Finns' in the *Daily Telegraph* to 'Snub For UK In Liner deal', in the *Daily Mirror*, as a stream of uninformed criticism came from the media. The hysteria even spilled over into Parliament where the shadow Secretary of State for Industry, and Labour's front bench spokesman on shipping, described the decision as 'outrageous' and 'appalling'.

However it soon became clear that British Ship-builders could not have met P&O's requirements. The only British shipyard which came close to meeting the order was Swan Hunter on the Tyne, but they had booked so many other contracts that P&O would have had to wait until 1985 for their ship. Harland & Wolff, the Belfast shipyard which built *Canberra*, did not even tender for the contract as they were now geared to building tankers and bulk carriers, and could not have met P&O's deadline of late 1984. It was a sad reflection on a once great industry, and once the facts became known the furore fell flat. Perhaps as surprising as the announcement itself from P&O, was an artists impression of the new ship. But, fortunately, the artist had been allowed a great deal of licence; when a model of Wartsila 464, as she was now known, was unveiled later that year it was clear that she would be similar in appearance to other ships built recently by Wartsila.

The formal contract for the new liner was signed on April 20 1982, and Lord Inchcape, the group Chairman, handed over the initial payment, a one pound note, to Mr Tankmar Horn the president of Wartsila. It seemed that all was going well, and by April 1983 the design of the ship was nearing completion. Full size mock up cabins had been built at the shipyard, and the interior designers were working on the decor and lighting of the public rooms. The shipyard had started production of the first steelwork units. Approximately 200 prefabricated units would be needed, and the first were due to enter Wartsila's giant building shed to be welded together during the following few months.

On April 28 1983 P&O announced that Wartsila 464 was to be named *Royal Princess*, and that the Princess of Wales had indicated that she hoped to name the ship in November 1984, at a ceremony to be held at Southampton Docks. It was a momentous announce-ment, for the last P&O liner to be launched and named by a member of the royal family was in April 1935, when *Strathmore* had been launched by the Duchess of York. But suddenly on May 24 1983 the future of the company itself was in doubt, when Trafalgar House, the property, shipping and construction group, launched a £290 million takeover bid for P&O. Although the board described the terms as 'derisory', they were faced with a long battle to keep their independence. In the minds of many people the takeover battle became a Cunard — P&O contest, and in the first broadside to be fired Mr Nigel Broakes,

Trafalgar's Chairman, criticised P&O's management. However, many people in the shipping world could recall Cunard's troubles with its passenger fleet in the 1960s, and their more recent problems with their smaller cruise-ships, and were not convinced. As the battle hotted up, full-page advertisments appeared in national newspapers as both sides addressed the P&O stockholders. P&O headed theirs, 'Stand By To Repel Boarders', and underneath printed a large 'Jolly Roger'. The Department of Trade referred the bid to the Monopolies Commission and, as it had been conditional on there being no such inquiry, the bid lapsed. As the wheels of government turn slowly, the results of the commission's deliberations were not expected for six months, thus giving P&O time to prepare its defences in the event of the bid being renewed.

Soon after P&O announced her name, the keel of *Royal Princess* was laid at the Wartsila shipyard, or at least the 1980s version of a keel laying. For the keel consisted of several 224 ton prefabricated sections of hull being manoeuvred into place. Before the first one was laid a selection of Finnish and British coins was placed underneath including for the first time, a one pound coin. During the next few months work progressed well, and in September 1983 the small section of the hull which had been completed was floated out of the building shed, to allow a small ship being built behind her to be towed out. A few weeks later the first of the four Pielstick PC4-2 six-cylinder diesel engines was refitted. Then on November 1 that year came the first big change on the board of directors, which was a direct result of the Trafalgar House takeover bid. Lord Inchcape was succeeded as Chairman of the company by Mr Jeffrey Sterling, and the previous Chairman-elect, Mr J.F. Denholm, became the Deputy Chairman.

On February 18 1984, the now recognisable hull of *Royal Princess* was floated out of the building dock to the icy waters of Helsinki's western harbour. It was a tricky operation which had started one day earlier when the flooding of the drydock had commenced. First she had to be moved a short distance astern to allow a small bow section to be welded on, then four ice-breaking tugs eased *Royal Princess* slowly out into the cold, clear winter's day. With only a few feet of clearance on either side and under the roof it was a slow-process, but it was successfully completed and she was turned and berthed alongside a newly-built fitting out complex. Four months later on June 15, with most of the external work on her superstructure completed, *Royal Princess* undertook preliminary sea trials in the Baltic. All the main machinery systems and the ship's storerooms were completed. The public rooms were far from ready, but work was proceeding steadily. During the trials the main engines were run at full power, and the hull and machinery were checked for vibrations and noise, both of which were found to be very low. The ship came through the trials with flying colours, and everything was on schedule for her owner's sea trials in September 1984.

By this time, although the Department of Trade had given the Trafalgar House takeover bid the go-ahead, it had become clear that the company's interest in P&O had gone. In early September Trafalgar House announced that it had sold its 7.08 per cent of P&O deferred stock to Sterling Guarantee Trust, which for P&O was a most satisfactory outcome of the activities of the past 18 months. Ten days later on Thursday September 20 1984, *Royal Princess* began her main sea trials in the Baltic and when they were completed three days later she returned to Wartsila's shipyard for the final stages of fitting out. She was handed over to P&O on Tuesday October 30 1984 at Wartsila's yard in Helsinki, ready for her positioning voyage to Southampton.

Royal Princess certainly lives up to P&O's claim that she is the 'world's most advanced cruise-ship'. She has nine passenger decks, from the uppermost 'Observation' deck down to the 'Plaza ' deck. Directly beneath the 'Observation' deck is the 'Sun' deck, with the 'Horizon Lounge' at the base of the funnel. This magnificent room with large panoramic windows has spectactular views over both sides and astern. By night, through the use of highly sophisticated lighting and sound techniques the room is converted into a discotheque. Amidships on this deck are swimming pools and the spa, which consists of gymnasium, beauty salon and sauna. The next deck down is the 'Lido' deck with 12 deluxe suites situated forward as well as 24 deluxe cabins and two luxury deluxe suites. Aft of this accommodation are more swimming pools, and the 'Lido Cafe', which is directly beneath the 'Horizon Lounge'. Beneath the 'Lido' deck are 'Aloha' and 'Baja' decks which are given over almost completely to passenger accommodation, as are the next two decks, 'Caribe' deck and 'Dolphin' deck ('Promenade' deck). All the cabins are situated along the side of the ship with large picture windows, and are twin-bedded with bath, shower, toilet and individually controlled air-conditioning.

Most of the public rooms are on the 'Riviera' deck, the main area being the 'International Lounge' which seats 612. It is an attractive room, with its imaginative interior design of glass murals and gesso and gold leaf panels, created by Mr Anthony Benjamin. By day many different activities can be organised and each evening it is the venue for lavish Broadway style shows. Aft of this, on the port side, is the library and photograph gallery. The 'Princess Theatre' and the 'Bridge Lounge', which seats 66 card players, are on the starboard side. Aft again is the 'Princess Court', which is a circular central lounge overlooking the Plaza. On the forward bulkhead is a portrait of *Royal Princess*' sponsor, the Princess of Wales, with a silver inscription plate. Also on this deck are the casino and boutique, and finally the 'Riviera Club'. This is a sophisticated nightclub area decorated in pastel shades with tufted wool murals designed by Mr Rib Bloomfield. The lowest passenger deck is the 'Plaza' deck, where the main foyer features a sweeping staircase leading to the circular balcony of the Princess Court. The foyer is dominated by an 11 ft seagull sculpture, 'Spindrift', by Mr David Norris. It takes the form of an elegant spiral in polished steel, carrying three groups of Herring Gulls in green patinated bronze. The sculpture can be seen from many angles and every view brings a different perspective to the sweep and flow of the design. At the forward end of the plaza area is the purser's bureau and more passenger cabins, and aft of it is the magnificent 'Continental Dining Room'. This is an elegant room decorated in beige and turquoise with large outside windows and seating for 616 passengers. The central feature of the room is an elaborate tapestry wall-hanging by Maggie Riegler. Altogether there are some 800 pot plants on board and £250,000 of original artwork by 29 British and American artists has been commissioned for the new ship.

Royal Princess arrived in Southampton's 106 berth in the Western Docks on the morning of Monday November 5 1984. It was a bleak day, but she was welcomed by a fire boat and siren blasts from ships in the port. On the day of her naming ceremony security in the docks was tight, following a recent assassination attempt on the British Prime Minister and members of the government in Brighton, and a naval diving team even went down to check the underwater hull. Fortunately it did not spoil the occasion, and at noon on Thursday November 15 Her Royal Highness The Princess of Wales pulled a lever to break a bottle of champagne against the side of *Royal Princess*, thus officially naming her. Following the ceremony, the Princess of Wales was escorted round the ship by Mr Jeffrey Sterling, meeting members of the ship's company. She was entertained to lunch on board and before disembarking she was presented with gifts by both P&O and Wartsila.

Four days later, on Monday November 19 1984, *Royal Princess* sailed from Southampton to Miami on her inaugural voyage. It was a cold, clear day as she left the UK to take her place in the US cruise market, and it augers well for her that she is fully booked for her first 12 months of service. She will spend 1985 cruising to a host of glamorous destinations along the Mexican Riviera, among the islands of the Caribbean, and to the majestic coasts of Canada and Alaska.

In the 81 years since the *Moldavia* sailed 'East of Suez' the role of the passenger liner has undergone a dramatic change. Now the very existence of these ships depends solely on the whims of the leisure industry. But it is good to see that not only has a British shipping company successfully weathered this change, but has remained one of the leaders in the cruise business, and possesses one of the largest passenger fleets in the world.

Technical data

Gross tonnage: 44,348
Net tonnage: 19,646
Length overall: 758 ft 5 in (231 m)
Breadth: 95 ft 8 in (29.2 m)
Draught: 21 ft 4 in (7.8 m)
Main engines: Twin screw, four Wartsila Pielstick 6PC4-2L diesel engines, each developing 7,290 Kw (9,900 HP). Arranged in pairs each pair driving a heavily skewed CP propeller through reduction gearing. Each engine also driving an alternator through the same gearing. Engines designed to burn heavy fuel of up to 600 CST viscosity at speeds up to 22 knots.
Ship's company: 498
Passengers: 1,260 maximum

Above *An artist's impression of the new liner, 'Wartsila 464'; fortunately the artist had been allowed a great deal of licence* (P&O).

Below *Looking much more like the* Royal Princess, *a scale model of the new ship* (P&O).

Above *On February 17 1984, the now recognisable hull of* Royal Princess *was floated out of the building dock to the icy waters of Helsinki's western harbour* (P&O).

Below Royal Princess *on her initial sea trials, June 15 1984* (P&O).

Above Royal Princess *on her owner's sea trials, September 20 1984* (P&O).

Below Royal Princess *on her way to Southampton following her delivery to P&O in Helsinki on October 30 1984* (P&O).

Above *A twin bedded deluxe suite with verandah, 'Lido' deck* (P&O).

Below *The plaza area dominated by the 'Spindrift' sculpture* (P&O).

Above *The portrait of the Princess of Wales in the 'Princess Court', it is from a photograph taken by Tim Graham in the drawing room of Kensington Palace* (author's collection).

Below *The 'Horizon Lounge' with its magnificent panoramic windows* (author's collection).

Above *The 'Lido Cafe'* (author's collection).

Below *The 'International Lounge', the venue for lavish Broadway-style shows* (author's collection).

Royal Princess *leaves Southampton on her maiden voyage to Miami, November 19 1984* (author's collection).

Bibliography

Lord Inchcape, Hector Bolitho, John Murray 1936.
Merchant Adventurers 19141918, F. A. Hook, A. & C. Black 1920.
A Hundred Year History of the P&O, Boyd Cable, Ivor Nicholson & Watson 1937.
These Splendid Ships, David Divine, Frederick Muller Ltd 1960.
Business In Great Waters, George F. Kerr, Faber & Faber Ltd 1951.
A Sea Affair, D. G. O. Baillie, Hutchinson 1957.
Axis Blockade Runners of World War Two, Martin Brice, B. T. Batsford Ltd 1981.
The Blockaders, A. Cecil Hampshire, William Kimber Ltd 1980.
Warships of World War Two, Denton & Colledge, Ian Allan 1964.
North Star to Southern Cross, John M. Maber, T. Stephenson & Sons Ltd 1967.
The Eye of the Wind, Peter Scott.
Merchant Fleets in Profile Vol One, The Ships of the P&O, Orient and Blue Anchor Lines, Duncan Haws, Patrick Stephens Ltd 1978.
Great Passenger Ships of the World, Volumes One to Five, Arnold Kludas, Patrick Stephens Ltd 1977.
British Vessels Lost at Sea 19141918, HMSO, Patrick Stephens Ltd 1980.
British Vessels Lost at Sea 19391945, HMSO, Patrick Stephens Ltd 1980.

Unpublished Sources

P&O records held at the National Maritime Museum.
Admiralty records held at the Public Records Office (Logs of AMCs).
Admiralty records held at the Ministry of Defence, Naval Historical Section and the Naval Historical Library.

Newspapers

The Times; Daily Telegraph; Daily Mirror; Southern Evening Echo; The Birkenhead News; The Greenock Telegraph & Clyde Shipping Gazette; Sydney Morning Herald; Dunedin Evening Star; South China Morning Post; The Belfast Newsletter; The Belfast Telegraph; North Western Daily Mail; Newcastle Daily Journal; The Straits Times.

Acknowledgements

Thanks to: Stephen Rabson, P&O Group Librarian; Keith Byass; Mike Smith, Public Relations Officer, Vickers Shipbuilding & Engineering Ltd; Alan Hedgley, Public Affairs Manager, Harland & Wolff Ltd; P. Colin Christie, University of Glasgow; Paul Pelowski, National Maritime Museum; W. K. Fox, Community Relations Officer, Cammell Laird Shipbuilders Ltd; A. J. Francis, Naval Historical Library, Ministry of Defence; Laurence Dunn; F. W. Manders, Librarian, City of Newcastle upon Tyne; John B. Hill, Loughton, Essex; John Clarkson, Preston, Lancashire; W. R. Wormersley, Singapore; Roger Chapman, Lutterworth, Leicestershire; Michael Cassar, Valletta, Malta; Staff of the British Newspaper Library, Colindale, London; Public Records Office, Kew, London; Scottish Records Office; Hong Kong Tourist Authority; and China Merchants Steam Navigation Ltd, Hong Kong.

Index

Royal Princess *is floated out of her building dock into the ice covered waters of Helsinki Harbour, February 1984* (P&O).